X-O MANOWAR

GENERAL

MATT KINDT | DOUG BRAITHWAITE | DIEGO RODRIGUEZ

CONTENTS

Collection Cover Art: Lewis LaRosa
with Brian Reber

Assistant Editors: Charlotte Greenbaum and Robert Meyers (#4)
Editor: Warren Simons

VALIANT.

X-O Manowar® (2017): General. Published by Valiant Entertainment LLC. Office
of Publication: 350 Seventh Avenue, New York, NY 10001. Compilation copyright
© 2017 Valiant Entertainment LLC. All rights reserved. Contains materials
originally published in single magazine form as X-O Manowar (2017) #4-6.
Copyright © 2017 Valiant Entertainment LLC. All rights reserved. All characters,
their distinctive likeness and related indicia featured in this publication are
trademarks of Valiant Entertainment LLC. The stories, characters, and incidents
featured in this publication are entirely fictional. Valiant Entertainment does not
read or accept unsolicited submissions of ideas, stories, or artwork.
Printed in the U.S.A. First Printing. ISBN: 9781682152171.

X O
MANOWAR
GENERAL ISSUE 04

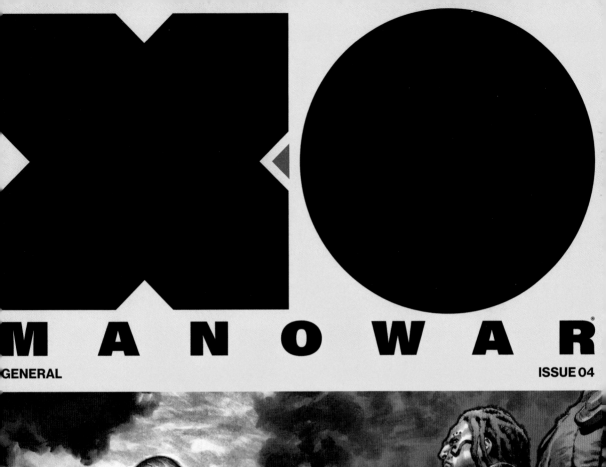

Matt Kindt
Doug Braithwaite
Diego Rodriguez

MANOWAR

ARIC OF EARTH

Once again into the fray. The warrior formerly known as X-O Manowar finds himself in the thick of the fight and leading a team in the heart of enemy territory.

SHANHARA

Aric has resisted donning the mystical X-O Manowar suit, but is unable to forget it entirely. Fashioned into a ring, the armor continues to speak to him, a small yet insistent voice that he cannot ignore.

WYNN

A young Azure soldier who followed Aric into battle in the initial assault on the Cadmium capital, what Wynn lacks in experience, he makes up for with a dogged devotion to his team leader.

CLUBB AND SCAR

The Azure twins forcefully drafted Aric and brought an end to his quiet life with Schon, but after some reluctance they have learned to trust the man they once looked down upon.

No matter where he goes, Aric is hailed as a once-in-a-lifetime warrior. On his new home planet, Gorin, this rings truer than ever as Aric continues to climb up the ranks of the Azure army.

Following his successful assault on The Cadmium Imperial City, Aric and his team have earned renown among the Azure forces, but their mission is incomplete. In the chaos of the attack, the Cadmium President managed to escape and now Aric must follow his trail through the mysterious lands of the deadly Burnt tribesmen.

CATT

A brutal and hardened warrior of the Burnt tribe, Catt is fierce fighter who takes no quarter with her enemy. She is a voice of reason and offers valuable insight to Aric.

BRUTO

A Cadmium turncoat, Bruto has supplied the Azure army with essential information for the siege of his former home. He may not be much of a fighter, but there is far more to Bruto than meets the eye.

SCHON

An Azure citizen working as a tavern maid, she longs to escape the yoke of Cadmium tyranny, but is distraught when Aric is forced to join the Azure army.

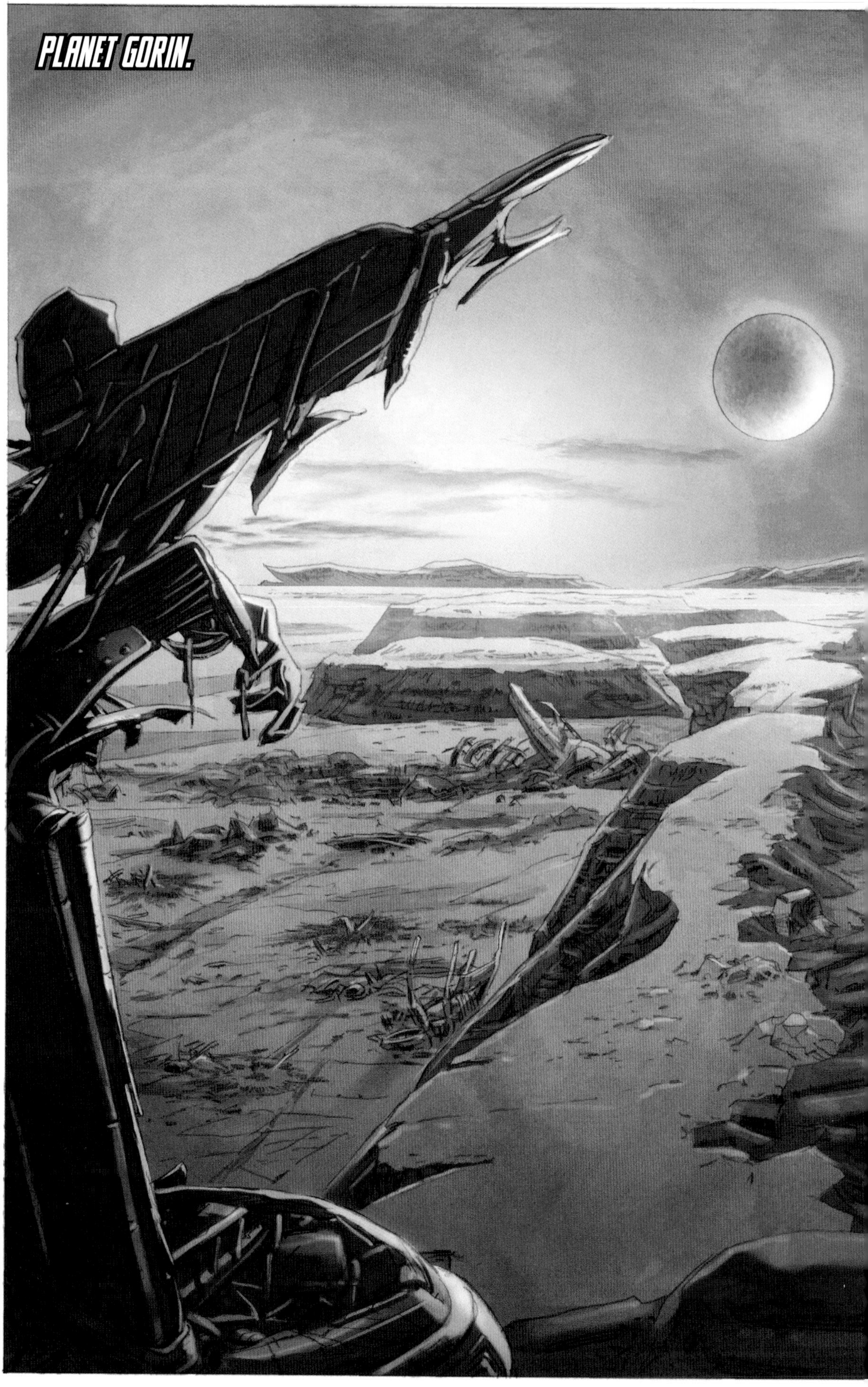
PLANET GORIN.

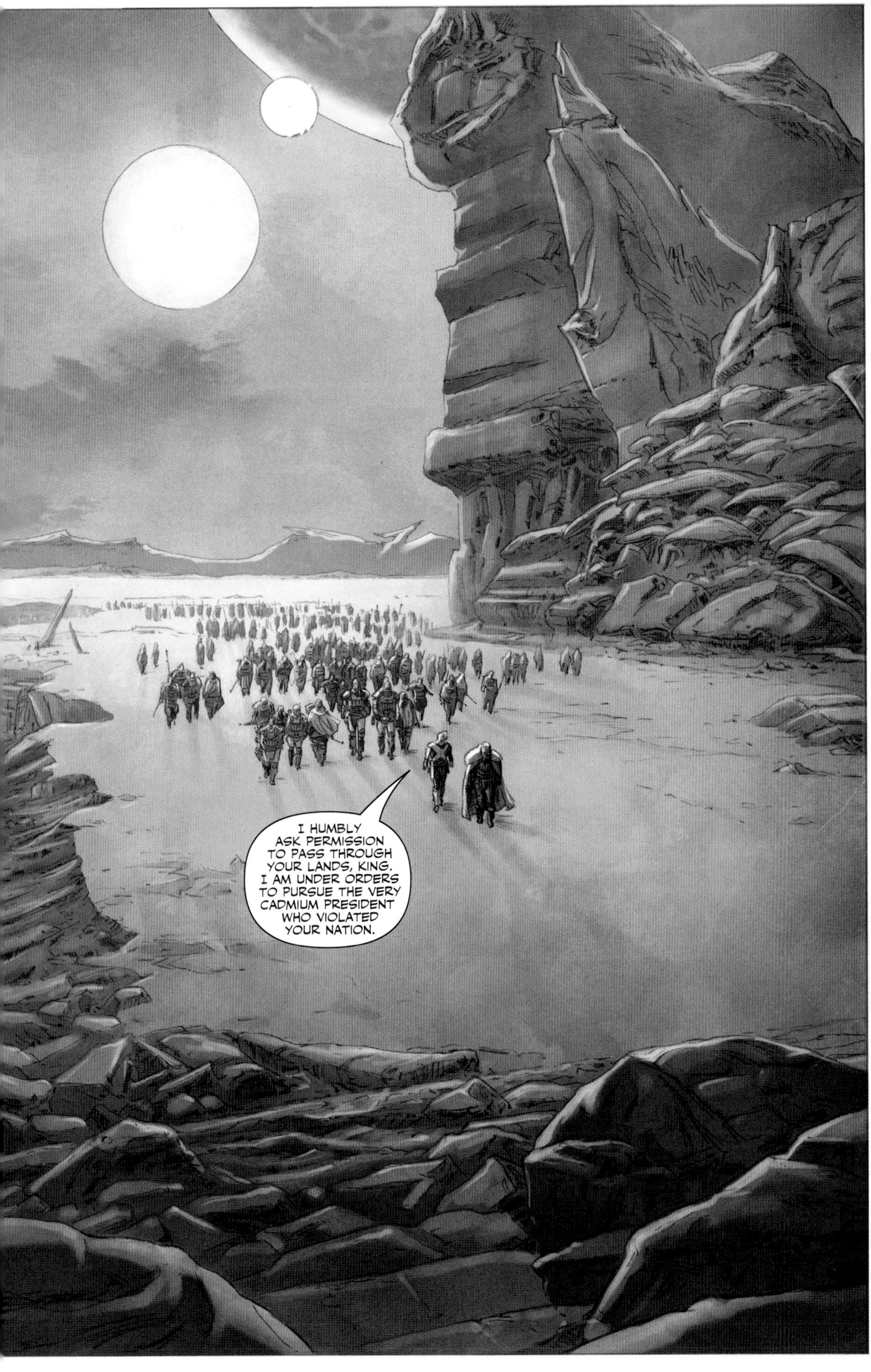
I HUMBLY ASK PERMISSION TO PASS THROUGH YOUR LANDS, KING. I AM UNDER ORDERS TO PURSUE THE VERY CADMIUM PRESIDENT WHO VIOLATED YOUR NATION.

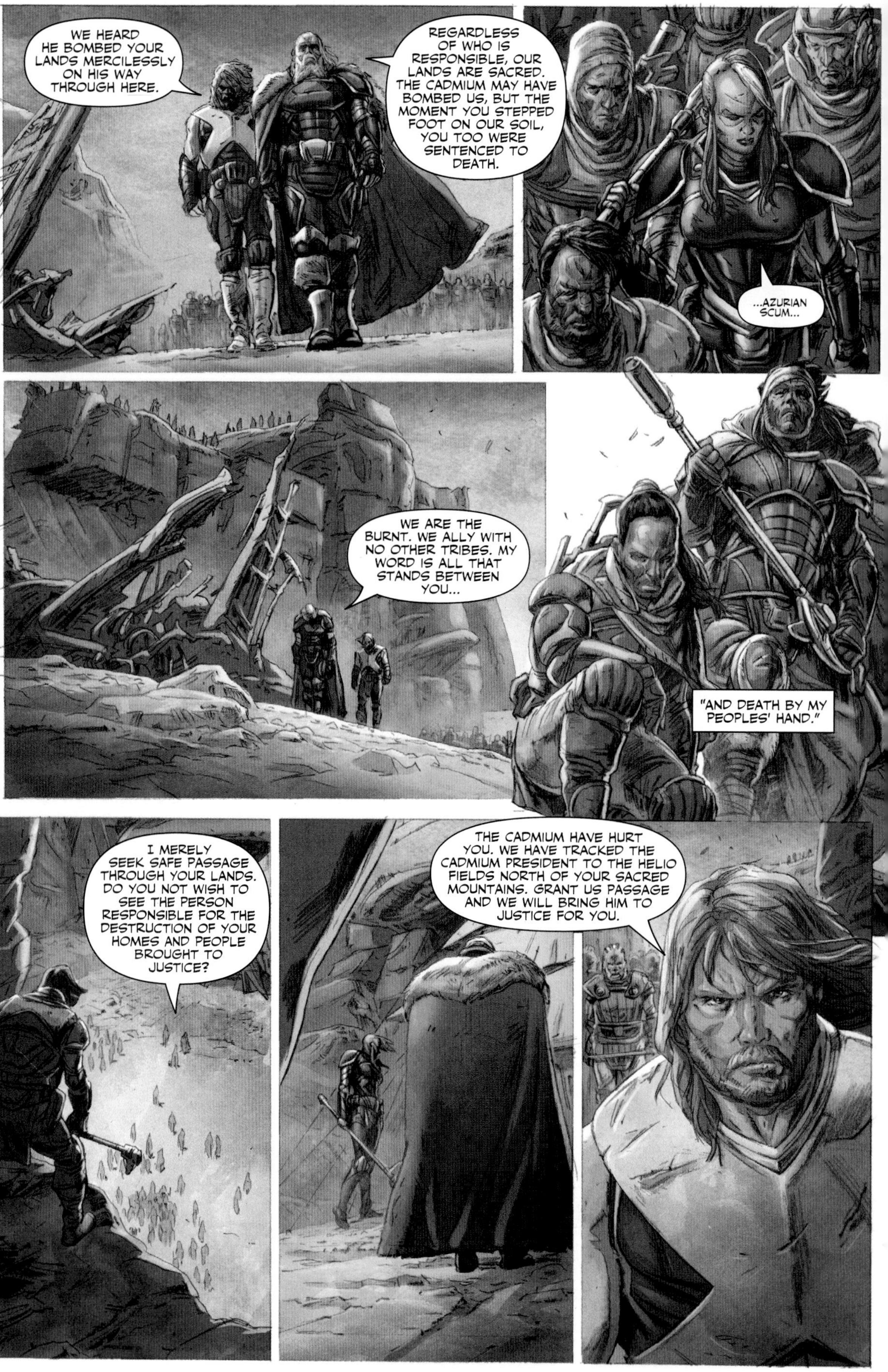
WE HEARD HE BOMBED YOUR LANDS MERCILESSLY ON HIS WAY THROUGH HERE.
REGARDLESS OF WHO IS RESPONSIBLE, OUR LANDS ARE SACRED. THE CADMIUM MAY HAVE BOMBED US, BUT THE MOMENT YOU STEPPED FOOT ON OUR SOIL, YOU TOO WERE SENTENCED TO DEATH.
...AZURIAN SCUM...
WE ARE THE BURNT. WE ALLY WITH NO OTHER TRIBES. MY WORD IS ALL THAT STANDS BETWEEN YOU...
"AND DEATH BY MY PEOPLES' HAND."
I MERELY SEEK SAFE PASSAGE THROUGH YOUR LANDS. DO YOU NOT WISH TO SEE THE PERSON RESPONSIBLE FOR THE DESTRUCTION OF YOUR HOMES AND PEOPLE BROUGHT TO JUSTICE?
THE CADMIUM HAVE HURT YOU. WE HAVE TRACKED THE CADMIUM PRESIDENT TO THE HELIO FIELDS NORTH OF YOUR SACRED MOUNTAINS. GRANT US PASSAGE AND WE WILL BRING HIM TO JUSTICE FOR YOU.

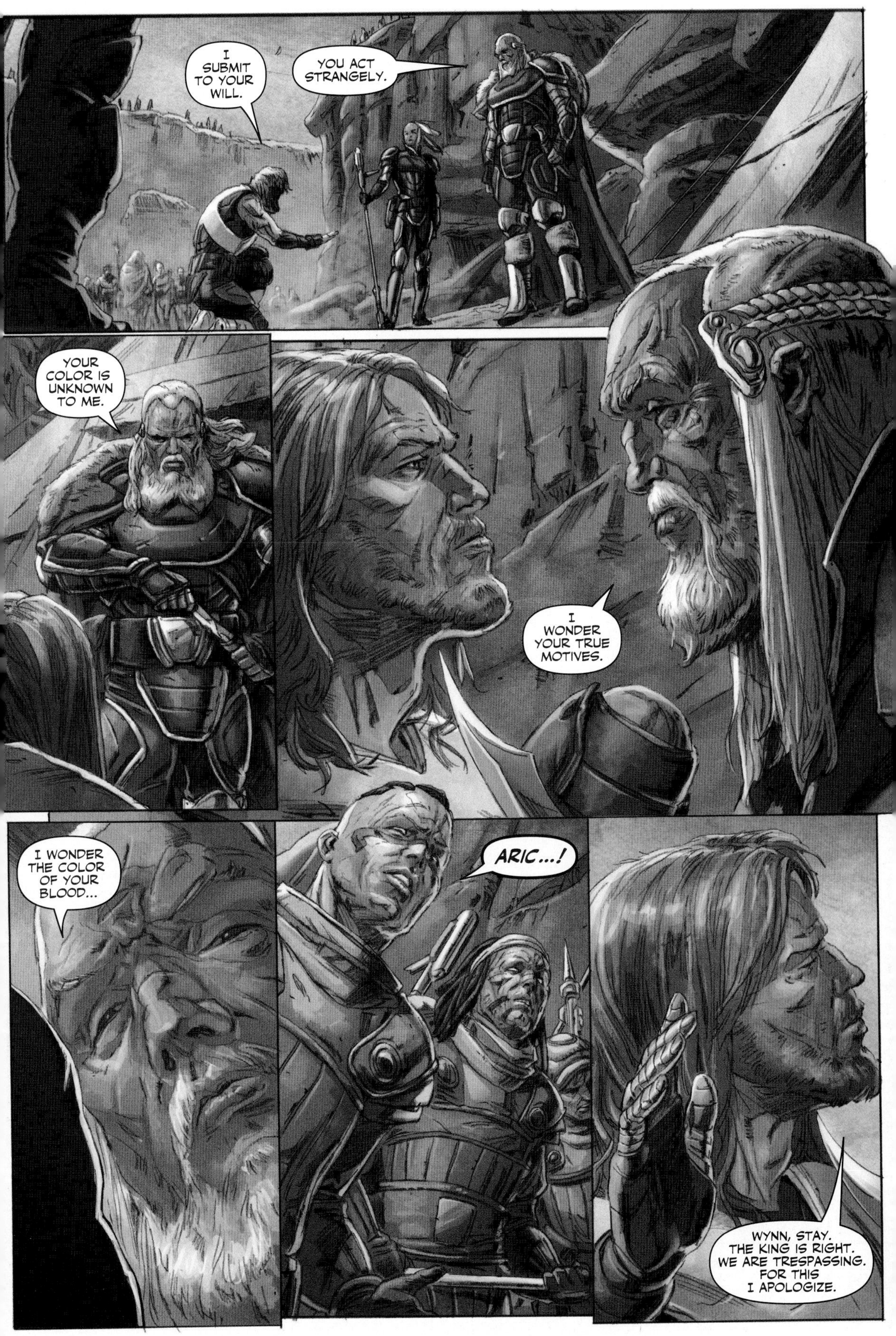
I SUBMIT TO YOUR WILL.
YOU ACT STRANGELY.
YOUR COLOR IS UNKNOWN TO ME.
I WONDER YOUR TRUE MOTIVES.
I WONDER THE COLOR OF YOUR BLOOD...
ARIC...!
WYNN, STAY. THE KING IS RIGHT. WE ARE TRESPASSING. FOR THIS I APOLOGIZE.

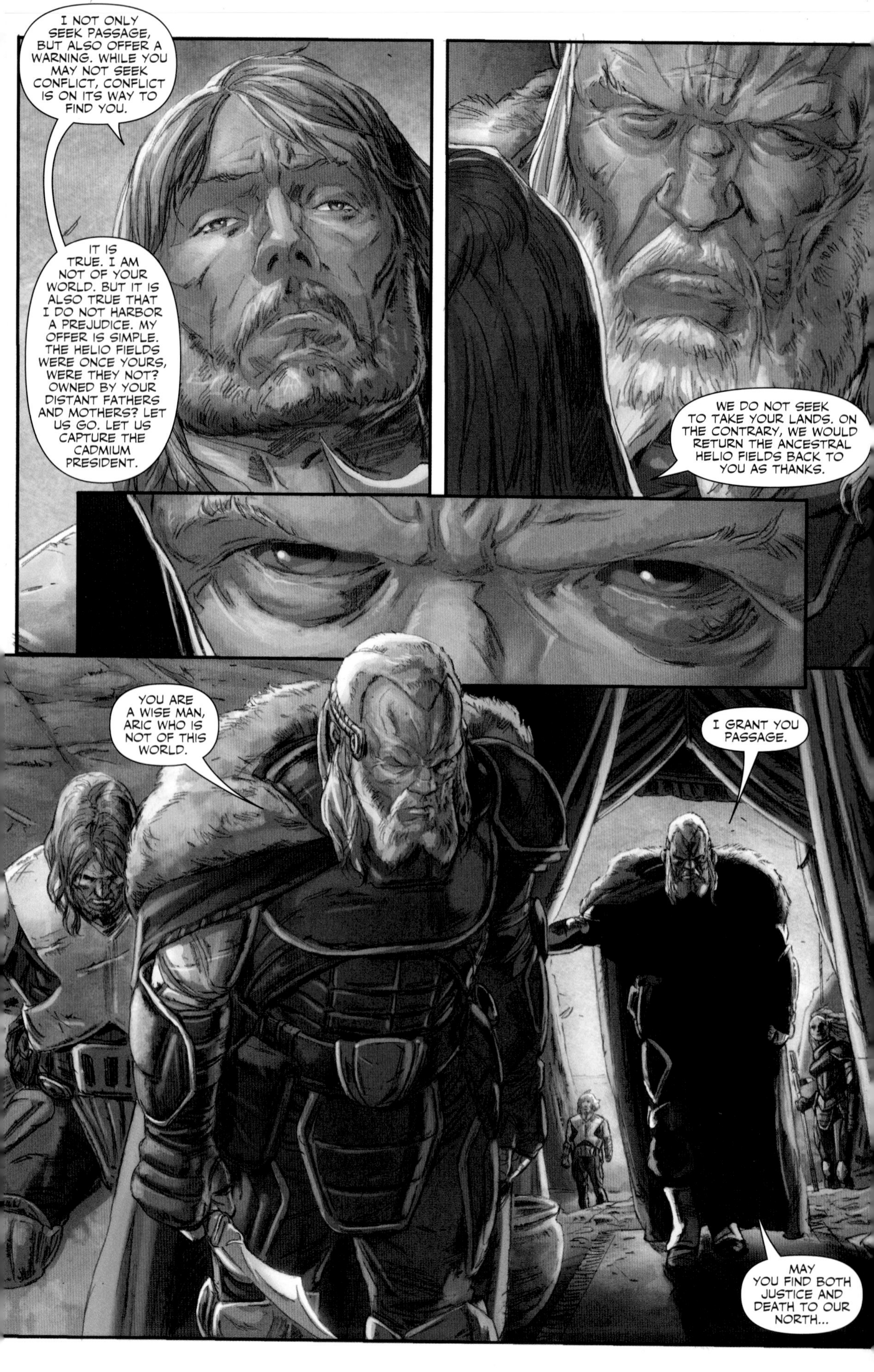
I NOT ONLY SEEK PASSAGE, BUT ALSO OFFER A WARNING. WHILE YOU MAY NOT SEEK CONFLICT, CONFLICT IS ON ITS WAY TO FIND YOU.
IT IS TRUE. I AM NOT OF YOUR WORLD. BUT IT IS ALSO TRUE THAT I DO NOT HARBOR A PREJUDICE. MY OFFER IS SIMPLE. THE HELIO FIELDS WERE ONCE YOURS, WERE THEY NOT? OWNED BY YOUR DISTANT FATHERS AND MOTHERS? LET US GO. LET US CAPTURE THE CADMIUM PRESIDENT.
WE DO NOT SEEK TO TAKE YOUR LANDS. ON THE CONTRARY, WE WOULD RETURN THE ANCESTRAL HELIO FIELDS BACK TO YOU AS THANKS.
YOU ARE A WISE MAN, ARIC WHO IS NOT OF THIS WORLD.
I GRANT YOU PASSAGE.
MAY YOU FIND BOTH JUSTICE AND DEATH TO OUR NORTH...

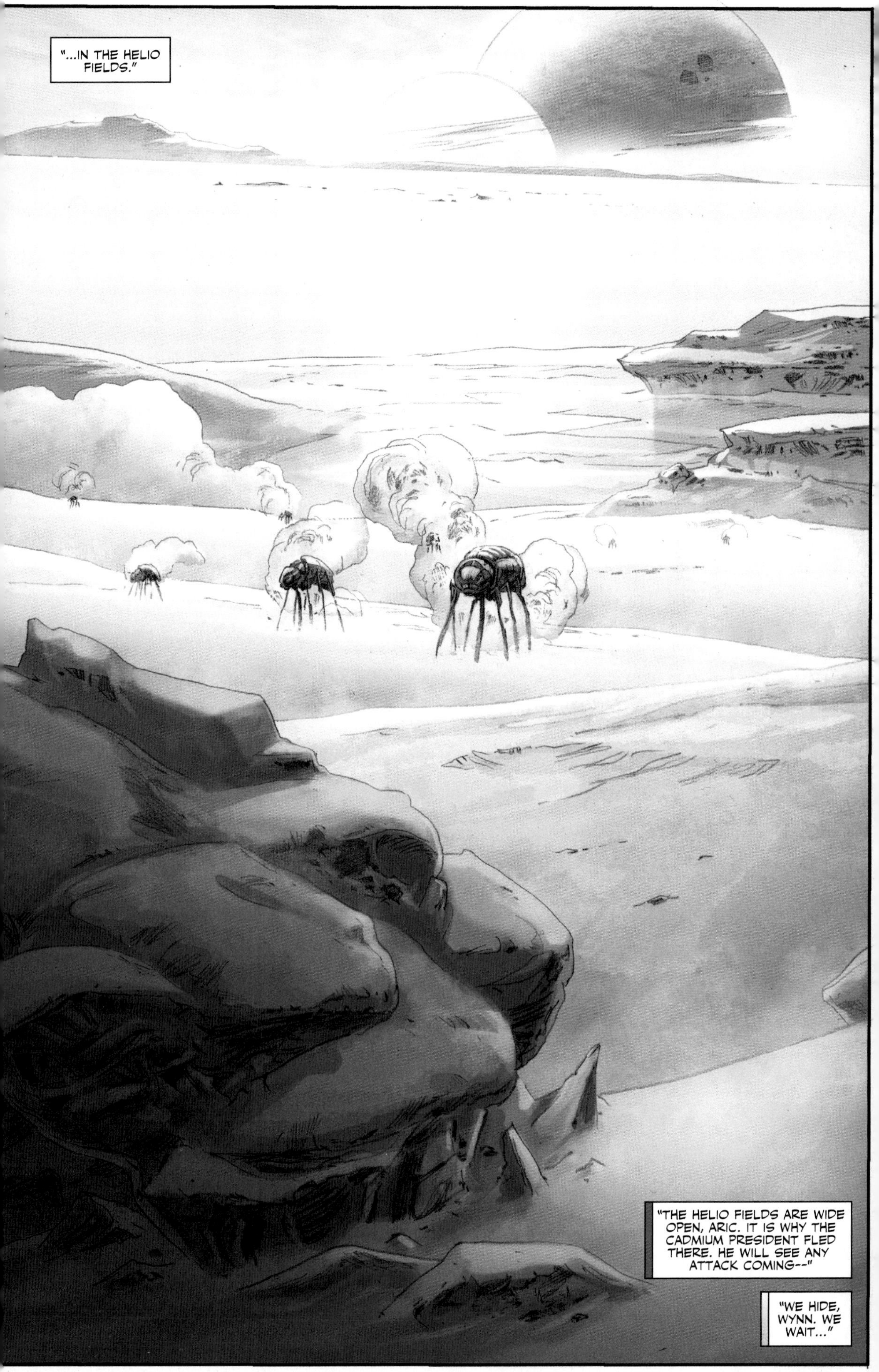
"...IN THE HELIO FIELDS."
"THE HELIO FIELDS ARE WIDE OPEN, ARIC. IT IS WHY THE CADMIUM PRESIDENT FLED THERE. HE WILL SEE ANY ATTACK COMING--"
"WE HIDE, WYNN. WE WAIT..."

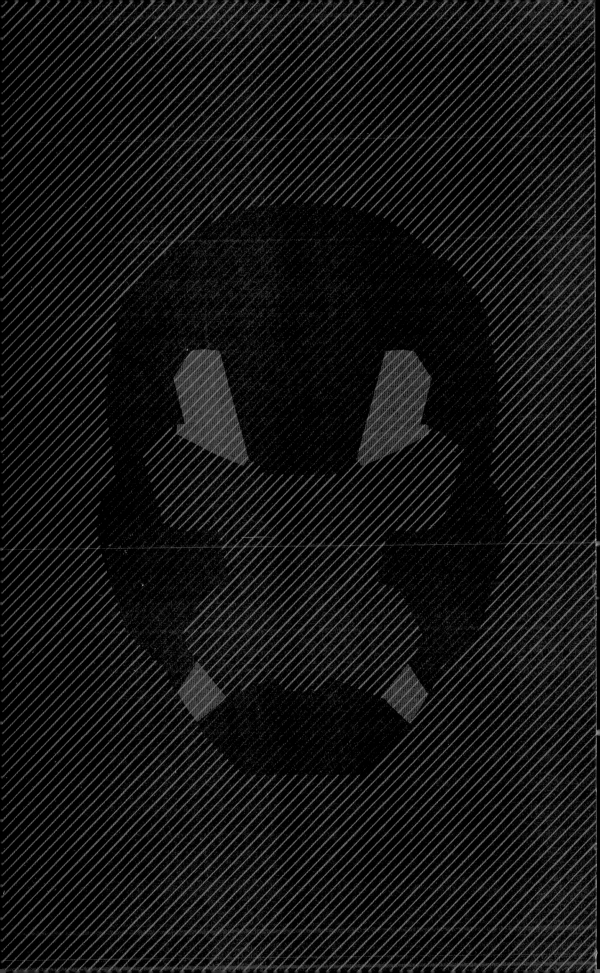

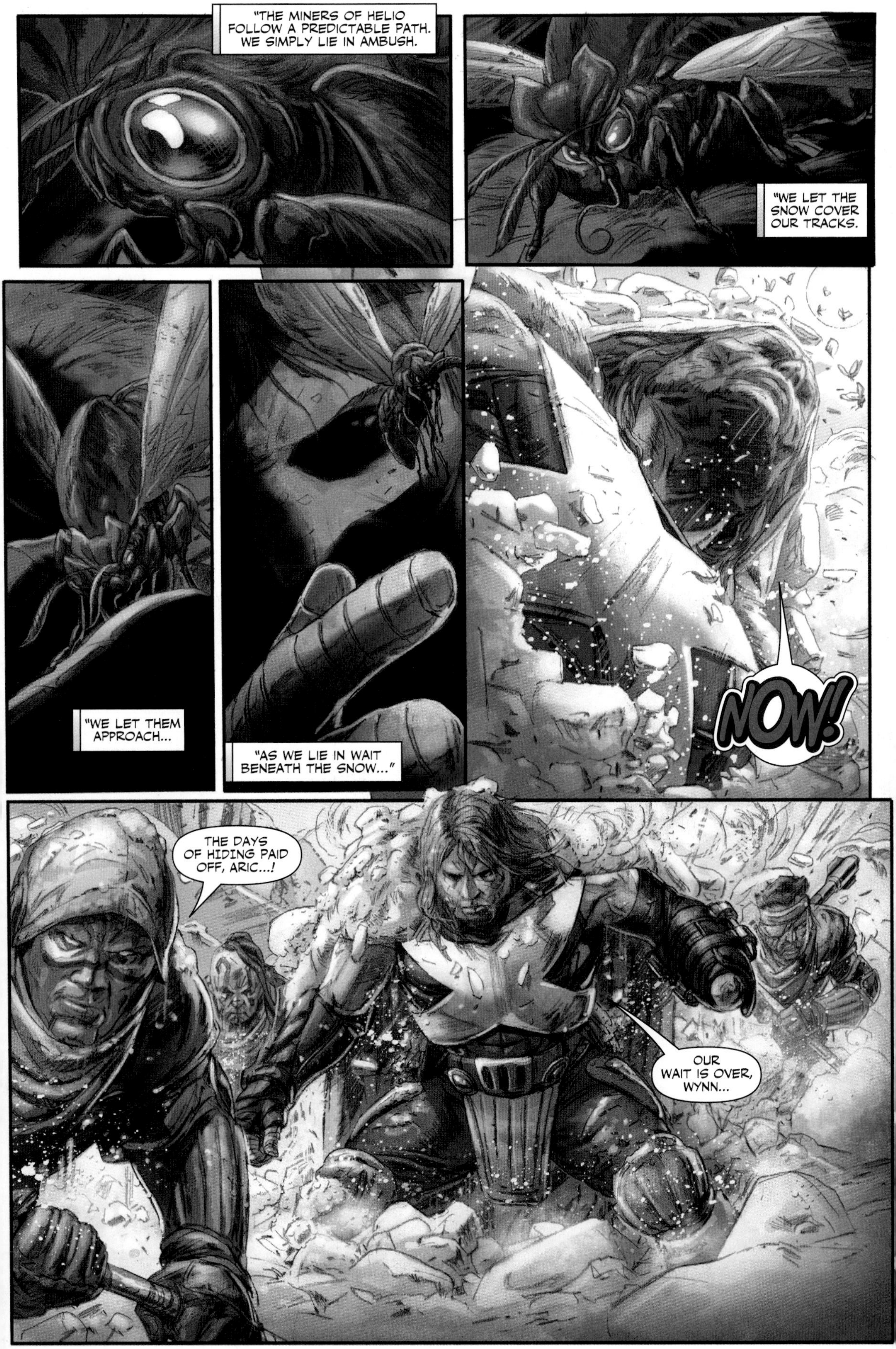
"THE MINERS OF HELIO FOLLOW A PREDICTABLE PATH. WE SIMPLY LIE IN AMBUSH.
"WE LET THE SNOW COVER OUR TRACKS.
"WE LET THEM APPROACH...
"AS WE LIE IN WAIT BENEATH THE SNOW..."
NOW!
THE DAYS OF HIDING PAID OFF, ARIC...!
OUR WAIT IS OVER, WYNN...

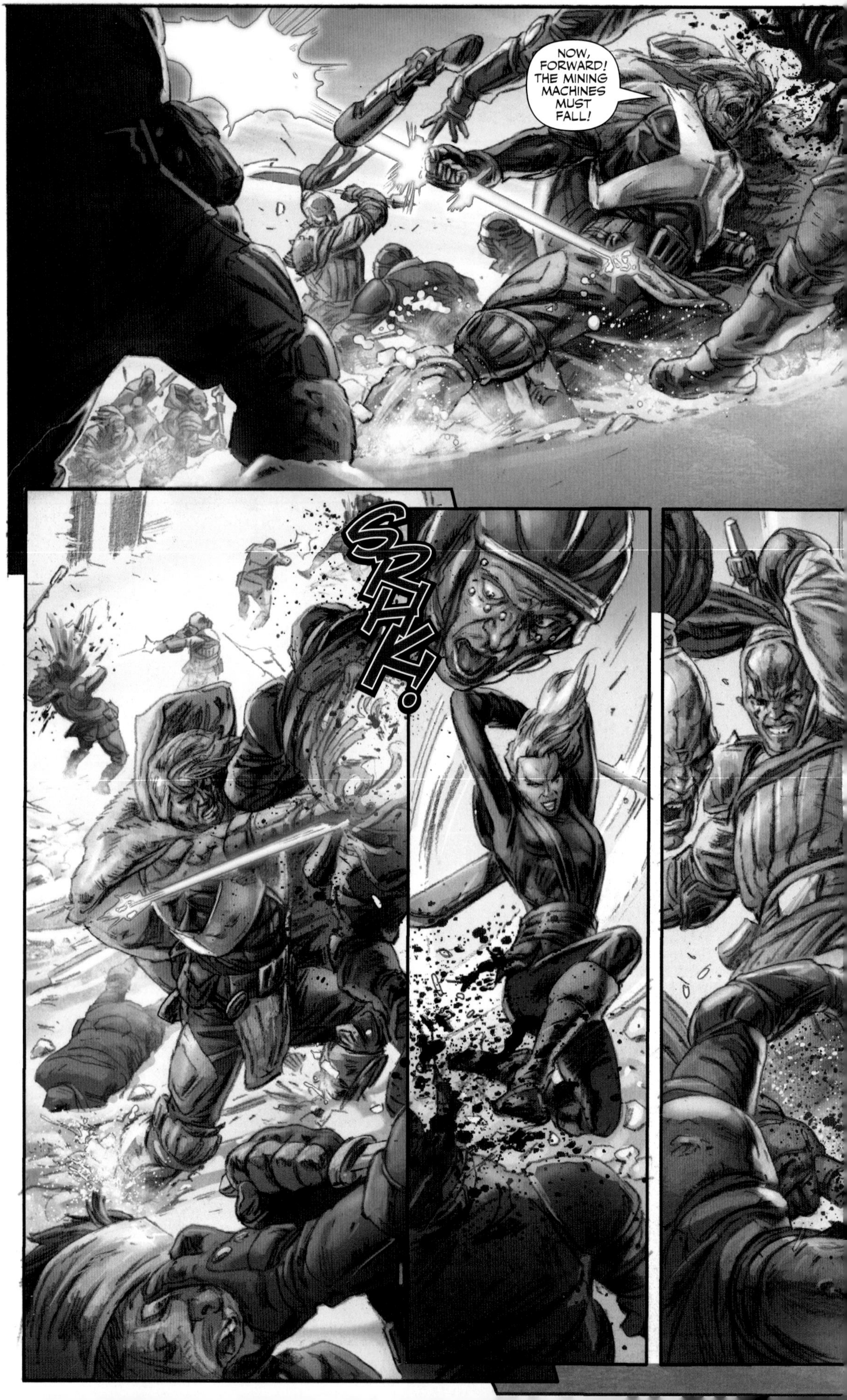
NOW, FORWARD! THE MINING MACHINES MUST FALL!
SSHHK!

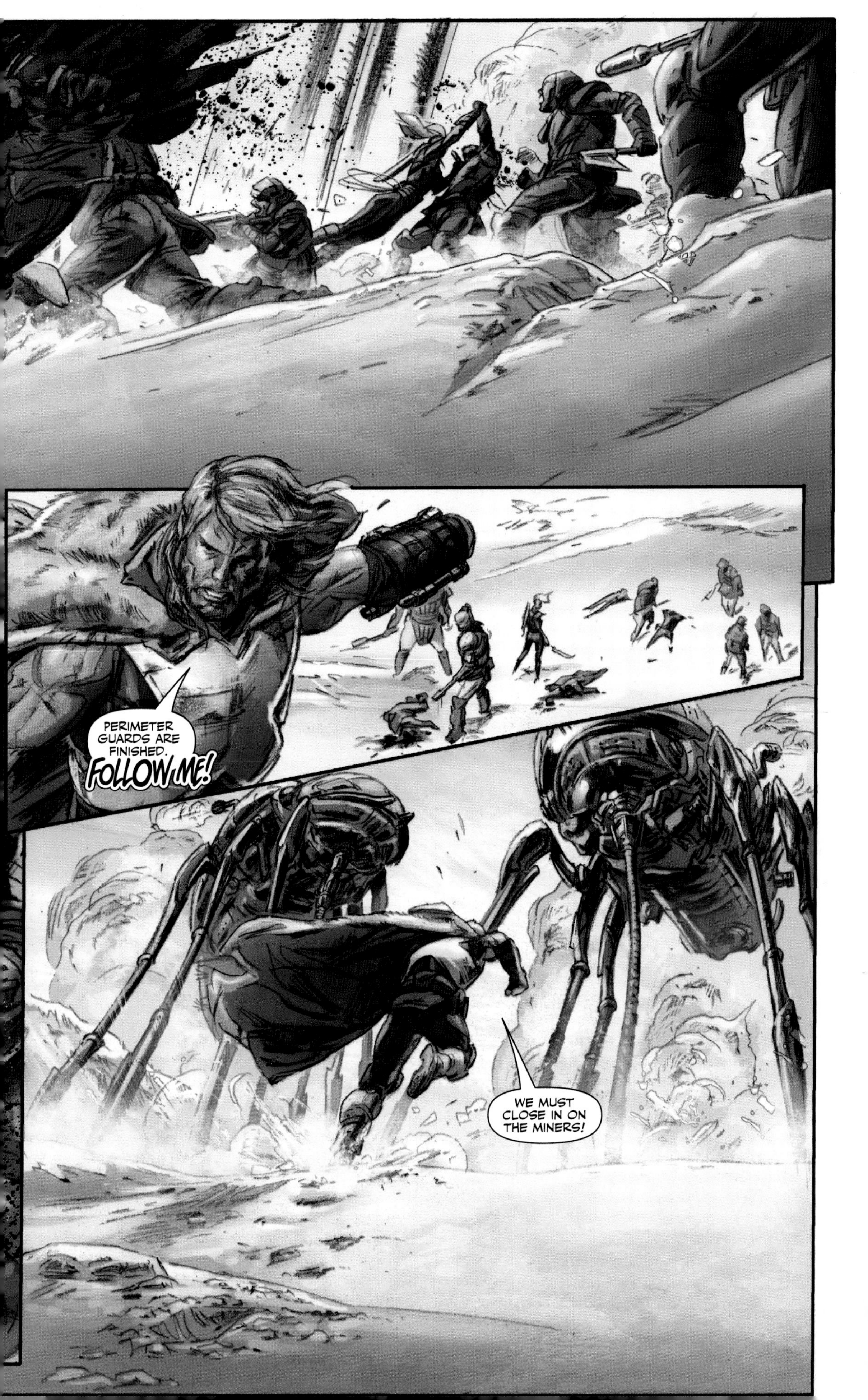
PERIMETER GUARDS ARE FINISHED. FOLLOW ME!
WE MUST CLOSE IN ON THE MINERS!

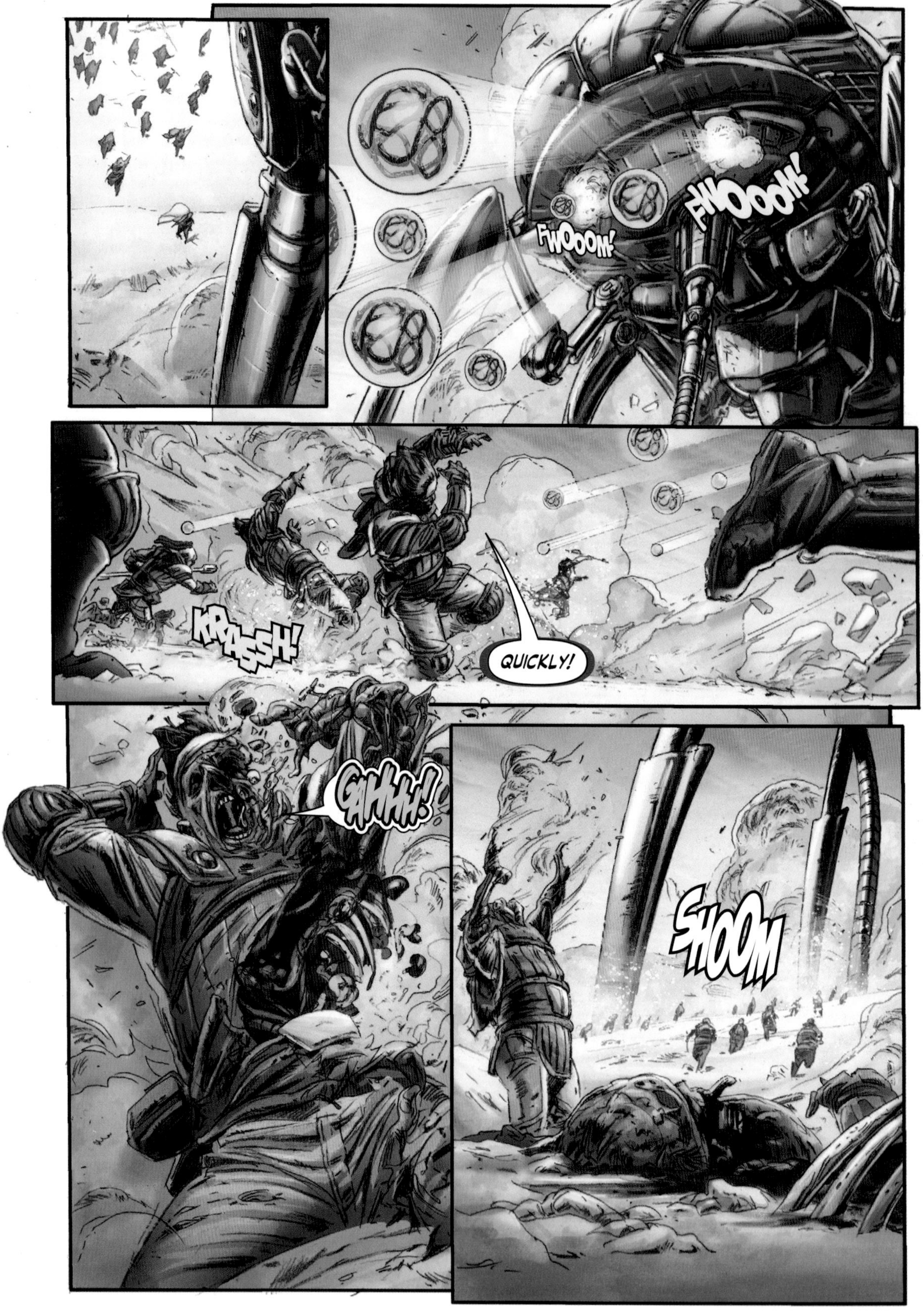
FWOOOM!
FWOOOM!
KRASSH!
QUICKLY!
GAHHHH!
SHOOM

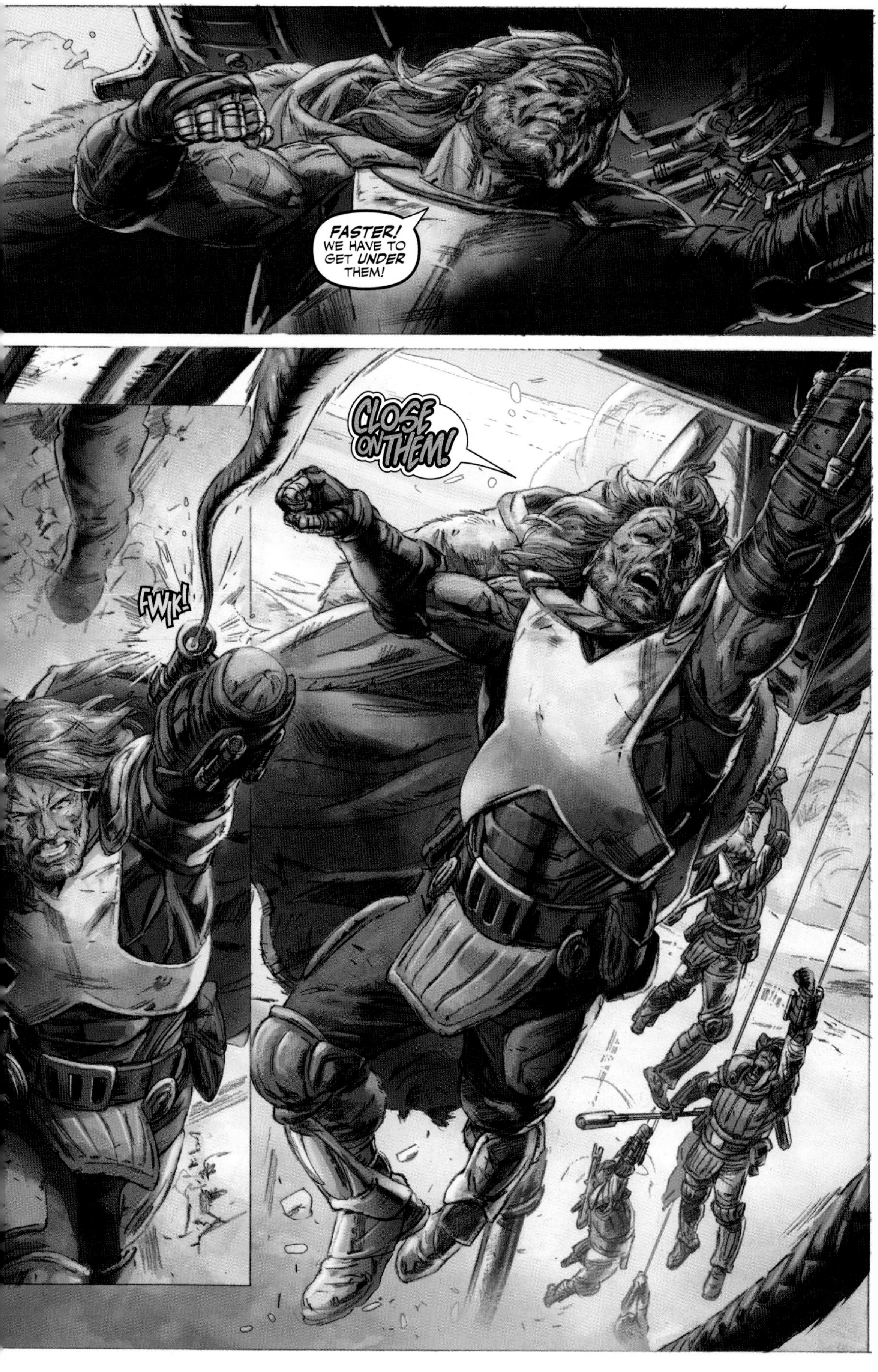
FASTER! WE HAVE TO GET UNDER THEM!
CLOSE ON THEM!
FWK!

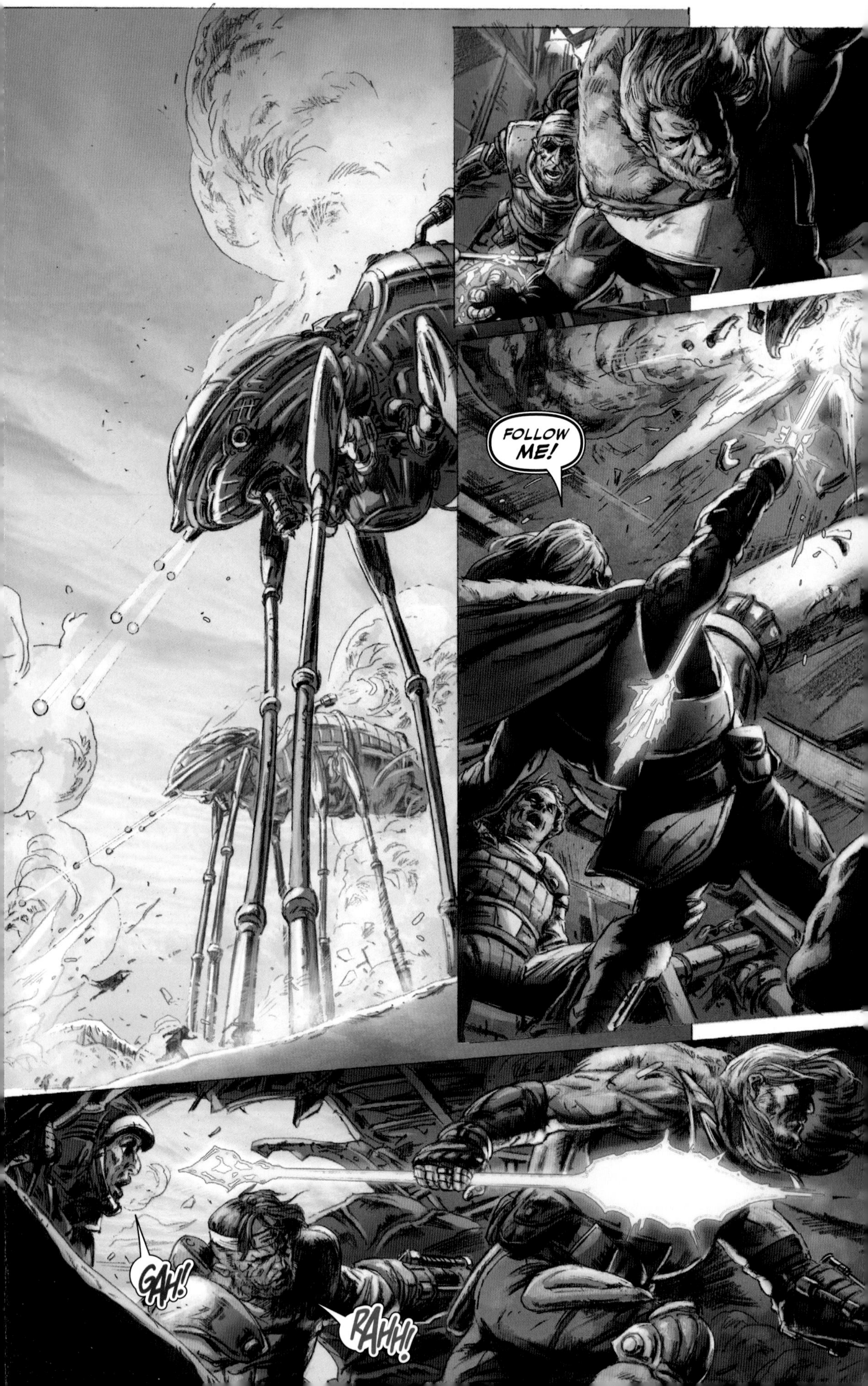
FOLLOW ME!
GAH!
RAHH!

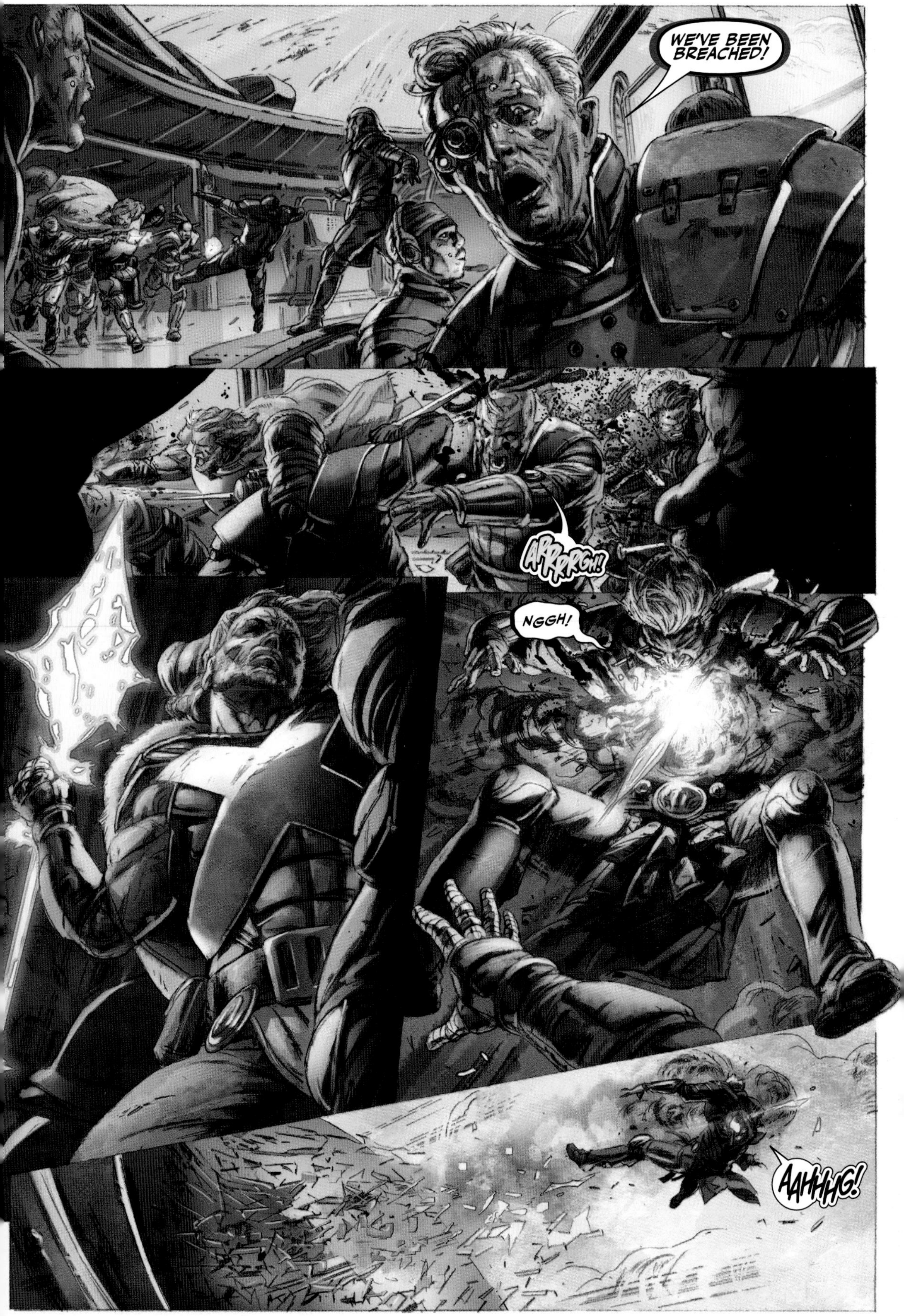
WE'VE BEEN BREACHED!
ARRRRGH!
NGGH!
AAHHHG!

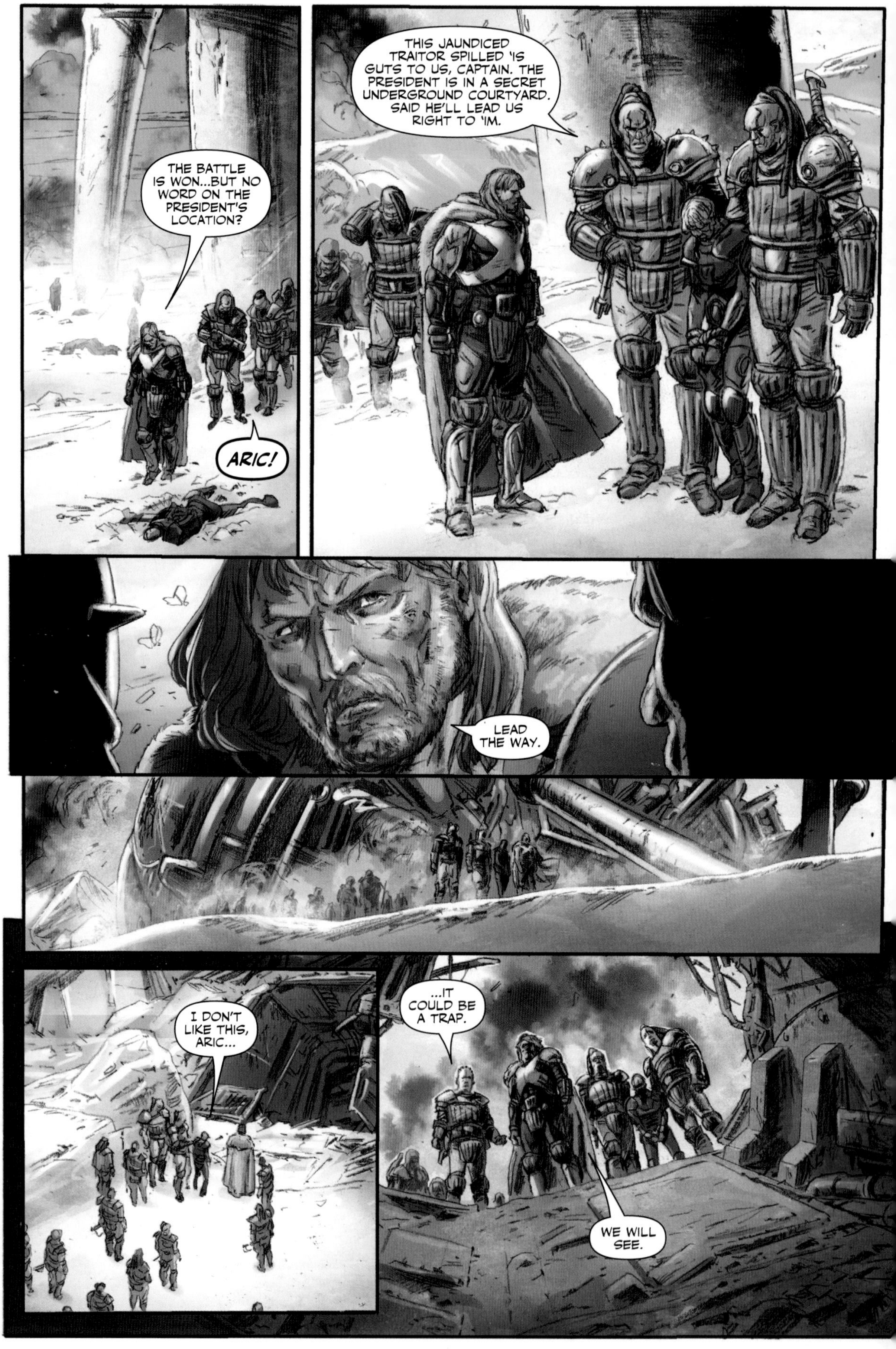
THE BATTLE IS WON...BUT NO WORD ON THE PRESIDENT'S LOCATION?
ARIC!
THIS JAUNDICED TRAITOR SPILLED 'IS GUTS TO US, CAPTAIN. THE PRESIDENT IS IN A SECRET UNDERGROUND COURTYARD. SAID HE'LL LEAD US RIGHT TO 'IM.
LEAD THE WAY.
I DON'T LIKE THIS, ARIC...
...IT COULD BE A TRAP.
WE WILL SEE.

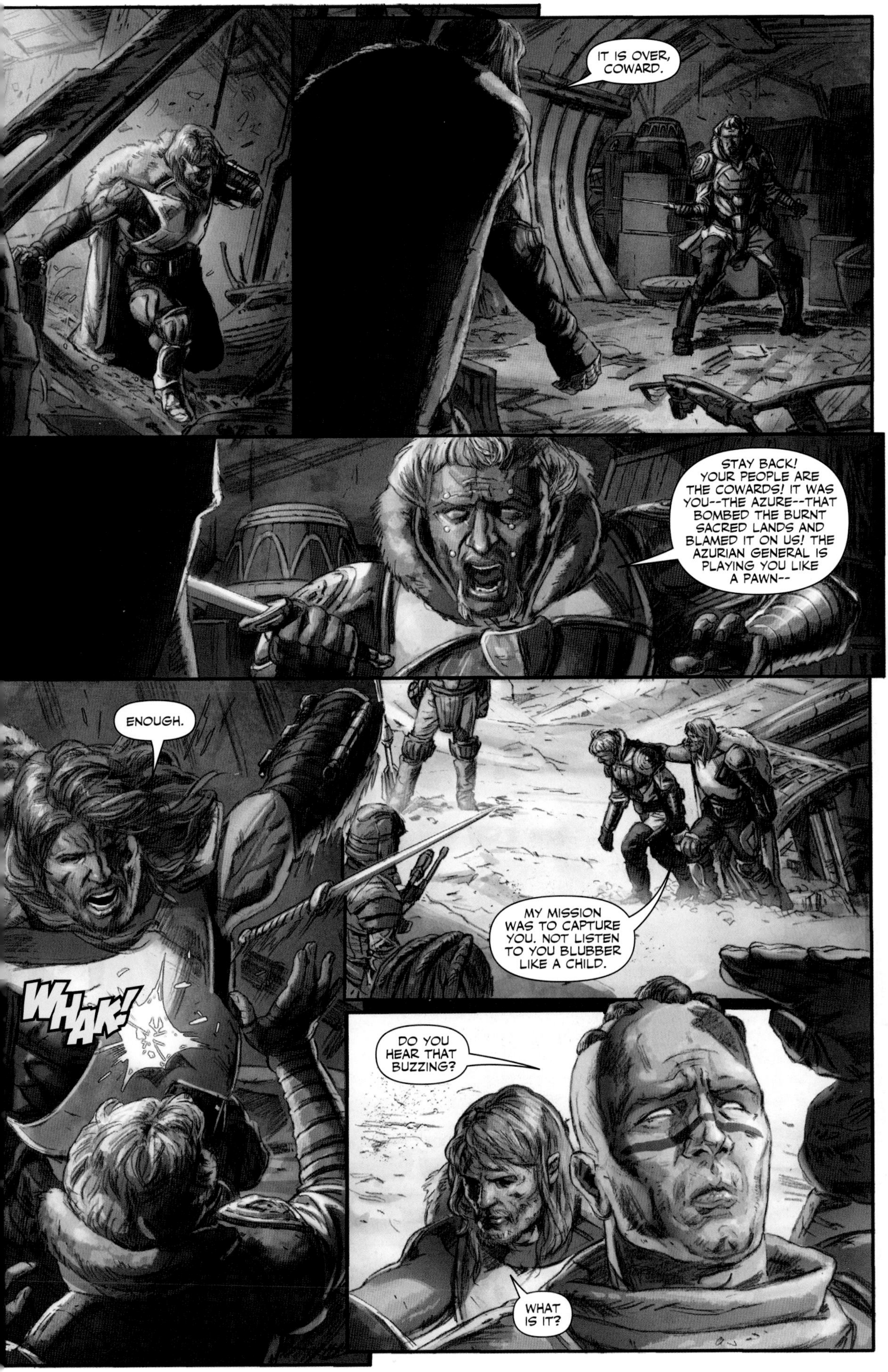
IT IS OVER, COWARD.
STAY BACK! YOUR PEOPLE ARE THE COWARDS! IT WAS YOU--THE AZURE--THAT BOMBED THE BURNT SACRED LANDS AND BLAMED IT ON US! THE AZURIAN GENERAL IS PLAYING YOU LIKE A PAWN--
ENOUGH.
WHAK!
MY MISSION WAS TO CAPTURE YOU. NOT LISTEN TO YOU BLUBBER LIKE A CHILD.
DO YOU HEAR THAT BUZZING?
WHAT IS IT?

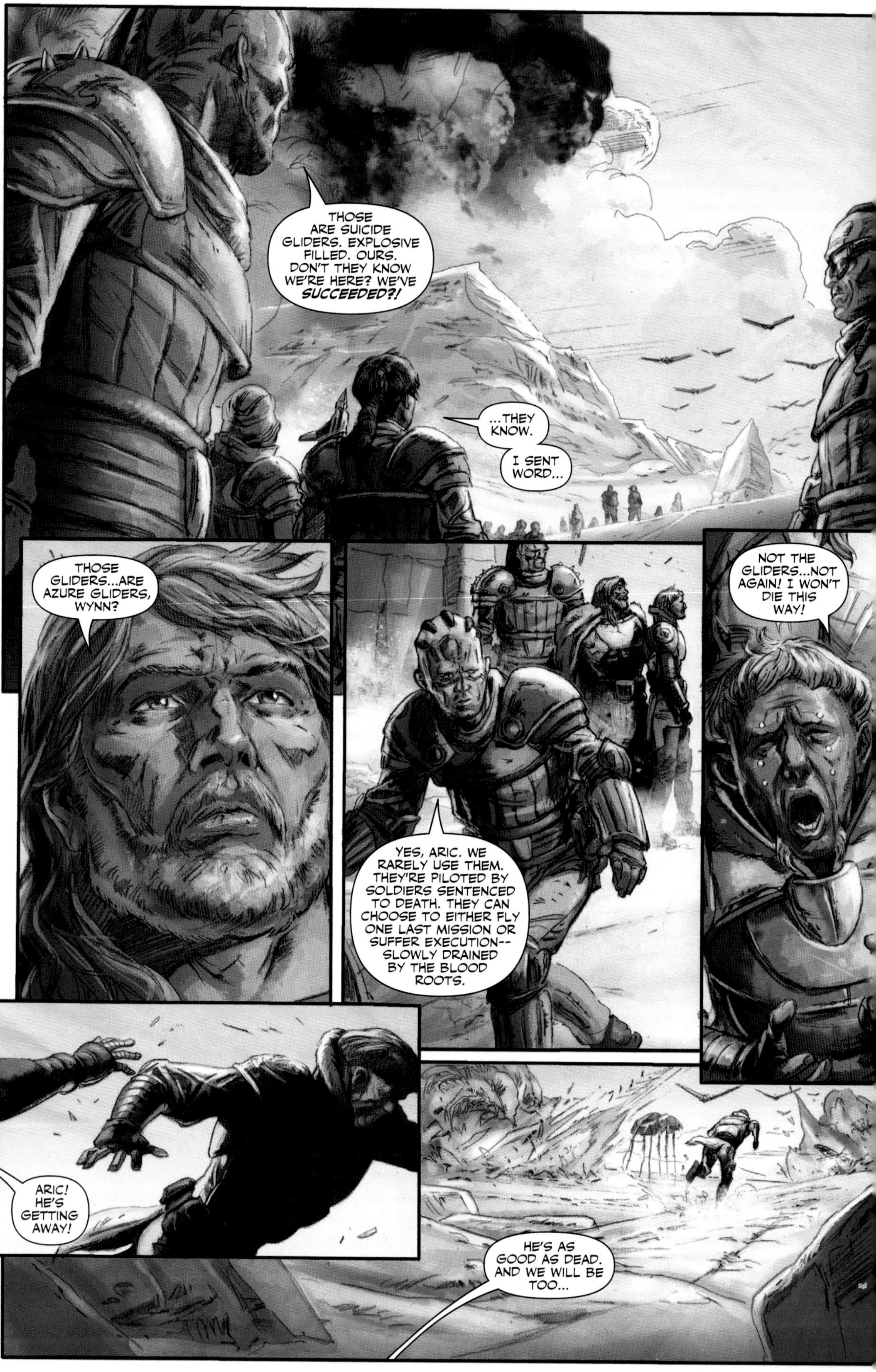
THOSE ARE SUICIDE GLIDERS. EXPLOSIVE FILLED. OURS. DON'T THEY KNOW WE'RE HERE? WE'VE *SUCCEEDED?!*
...THEY KNOW.
I SENT WORD...
THOSE GLIDERS...ARE AZURE GLIDERS, WYNN?
YES, ARIC. WE RARELY USE THEM. THEY'RE PILOTED BY SOLDIERS SENTENCED TO DEATH. THEY CAN CHOOSE TO EITHER FLY ONE LAST MISSION OR SUFFER EXECUTION-- SLOWLY DRAINED BY THE BLOOD ROOTS.
NOT THE GLIDERS...NOT AGAIN! I WON'T DIE THIS WAY!
ARIC! HE'S GETTING AWAY!
HE'S AS GOOD AS DEAD. AND WE WILL BE TOO...

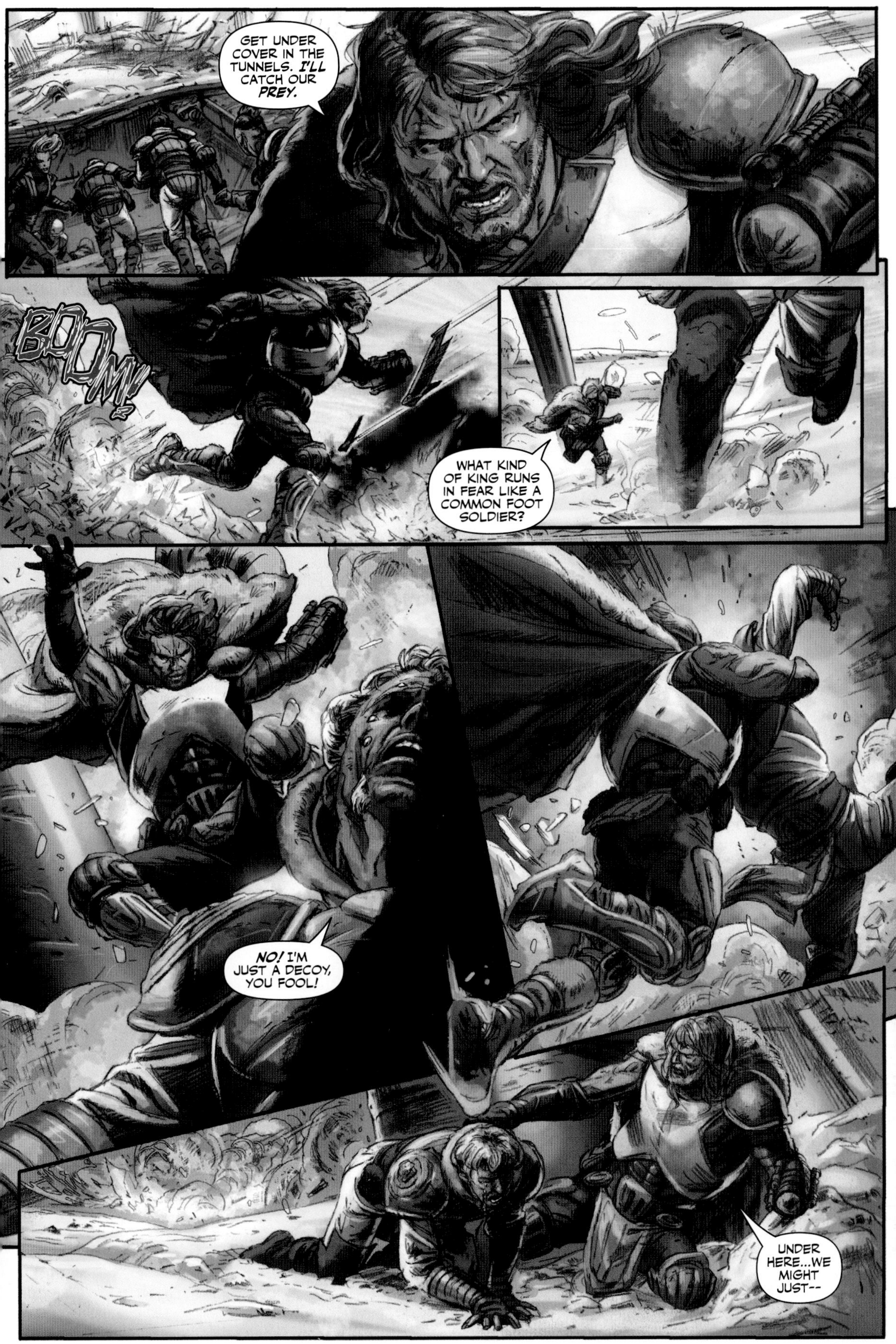
GET UNDER COVER IN THE TUNNELS. I'LL CATCH OUR PREY.
BOOM!
WHAT KIND OF KING RUNS IN FEAR LIKE A COMMON FOOT SOLDIER?
NO! I'M JUST A DECOY, YOU FOOL!
UNDER HERE...WE MIGHT JUST--

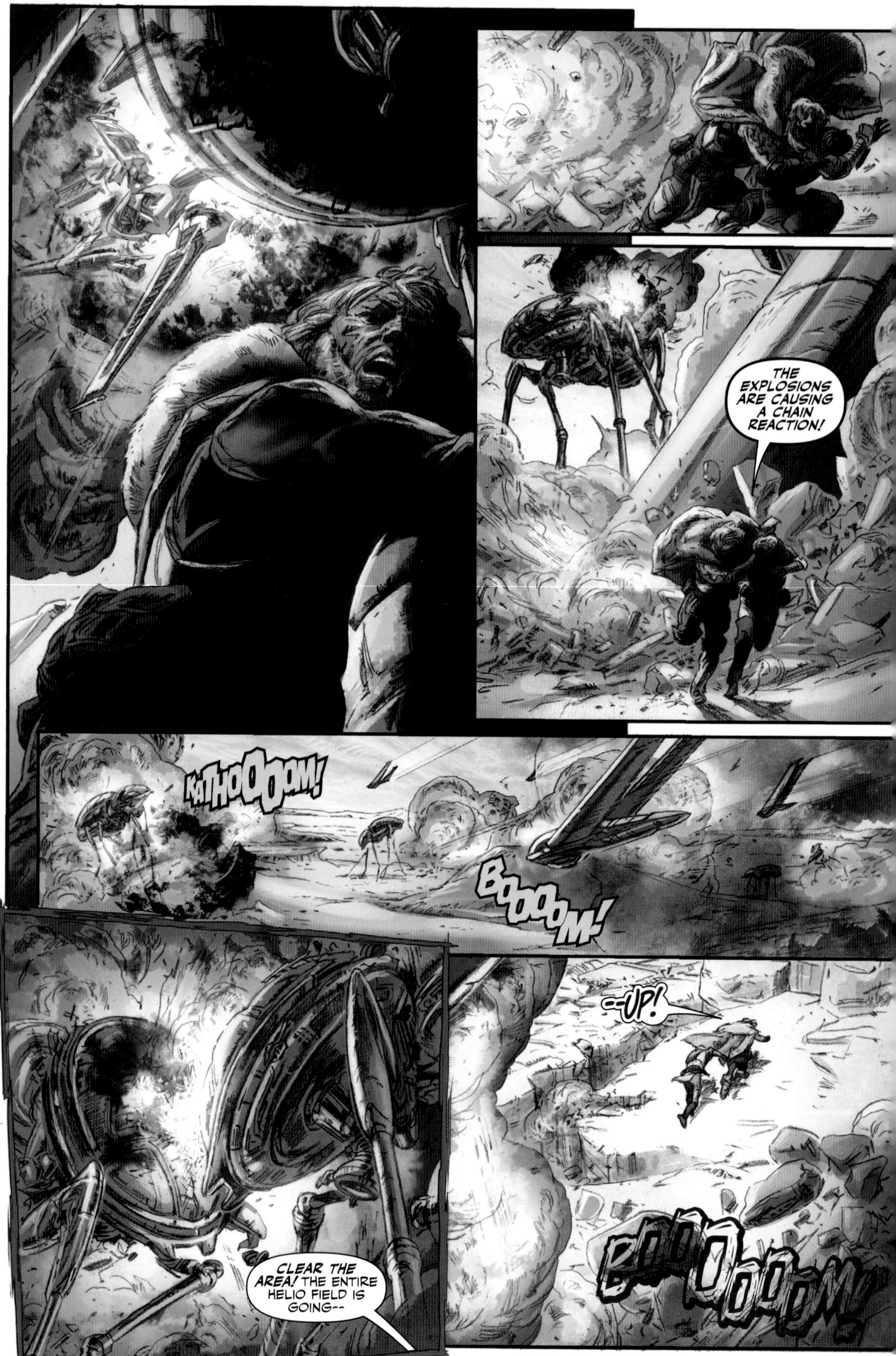
THE EXPLOSIONS ARE CAUSING A CHAIN REACTION!
KATHOOOOOM!
BOOOOOM!
CLEAR THE AREA! THE ENTIRE HELIO FIELD IS GOING--
--UP!
BOOOOOOOOM!

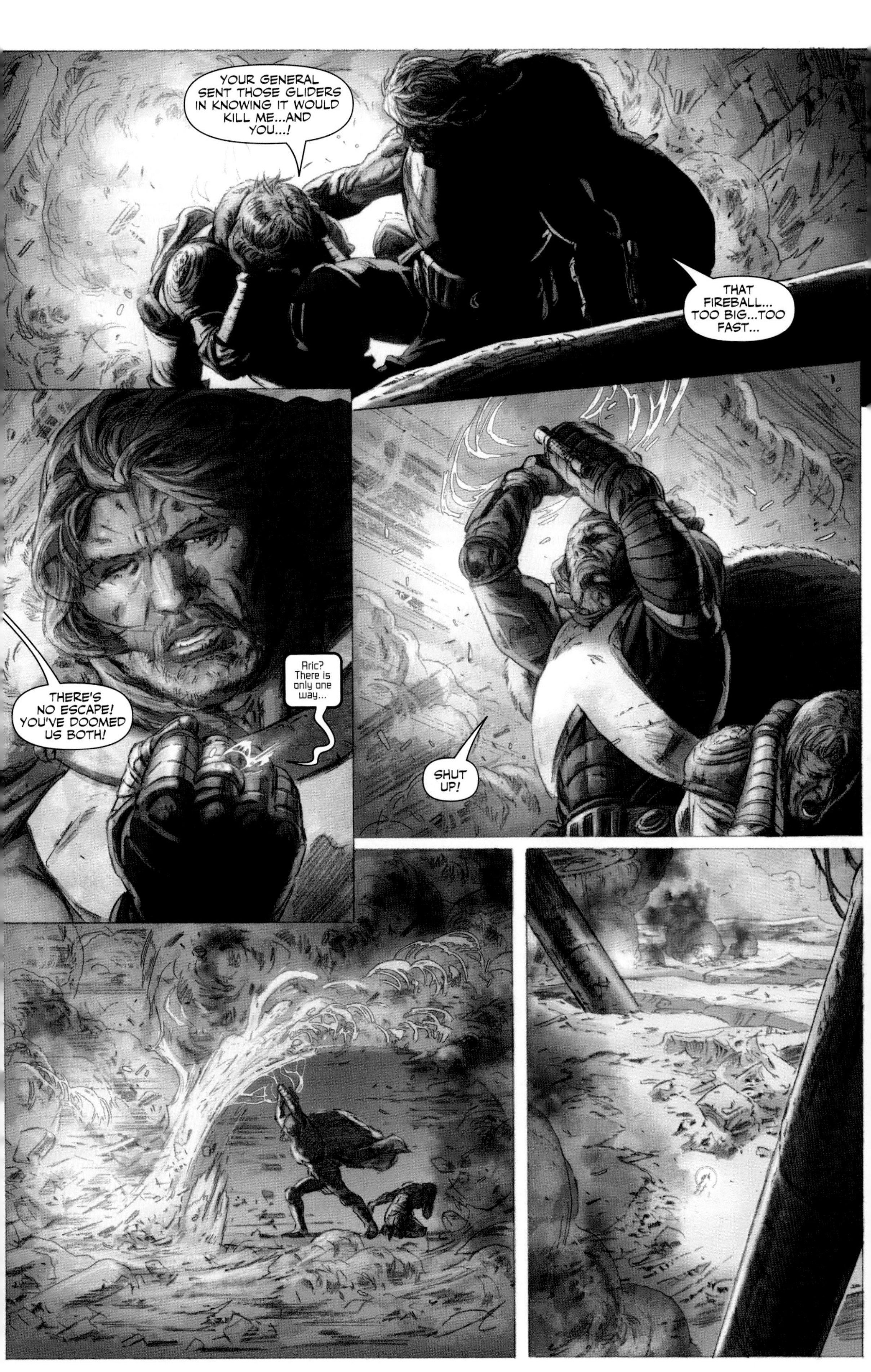
YOUR GENERAL SENT THOSE GLIDERS IN KNOWING IT WOULD KILL ME...AND YOU...!
THAT FIREBALL... TOO BIG...TOO FAST...
THERE'S NO ESCAPE! YOU'VE DOOMED US BOTH!
Aric? There is only one way...
SHUT UP!

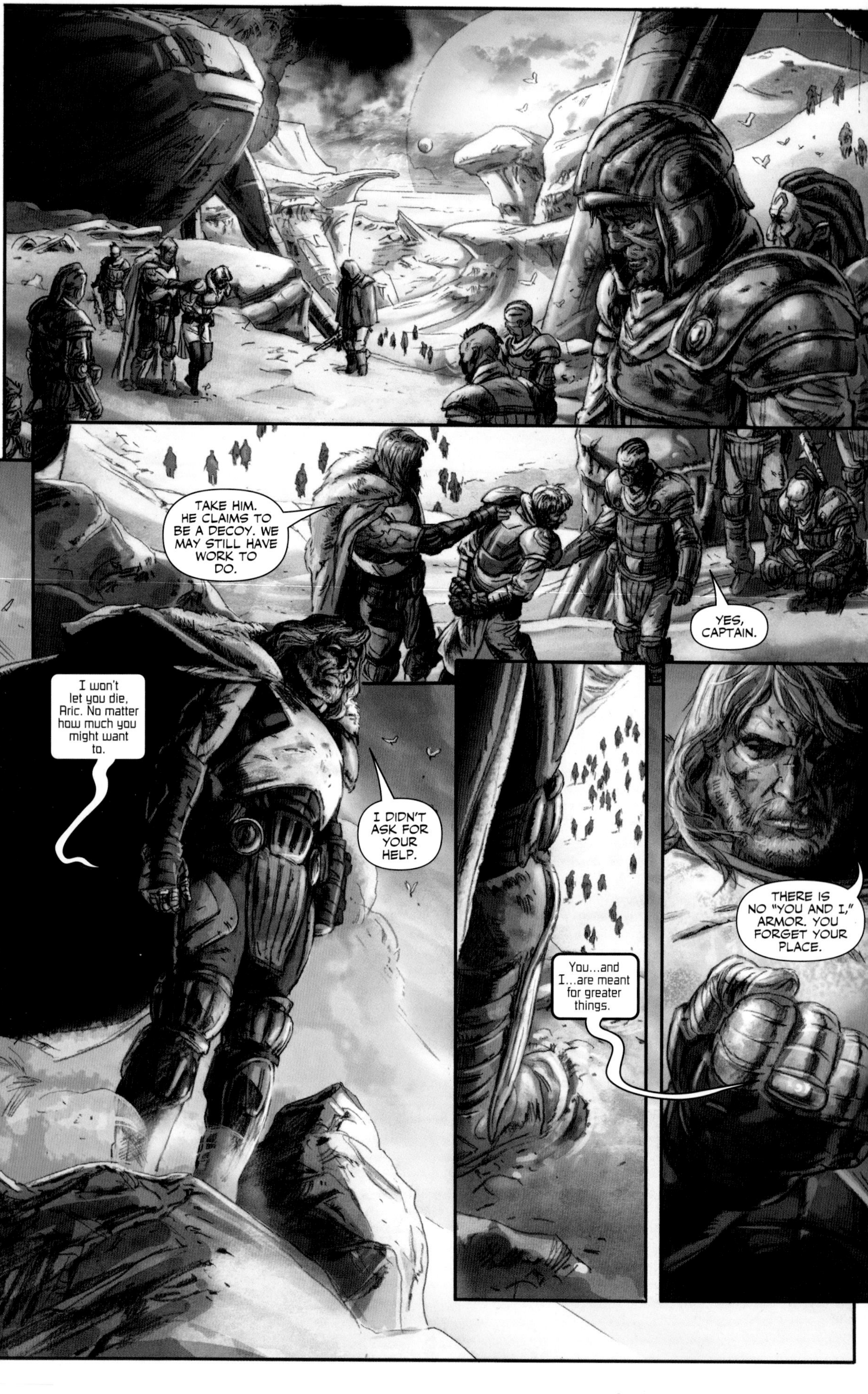
TAKE HIM. HE CLAIMS TO BE A DECOY. WE MAY STILL HAVE WORK TO DO.
YES, CAPTAIN.
I won't let you die, Aric. No matter how much you might want to.
I DIDN'T ASK FOR YOUR HELP.
You...and I...are meant for greater things.
THERE IS NO "YOU AND I," ARMOR. YOU FORGET YOUR PLACE.

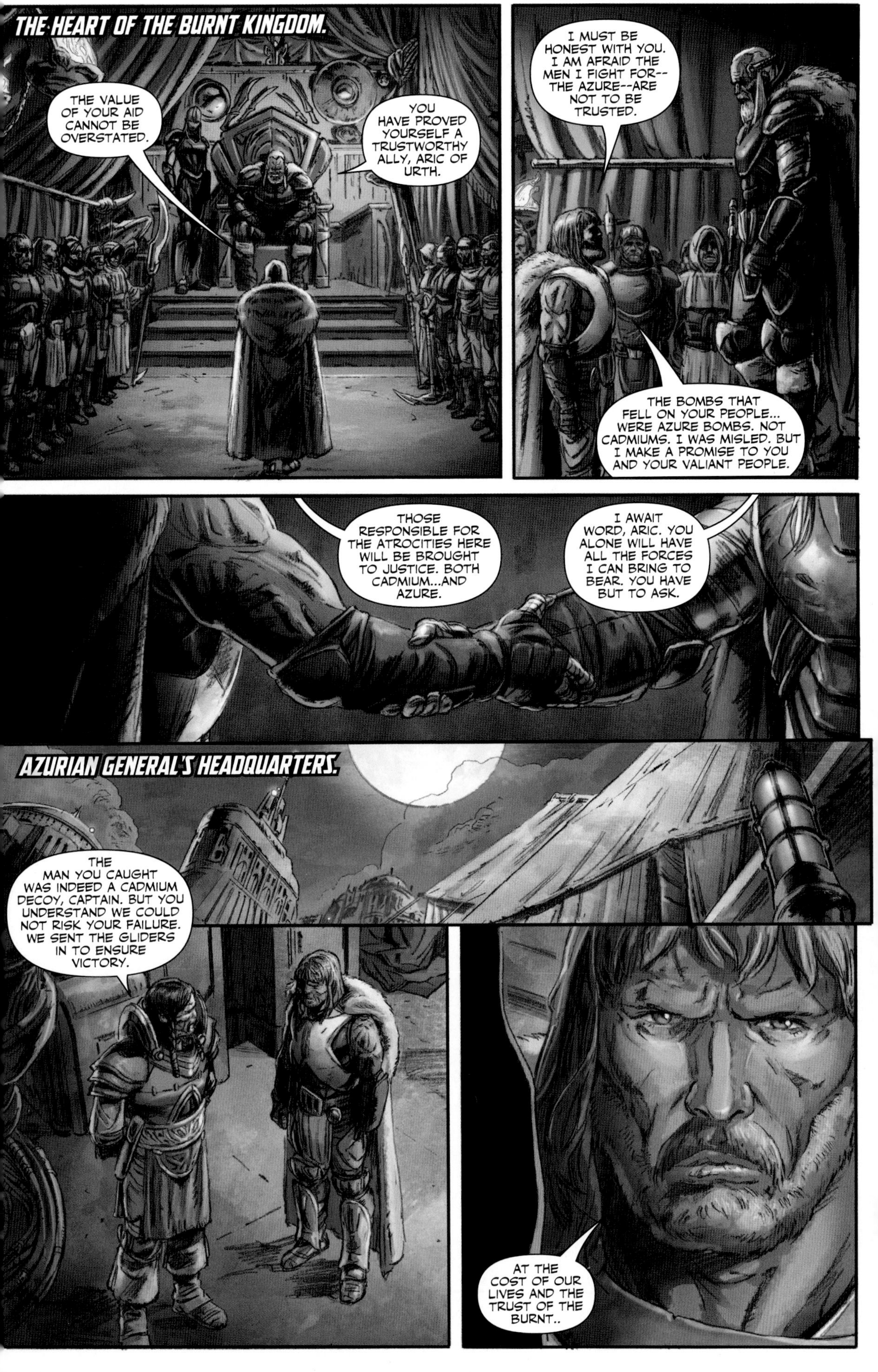
THE HEART OF THE BURNT KINGDOM.
THE VALUE OF YOUR AID CANNOT BE OVERSTATED.
YOU HAVE PROVED YOURSELF A TRUSTWORTHY ALLY, ARIC OF URTH.
I MUST BE HONEST WITH YOU. I AM AFRAID THE MEN I FIGHT FOR-- THE AZURE--ARE NOT TO BE TRUSTED.
THE BOMBS THAT FELL ON YOUR PEOPLE... WERE AZURE BOMBS. NOT CADMIUMS. I WAS MISLED. BUT I MAKE A PROMISE TO YOU AND YOUR VALIANT PEOPLE.
THOSE RESPONSIBLE FOR THE ATROCITIES HERE WILL BE BROUGHT TO JUSTICE. BOTH CADMIUM...AND AZURE.
I AWAIT WORD, ARIC. YOU ALONE WILL HAVE ALL THE FORCES I CAN BRING TO BEAR. YOU HAVE BUT TO ASK.
AZURIAN GENERAL'S HEADQUARTERS.
THE MAN YOU CAUGHT WAS INDEED A CADMIUM DECOY, CAPTAIN. BUT YOU UNDERSTAND WE COULD NOT RISK YOUR FAILURE. WE SENT THE GLIDERS IN TO ENSURE VICTORY.
AT THE COST OF OUR LIVES AND THE TRUST OF THE BURNT..

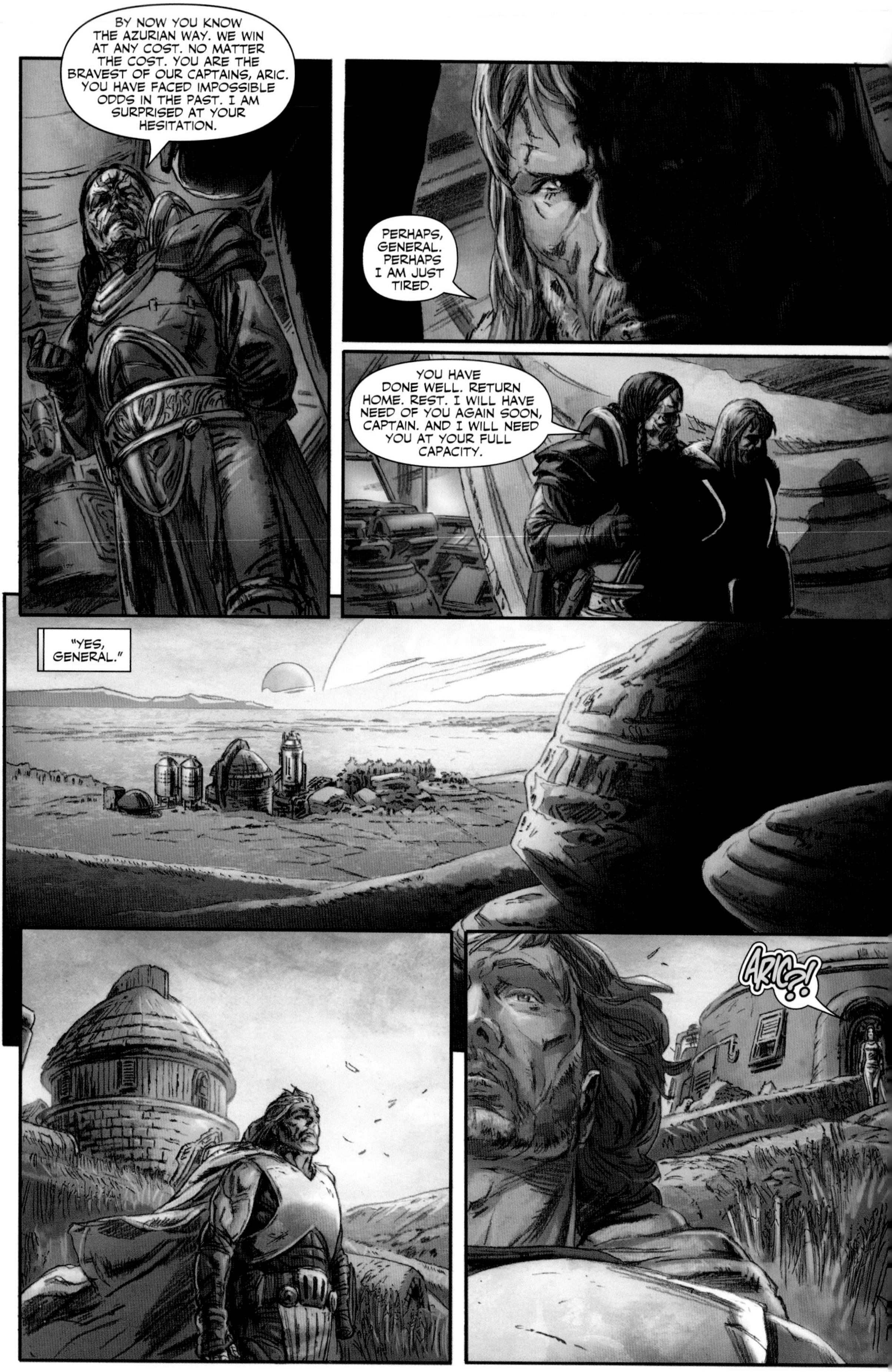
BY NOW YOU KNOW THE AZURIAN WAY. WE WIN AT ANY COST. NO MATTER THE COST. YOU ARE THE BRAVEST OF OUR CAPTAINS, ARIC. YOU HAVE FACED IMPOSSIBLE ODDS IN THE PAST. I AM SURPRISED AT YOUR HESITATION.
PERHAPS, GENERAL. PERHAPS I AM JUST TIRED.
YOU HAVE DONE WELL. RETURN HOME. REST. I WILL HAVE NEED OF YOU AGAIN SOON, CAPTAIN. AND I WILL NEED YOU AT YOUR FULL CAPACITY.
"YES, GENERAL."
ARIC?!

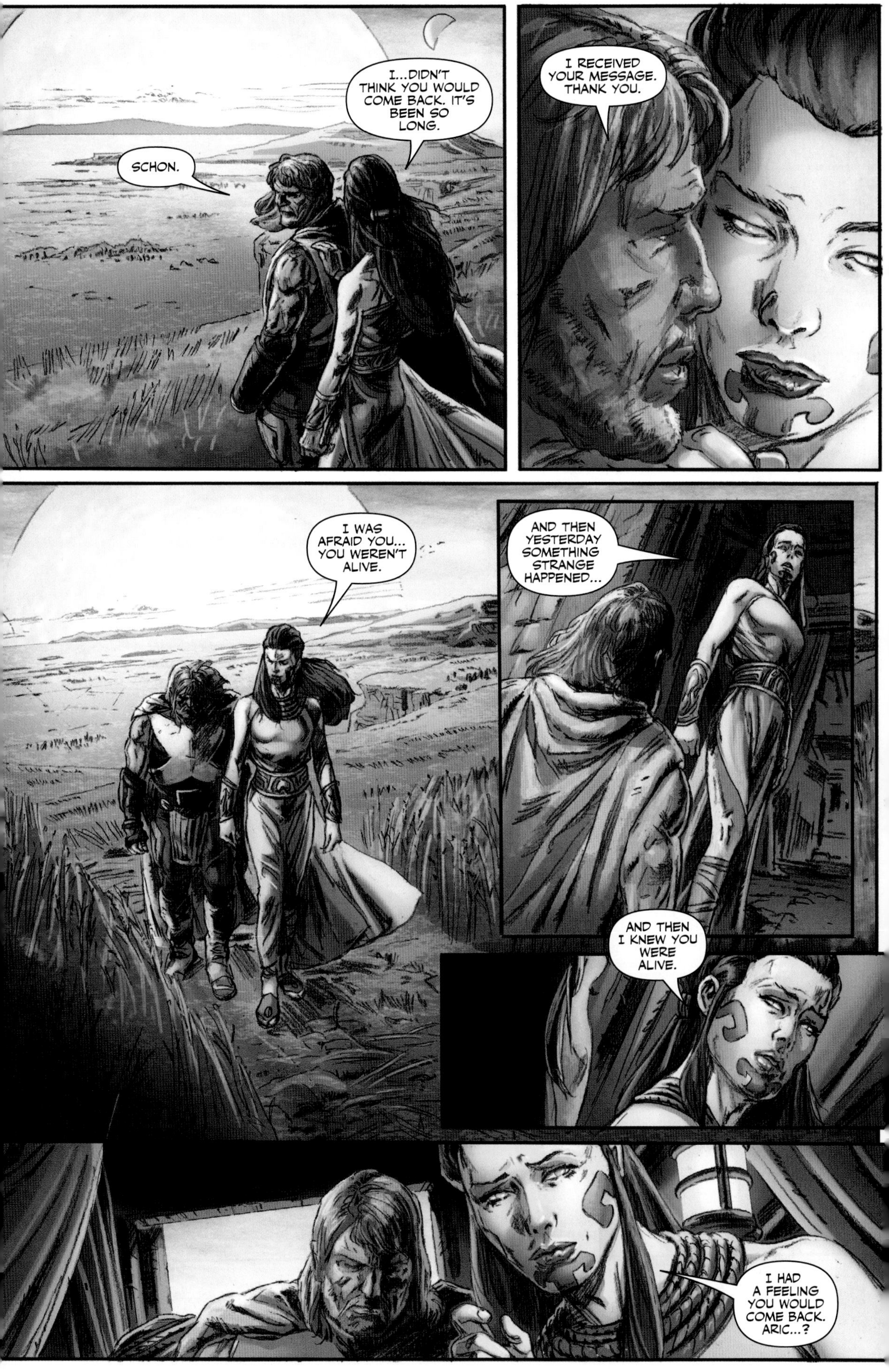
SCHON.
I...DIDN'T THINK YOU WOULD COME BACK. IT'S BEEN SO LONG.
I RECEIVED YOUR MESSAGE. THANK YOU.
I WAS AFRAID YOU... YOU WEREN'T ALIVE.
AND THEN YESTERDAY SOMETHING STRANGE HAPPENED...
AND THEN I KNEW YOU WERE ALIVE.
I HAD A FEELING YOU WOULD COME BACK. ARIC...?

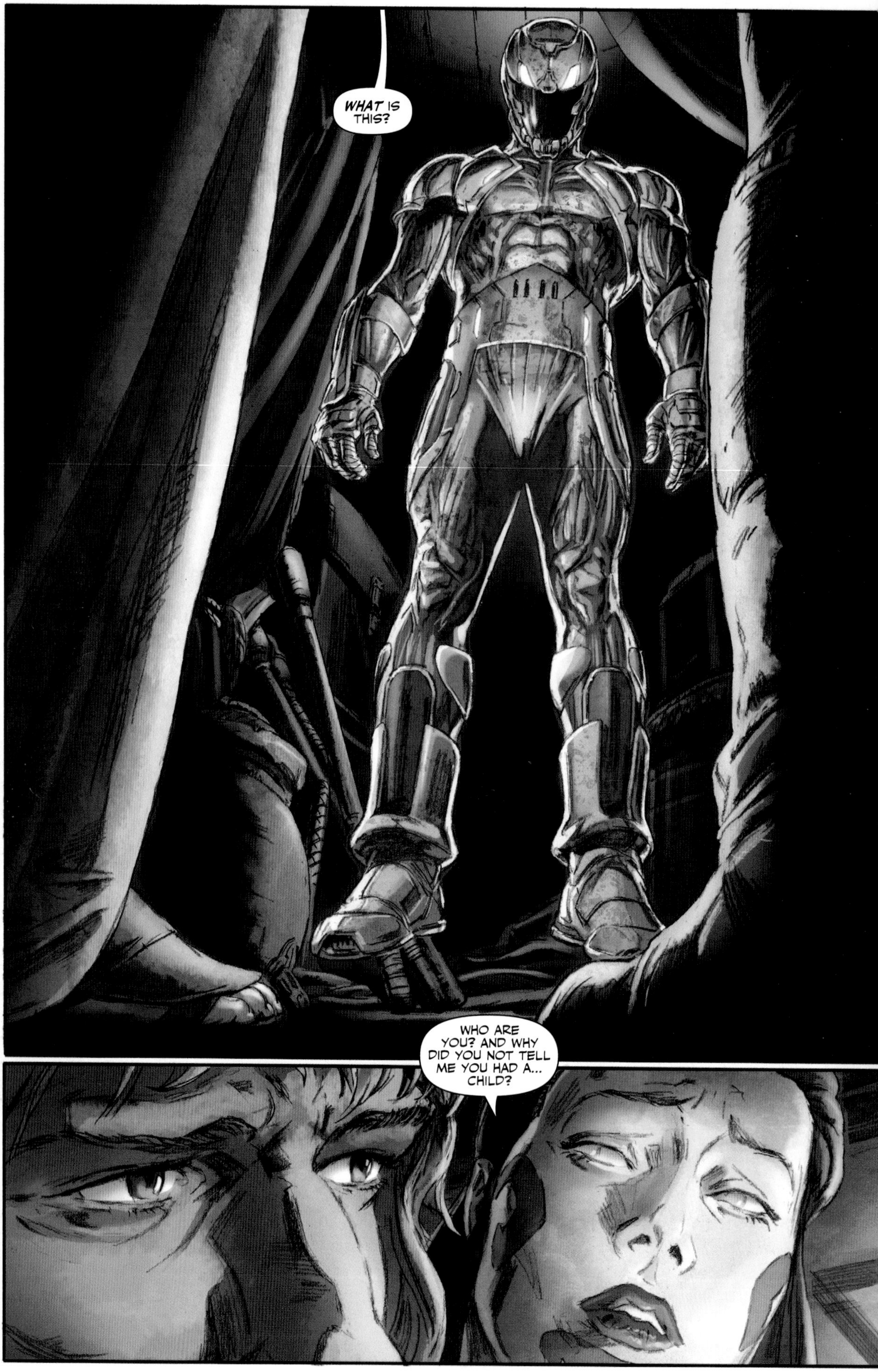

WHAT IS THIS?
WHO ARE YOU? AND WHY DID YOU NOT TELL ME YOU HAD A... CHILD?

X-O MANOWAR

GENERAL

ISSUE 05

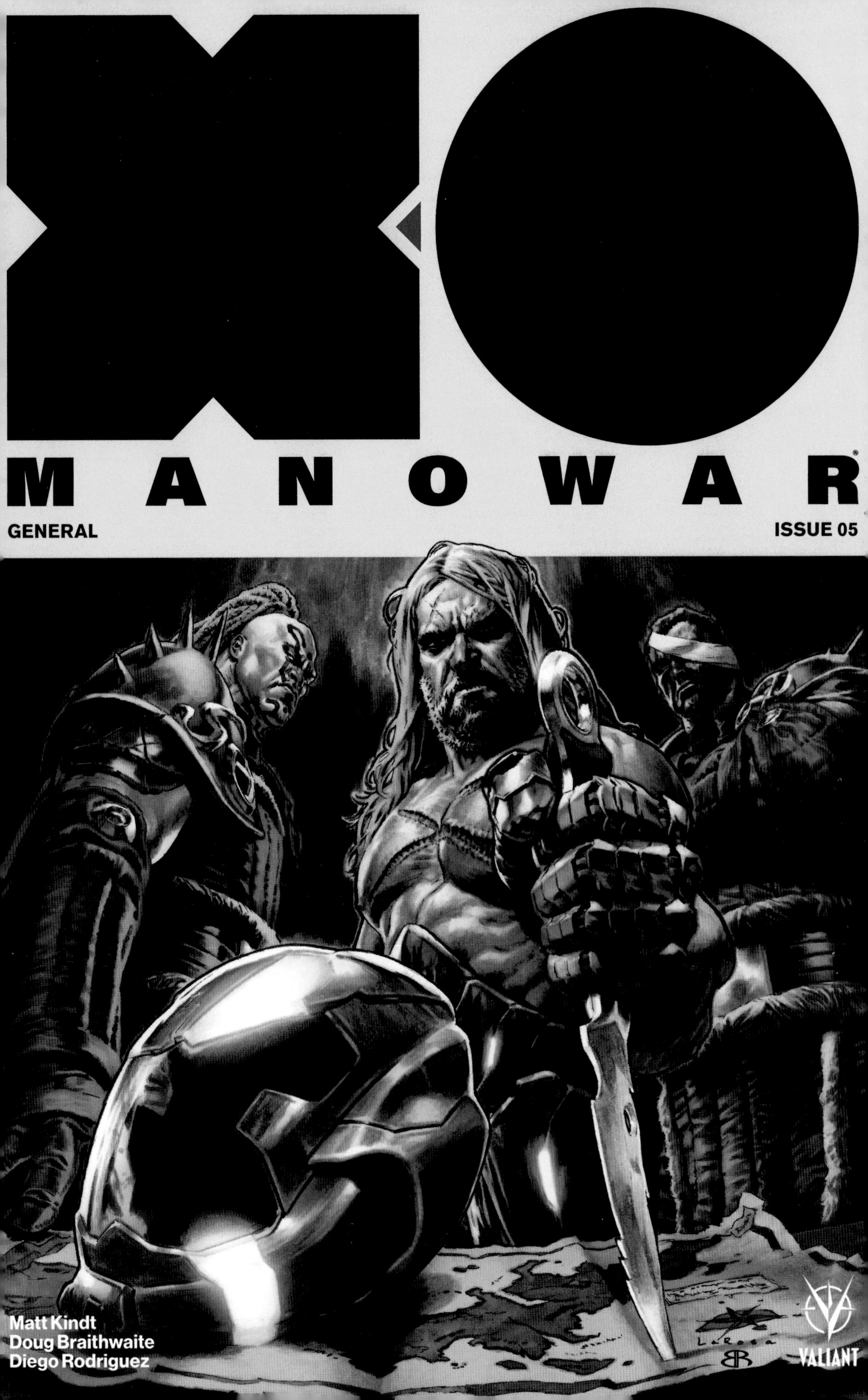
Matt Kindt
Doug Braithwaite
Diego Rodriguez
VALIANT

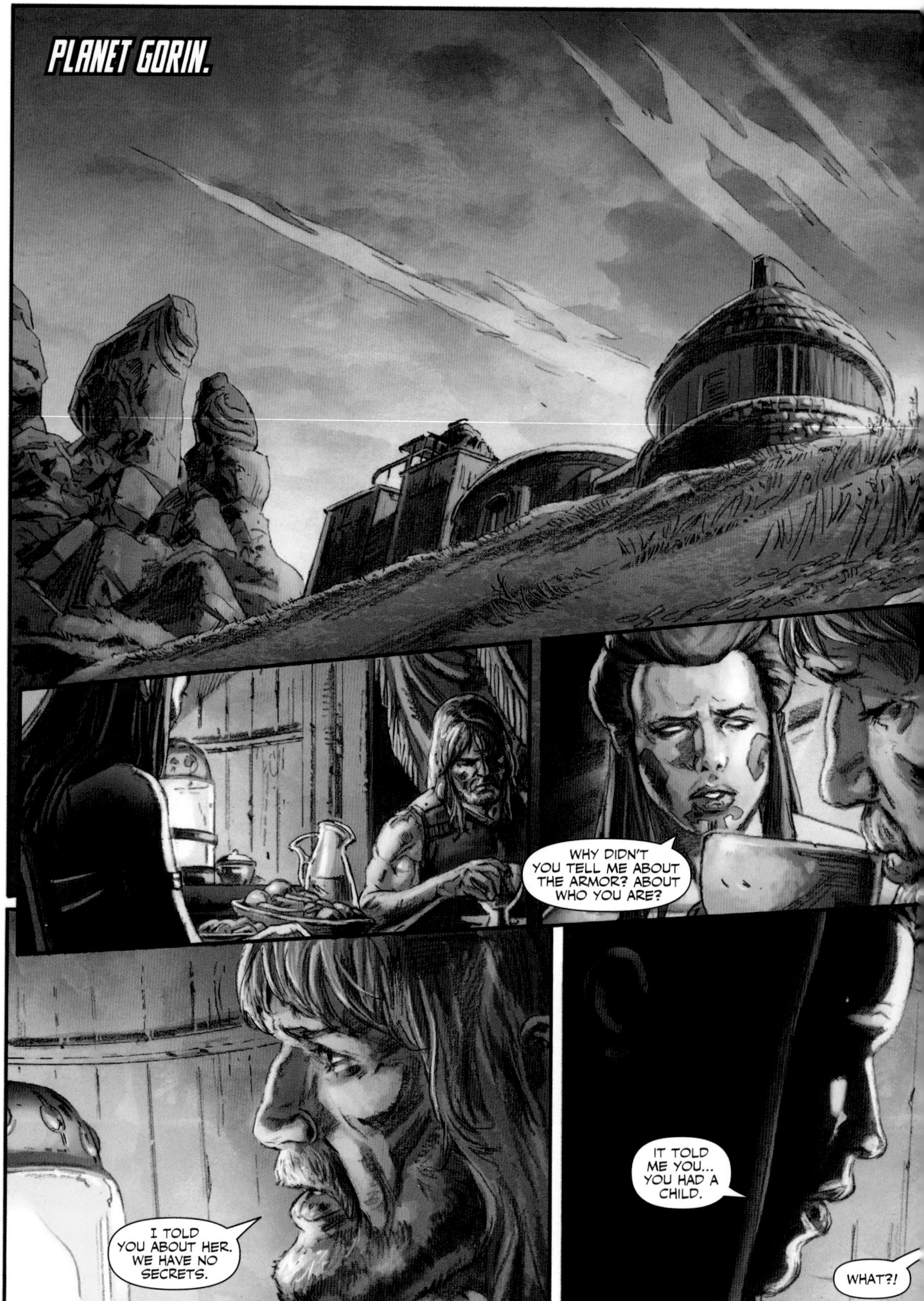
PLANET GORIN.
WHY DIDN'T YOU TELL ME ABOUT THE ARMOR? ABOUT WHO YOU ARE?
I TOLD YOU ABOUT HER. WE HAVE NO SECRETS.
IT TOLD ME YOU... YOU HAD A CHILD.
WHAT?!

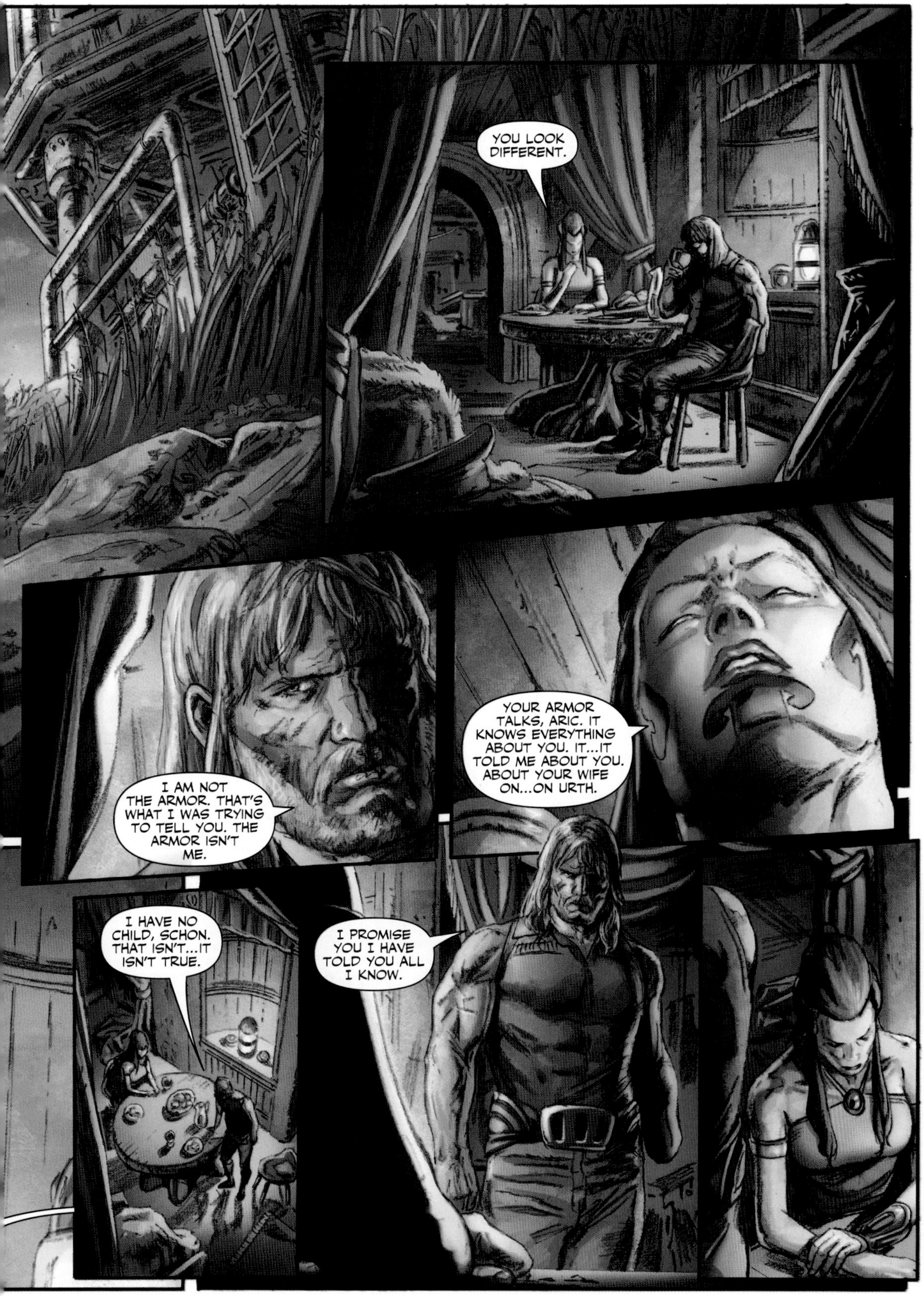
YOU LOOK DIFFERENT.
I AM NOT THE ARMOR. THAT'S WHAT I WAS TRYING TO TELL YOU. THE ARMOR ISN'T ME.
YOUR ARMOR TALKS, ARIC. IT KNOWS EVERYTHING ABOUT YOU. IT...IT TOLD ME ABOUT YOU. ABOUT YOUR WIFE ON...ON URTH.
I HAVE NO CHILD, SCHON. THAT ISN'T...IT ISN'T TRUE.
I PROMISE YOU I HAVE TOLD YOU ALL I KNOW.

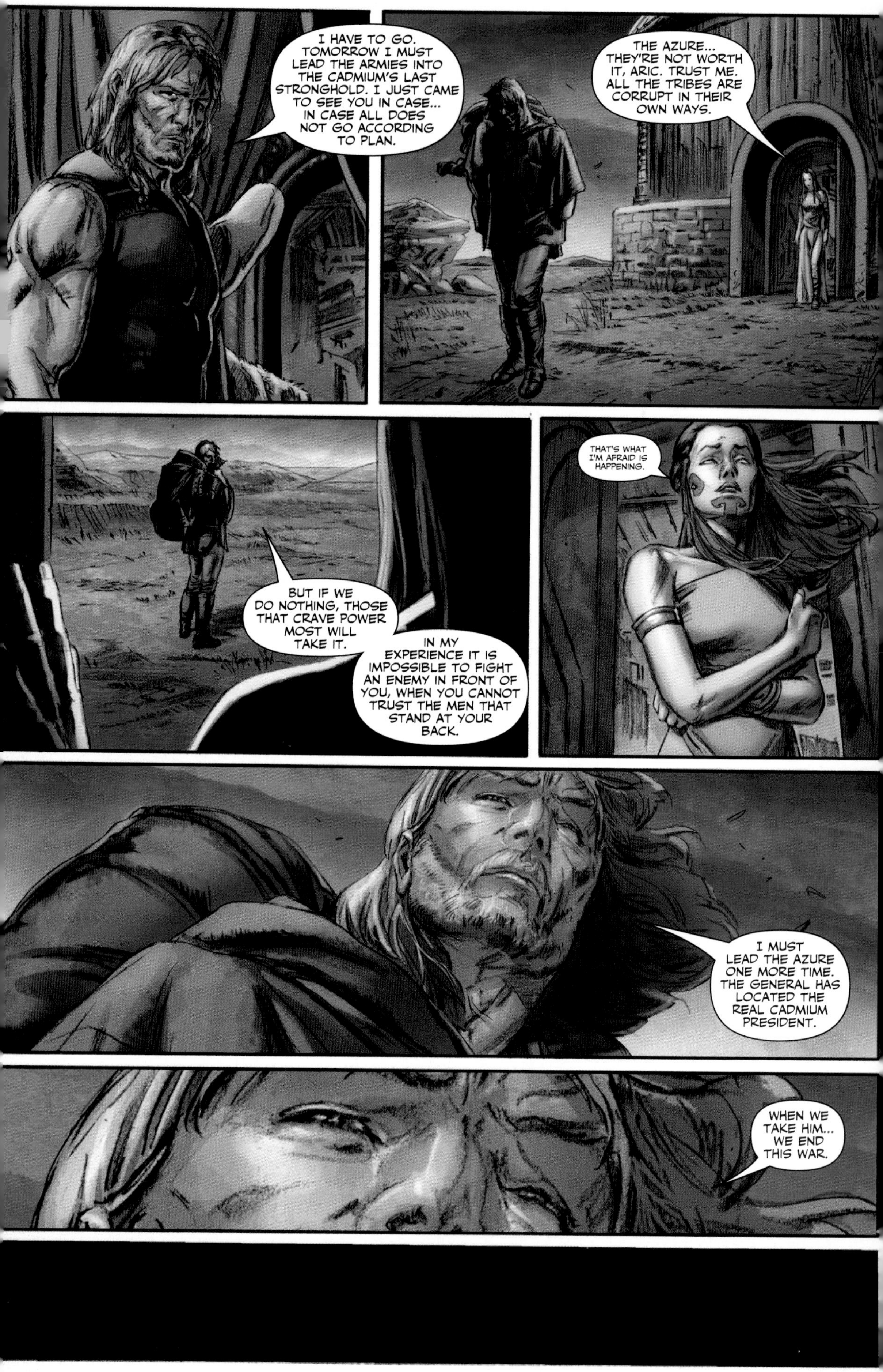
I HAVE TO GO. TOMORROW I MUST LEAD THE ARMIES INTO THE CADMIUM'S LAST STRONGHOLD. I JUST CAME TO SEE YOU IN CASE... IN CASE ALL DOES NOT GO ACCORDING TO PLAN.
THE AZURE... THEY'RE NOT WORTH IT, ARIC. TRUST ME. ALL THE TRIBES ARE CORRUPT IN THEIR OWN WAYS.
BUT IF WE DO NOTHING, THOSE THAT CRAVE POWER MOST WILL TAKE IT.
IN MY EXPERIENCE IT IS IMPOSSIBLE TO FIGHT AN ENEMY IN FRONT OF YOU, WHEN YOU CANNOT TRUST THE MEN THAT STAND AT YOUR BACK.
THAT'S WHAT I'M AFRAID IS HAPPENING.
I MUST LEAD THE AZURE ONE MORE TIME. THE GENERAL HAS LOCATED THE REAL CADMIUM PRESIDENT.
WHEN WE TAKE HIM... WE END THIS WAR.

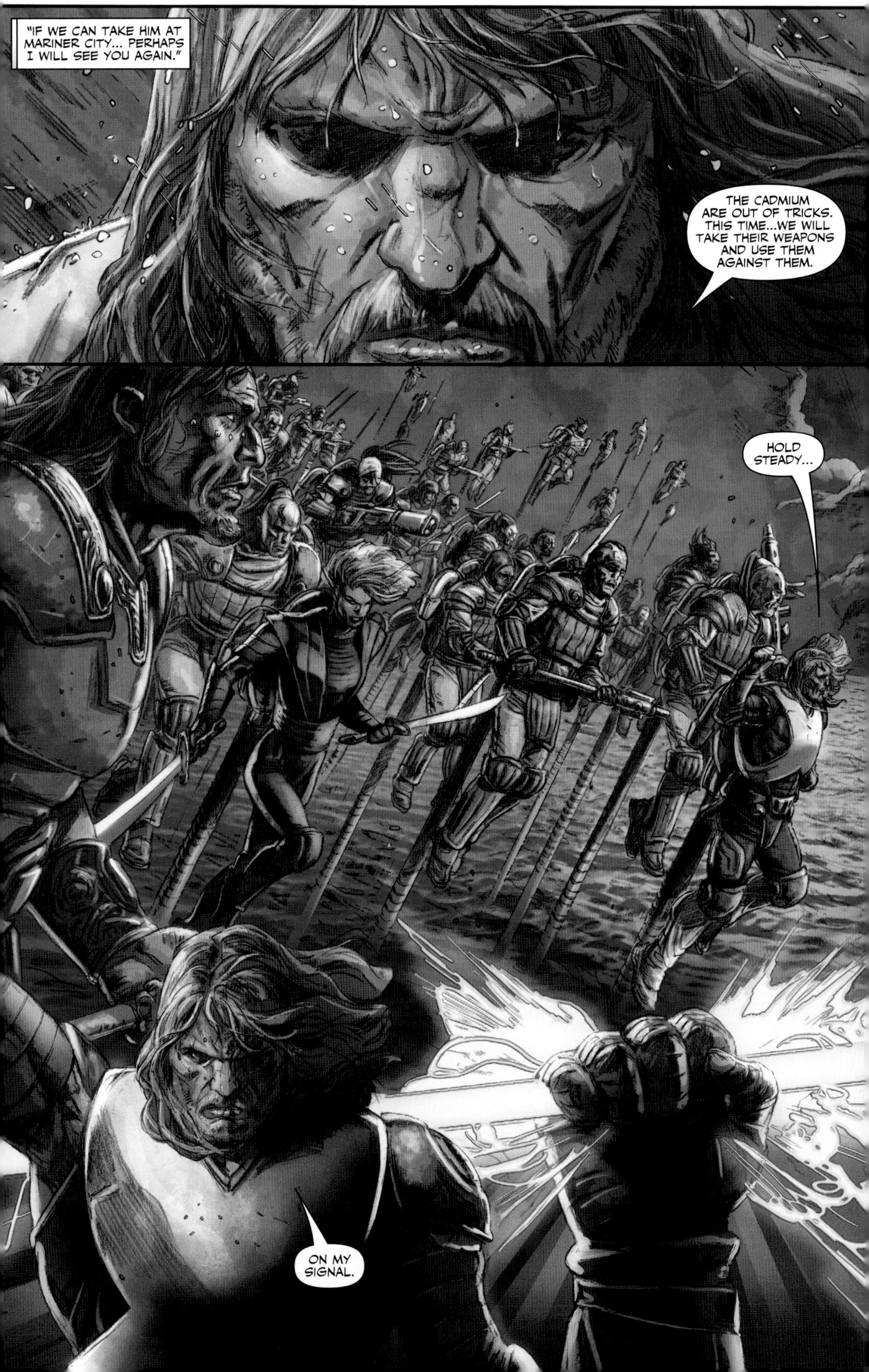
"IF WE CAN TAKE HIM AT MARINER CITY... PERHAPS I WILL SEE YOU AGAIN."
THE CADMIUM ARE OUT OF TRICKS. THIS TIME...WE WILL TAKE THEIR WEAPONS AND USE THEM AGAINST THEM.
HOLD STEADY...
ON MY SIGNAL.

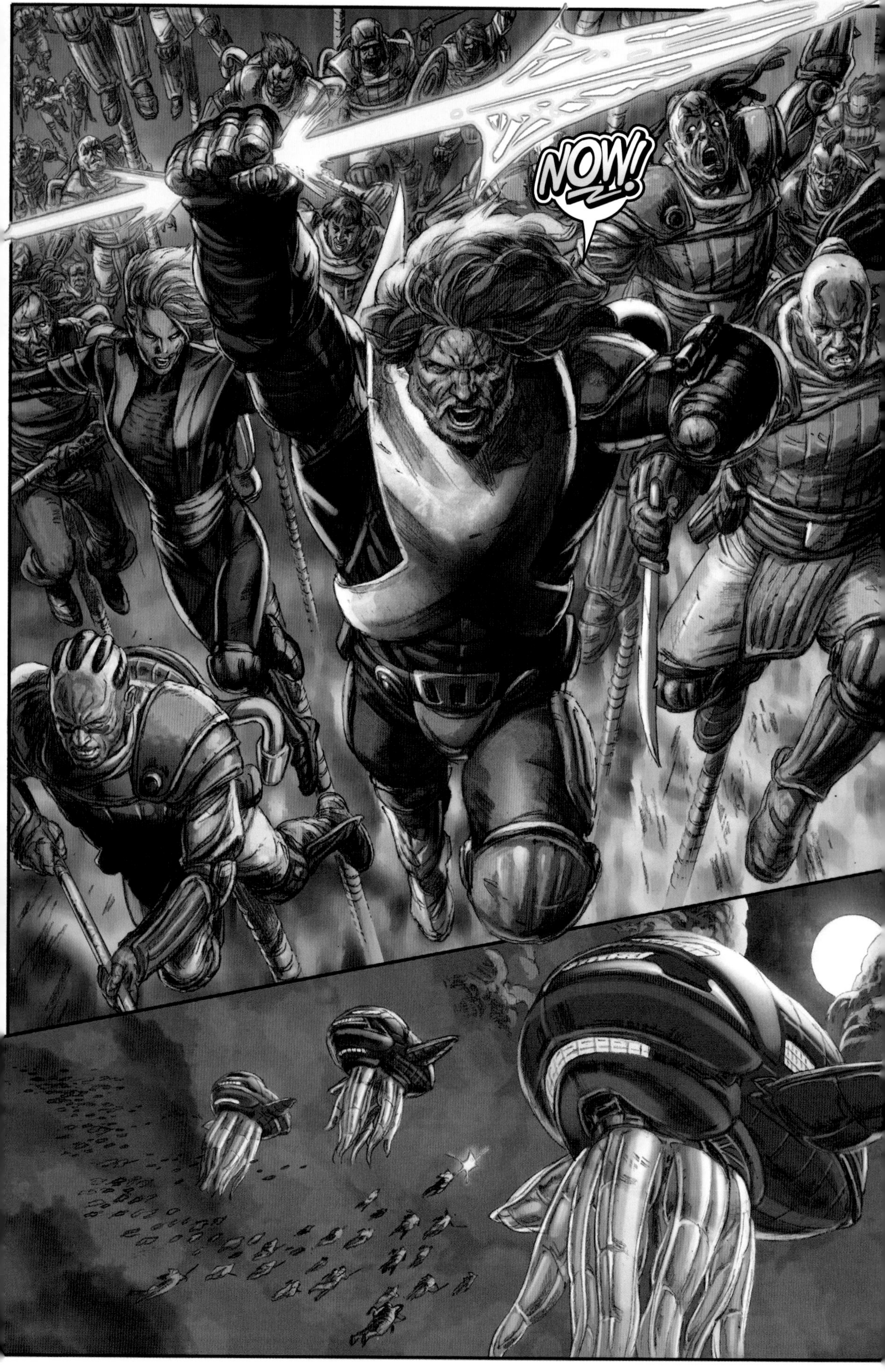
NOW!

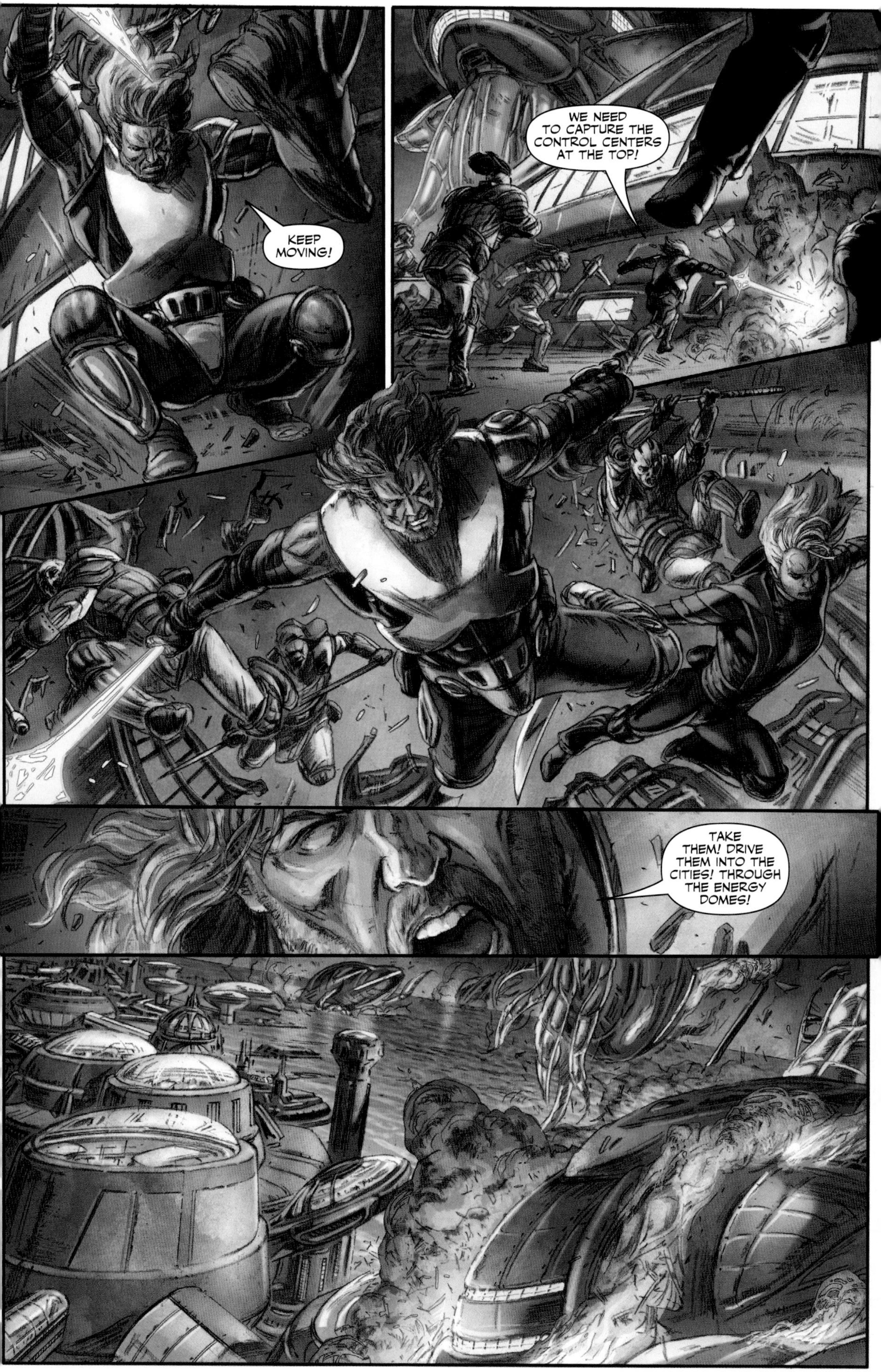
KEEP MOVING!
WE NEED TO CAPTURE THE CONTROL CENTERS AT THE TOP!
TAKE THEM! DRIVE THEM INTO THE CITIES! THROUGH THE ENERGY DOMES!

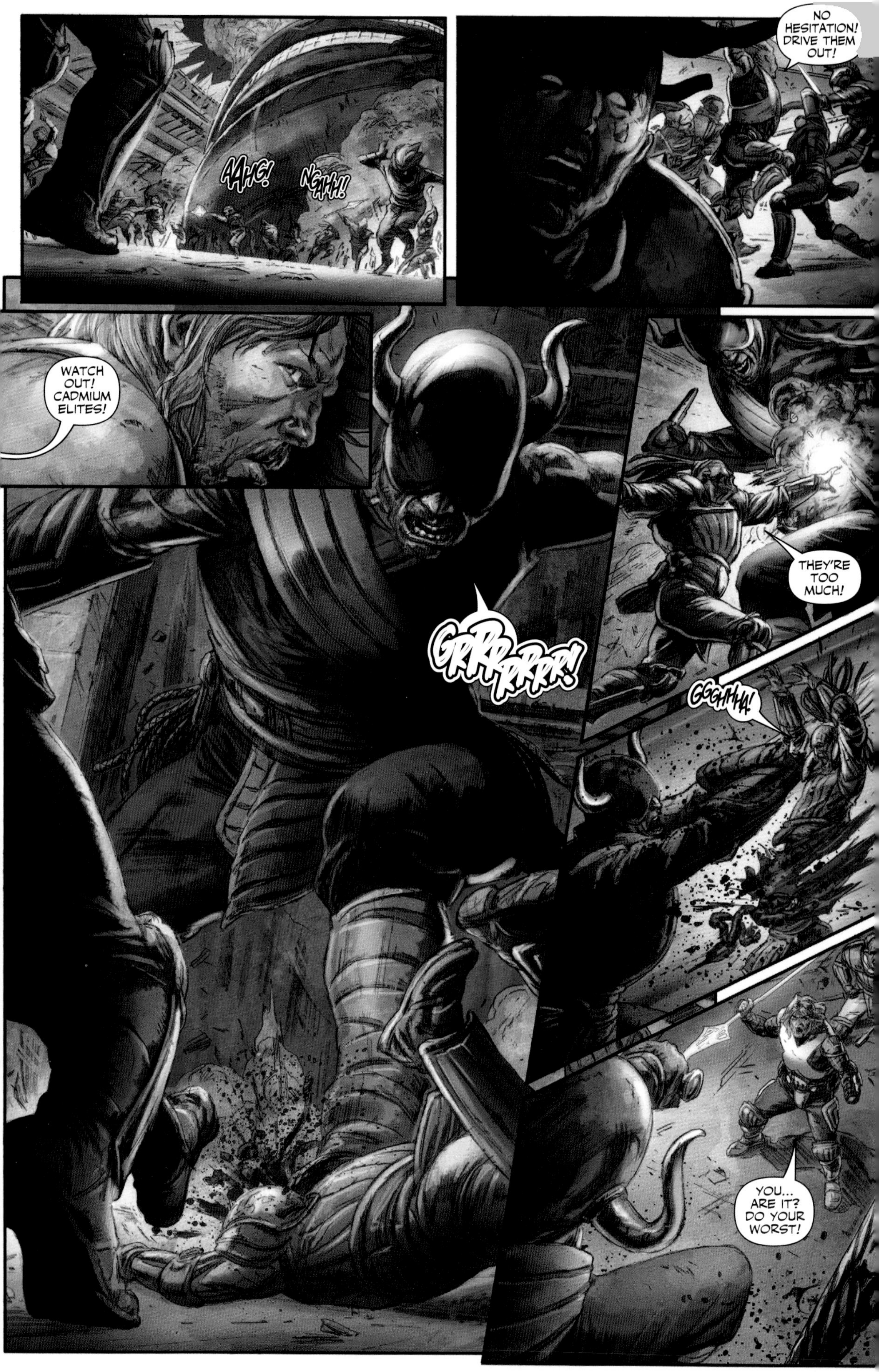
AAHG!
NGAHH!
NO HESITATION! DRIVE THEM OUT!
WATCH OUT! CADMIUM ELITES!
THEY'RE TOO MUCH!
GRRRRRRR!
GGGHHHA!
YOU... ARE IT? DO YOUR WORST!

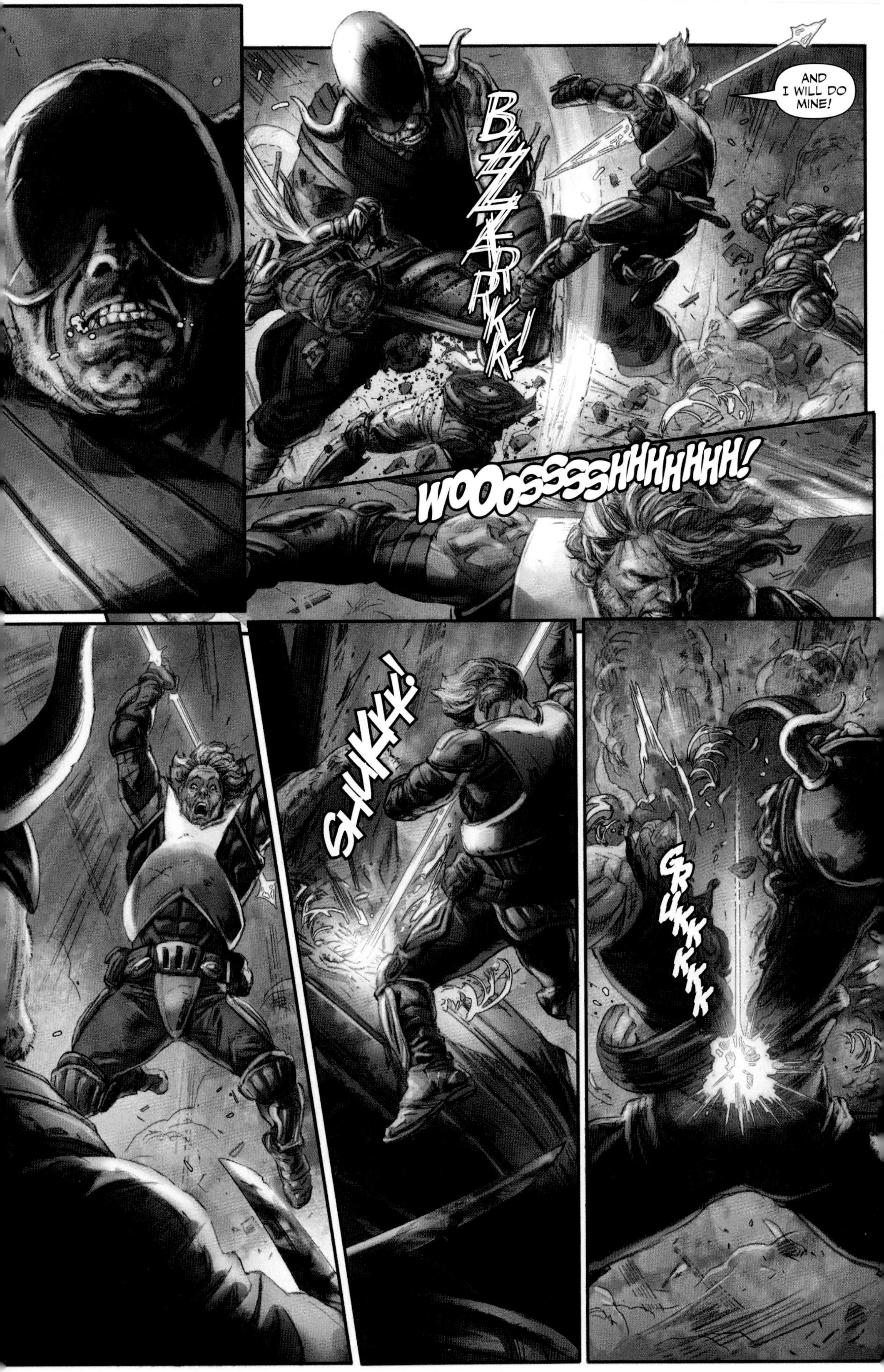

BZZZARRKK!
AND I WILL DO MINE!
WOOOSSSSSHHHHHHH!
SHUKKK!
GRUKKKK

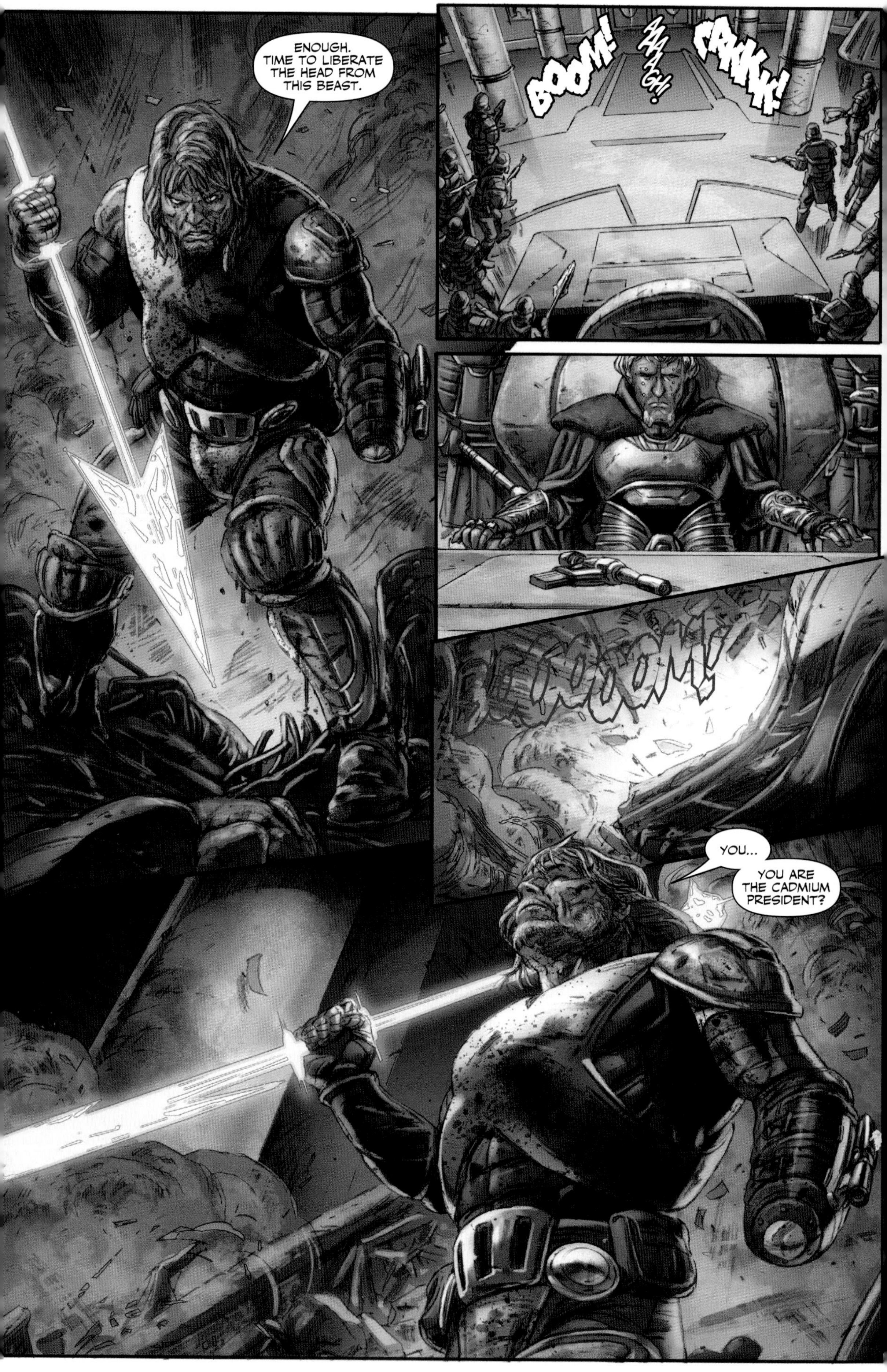
ENOUGH. TIME TO LIBERATE THE HEAD FROM THIS BEAST.
BOOM!
AAAAGH!
CRAKK!
YOU...
YOU ARE THE CADMIUM PRESIDENT?

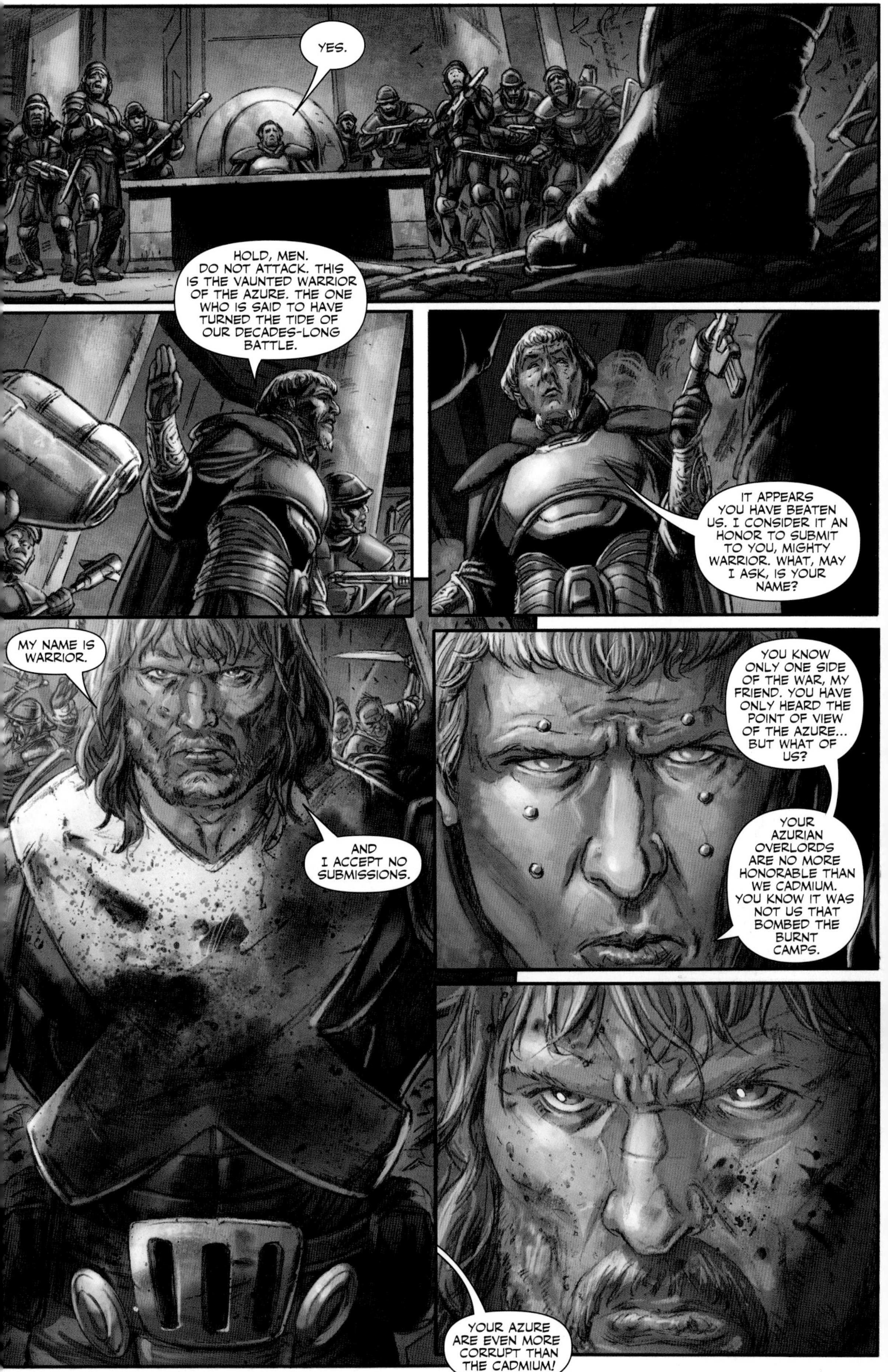
YES.
HOLD, MEN. DO NOT ATTACK. THIS IS THE VAUNTED WARRIOR OF THE AZURE. THE ONE WHO IS SAID TO HAVE TURNED THE TIDE OF OUR DECADES-LONG BATTLE.
IT APPEARS YOU HAVE BEATEN US. I CONSIDER IT AN HONOR TO SUBMIT TO YOU, MIGHTY WARRIOR. WHAT, MAY I ASK, IS YOUR NAME?
MY NAME IS WARRIOR.
AND I ACCEPT NO SUBMISSIONS.
YOU KNOW ONLY ONE SIDE OF THE WAR, MY FRIEND. YOU HAVE ONLY HEARD THE POINT OF VIEW OF THE AZURE... BUT WHAT OF US?
YOUR AZURIAN OVERLORDS ARE NO MORE HONORABLE THAN WE CADMIUM. YOU KNOW IT WAS NOT US THAT BOMBED THE BURNT CAMPS.
YOUR AZURE ARE EVEN MORE CORRUPT THAN THE CADMIUM!

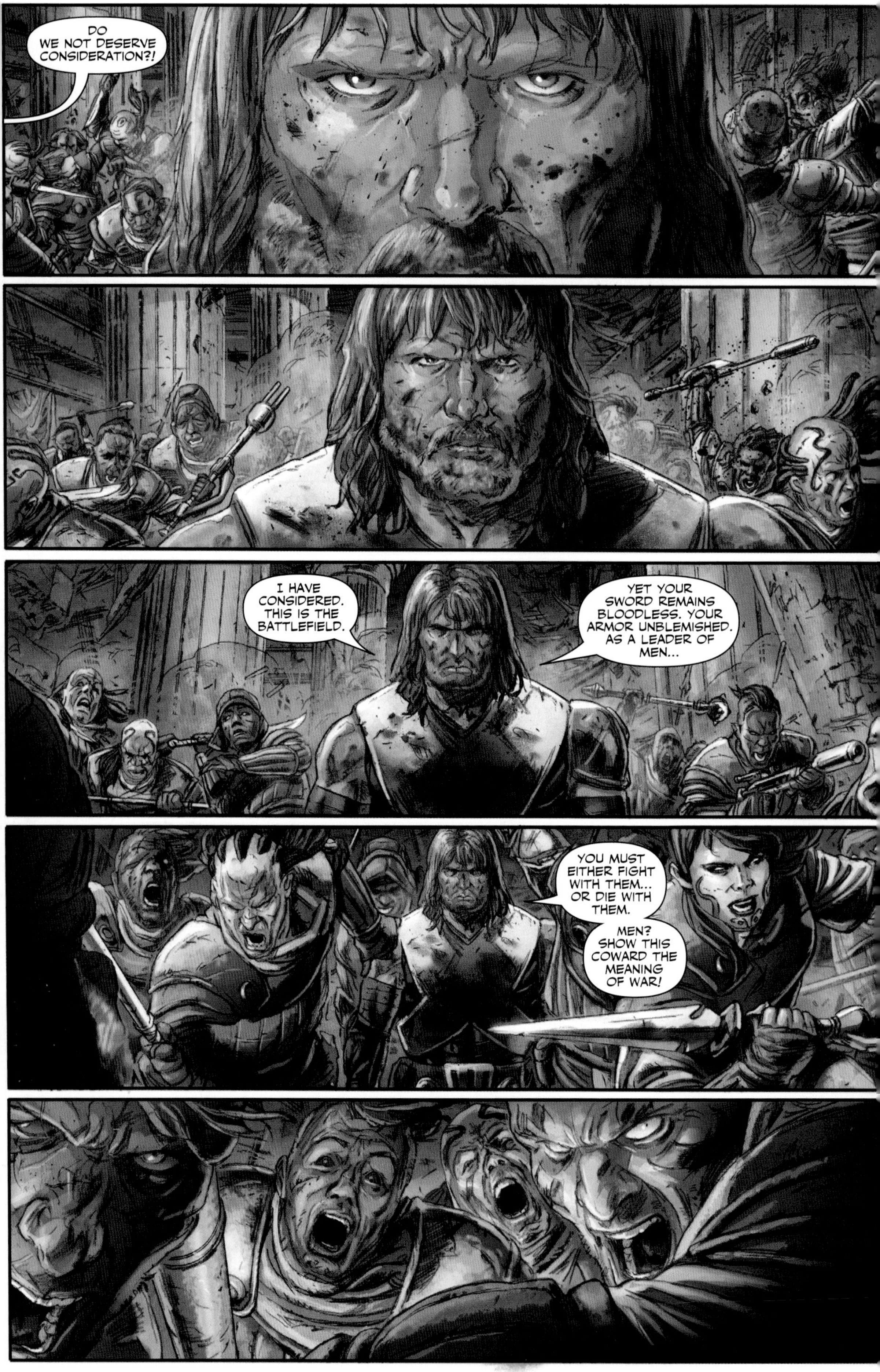
DO WE NOT DESERVE CONSIDERATION?!
I HAVE CONSIDERED. THIS IS THE BATTLEFIELD.
YET YOUR SWORD REMAINS BLOODLESS. YOUR ARMOR UNBLEMISHED. AS A LEADER OF MEN...
YOU MUST EITHER FIGHT WITH THEM... OR DIE WITH THEM.
MEN? SHOW THIS COWARD THE MEANING OF WAR!

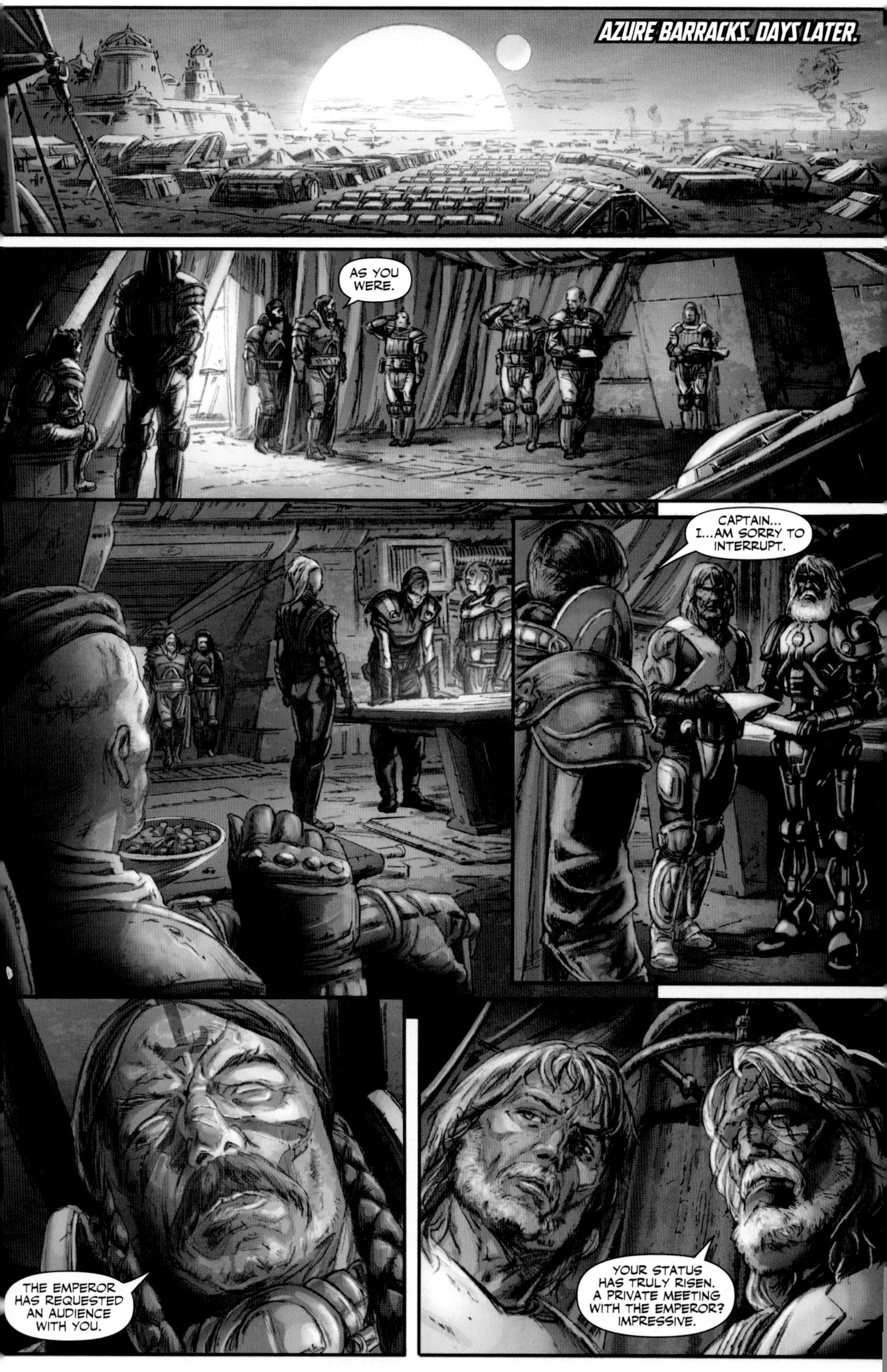
AZURE BARRACKS. DAYS LATER.
AS YOU WERE.
CAPTAIN... I...AM SORRY TO INTERRUPT.
THE EMPEROR HAS REQUESTED AN AUDIENCE WITH YOU.
YOUR STATUS HAS TRULY RISEN. A PRIVATE MEETING WITH THE EMPEROR? IMPRESSIVE.

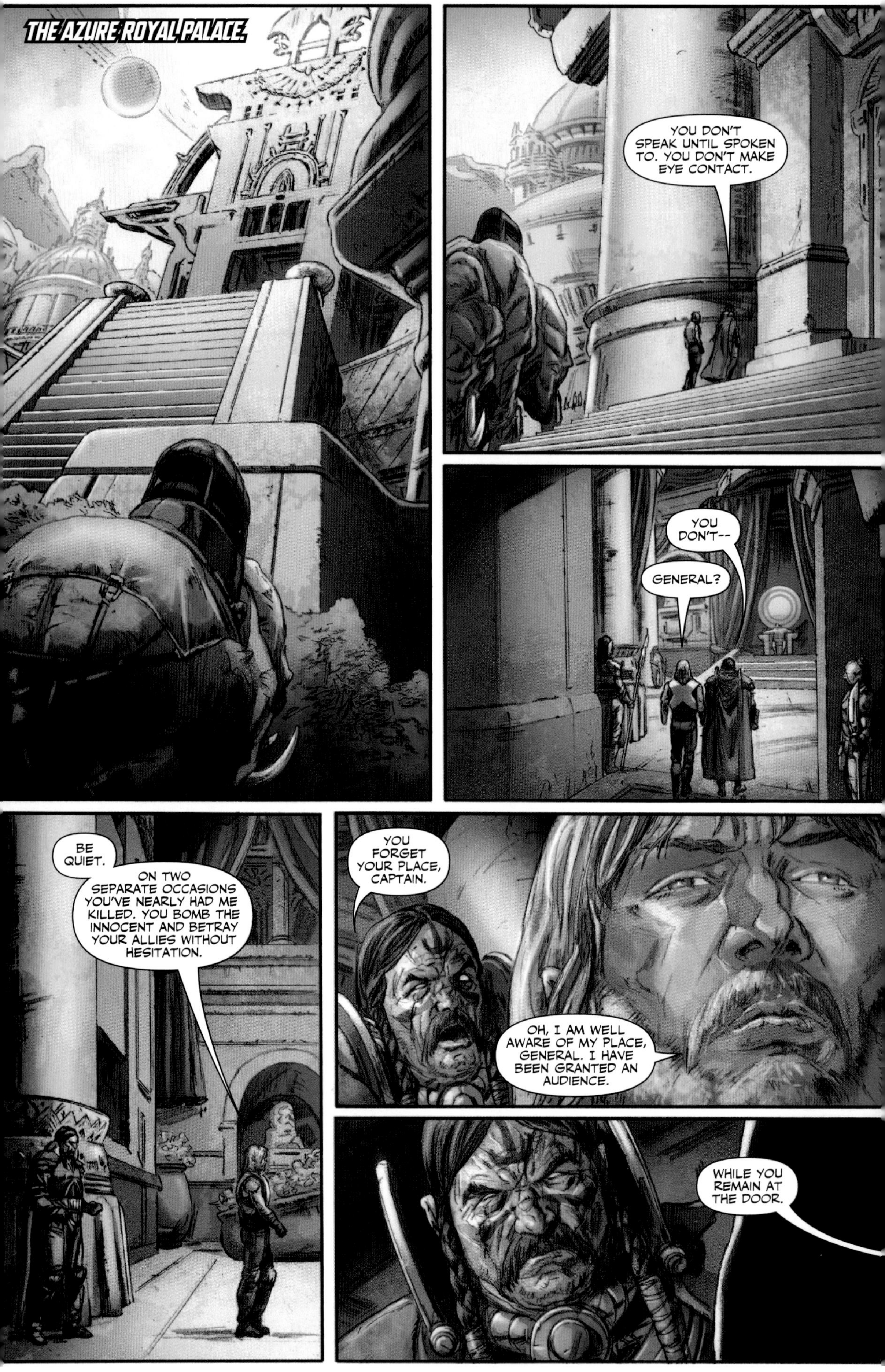
THE AZURE ROYAL PALACE.
YOU DON'T SPEAK UNTIL SPOKEN TO. YOU DON'T MAKE EYE CONTACT.
YOU DON'T--
GENERAL?
BE QUIET.
ON TWO SEPARATE OCCASIONS YOU'VE NEARLY HAD ME KILLED. YOU BOMB THE INNOCENT AND BETRAY YOUR ALLIES WITHOUT HESITATION.
YOU FORGET YOUR PLACE, CAPTAIN.
OH, I AM WELL AWARE OF MY PLACE, GENERAL. I HAVE BEEN GRANTED AN AUDIENCE.
WHILE YOU REMAIN AT THE DOOR.

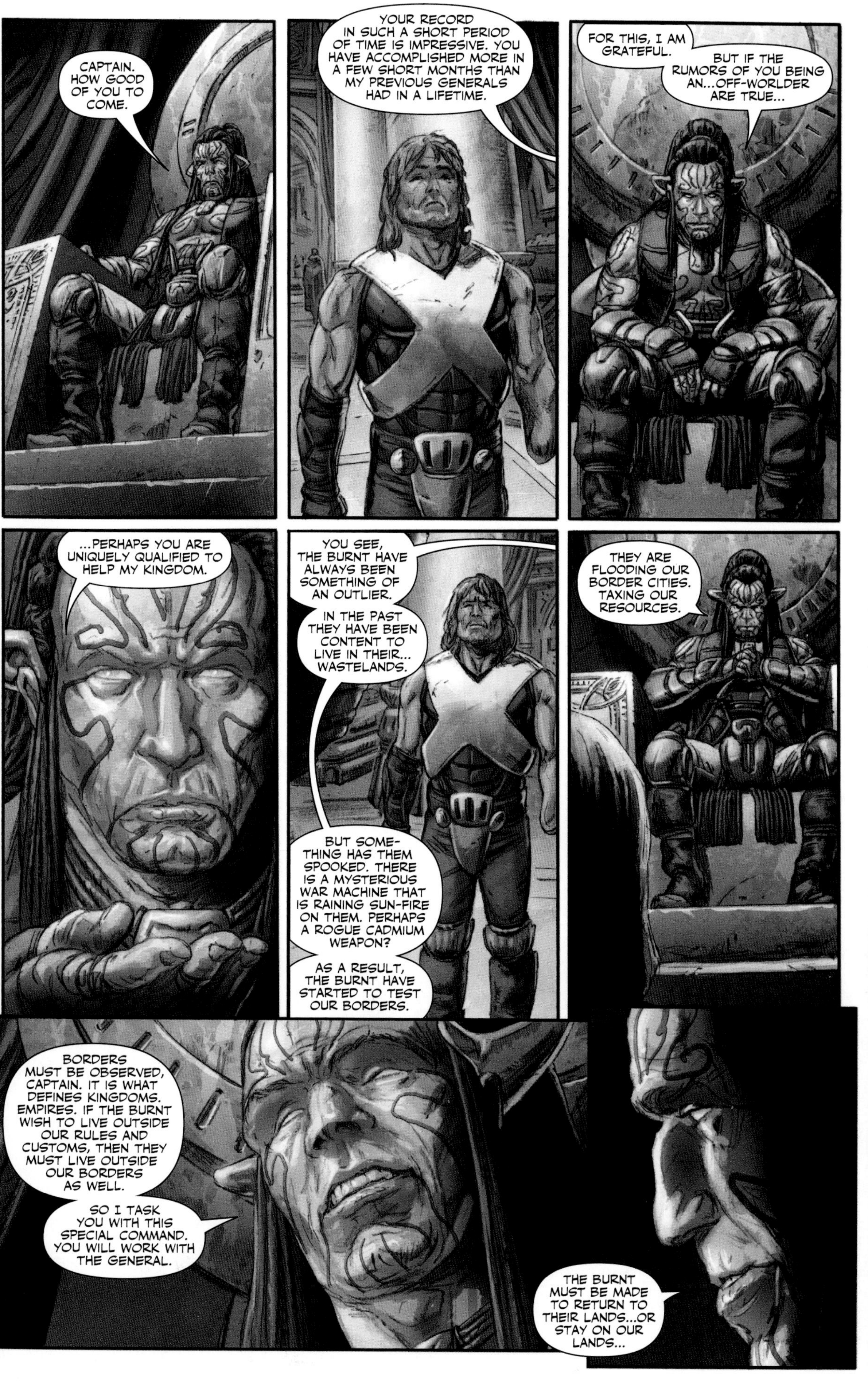
CAPTAIN. HOW GOOD OF YOU TO COME.
YOUR RECORD IN SUCH A SHORT PERIOD OF TIME IS IMPRESSIVE. YOU HAVE ACCOMPLISHED MORE IN A FEW SHORT MONTHS THAN MY PREVIOUS GENERALS HAD IN A LIFETIME.
FOR THIS, I AM GRATEFUL.
BUT IF THE RUMORS OF YOU BEING AN...OFF-WORLDER ARE TRUE...
...PERHAPS YOU ARE UNIQUELY QUALIFIED TO HELP MY KINGDOM.
YOU SEE, THE BURNT HAVE ALWAYS BEEN SOMETHING OF AN OUTLIER.
IN THE PAST THEY HAVE BEEN CONTENT TO LIVE IN THEIR... WASTELANDS.
BUT SOME-THING HAS THEM SPOOKED. THERE IS A MYSTERIOUS WAR MACHINE THAT IS RAINING SUN-FIRE ON THEM. PERHAPS A ROGUE CADMIUM WEAPON?
AS A RESULT, THE BURNT HAVE STARTED TO TEST OUR BORDERS.
THEY ARE FLOODING OUR BORDER CITIES. TAXING OUR RESOURCES.
BORDERS MUST BE OBSERVED, CAPTAIN. IT IS WHAT DEFINES KINGDOMS. EMPIRES. IF THE BURNT WISH TO LIVE OUTSIDE OUR RULES AND CUSTOMS, THEN THEY MUST LIVE OUTSIDE OUR BORDERS AS WELL.
SO I TASK YOU WITH THIS SPECIAL COMMAND. YOU WILL WORK WITH THE GENERAL.
THE BURNT MUST BE MADE TO RETURN TO THEIR LANDS...OR STAY ON OUR LANDS...

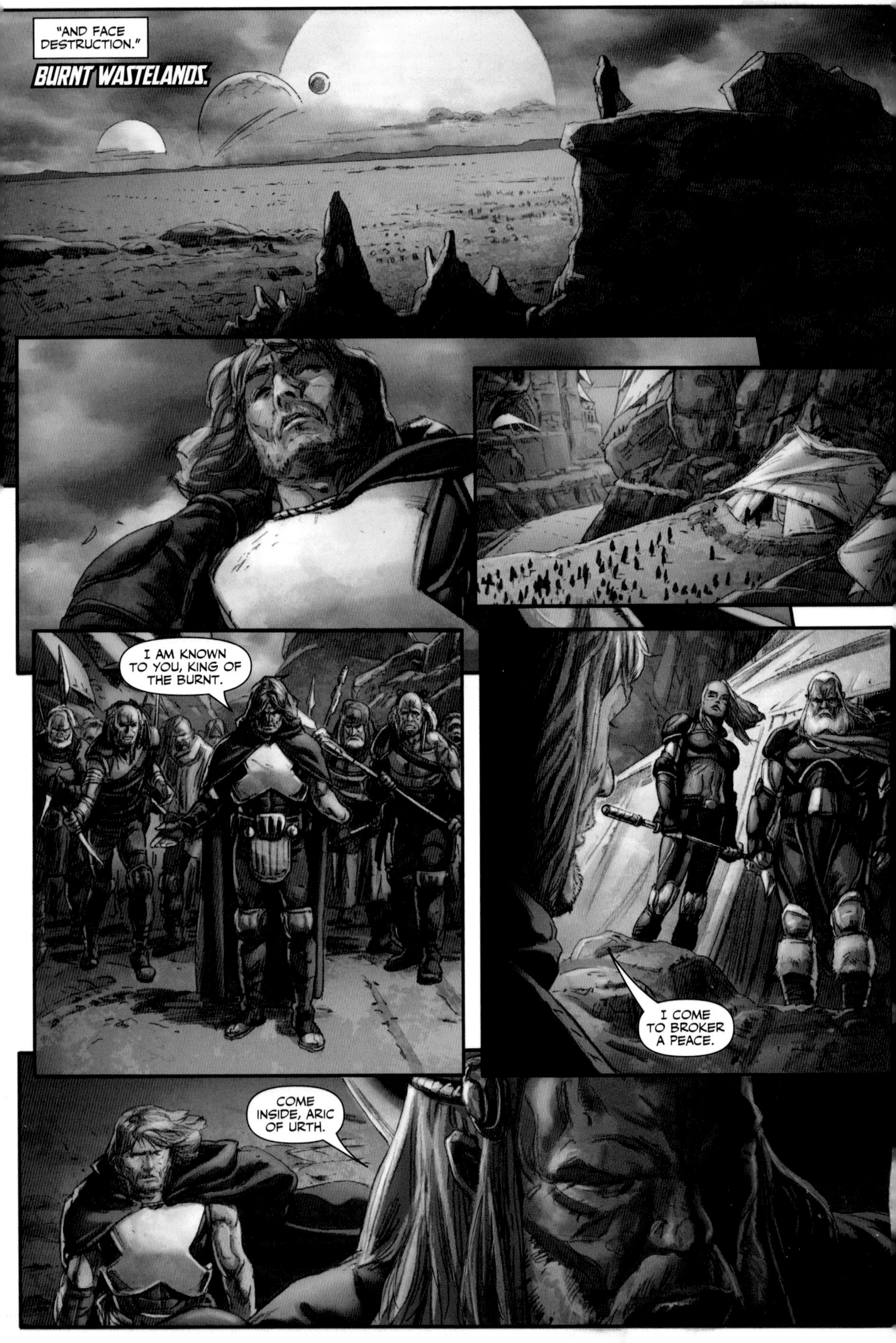
"AND FACE DESTRUCTION."
BURNT WASTELANDS.
I AM KNOWN TO YOU, KING OF THE BURNT.
I COME TO BROKER A PEACE.
COME INSIDE, ARIC OF URTH.

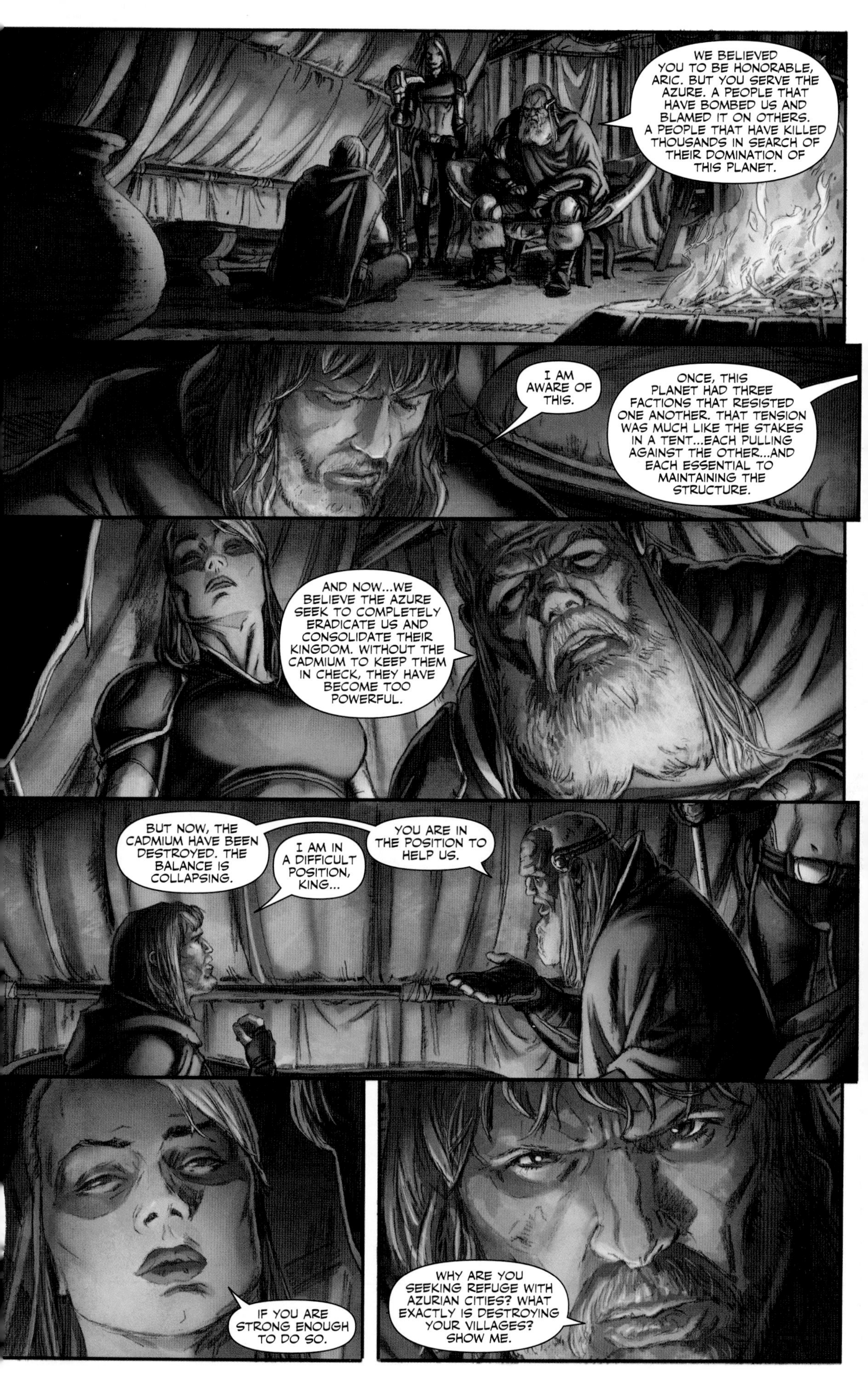
WE BELIEVED YOU TO BE HONORABLE, ARIC. BUT YOU SERVE THE AZURE. A PEOPLE THAT HAVE BOMBED US AND BLAMED IT ON OTHERS. A PEOPLE THAT HAVE KILLED THOUSANDS IN SEARCH OF THEIR DOMINATION OF THIS PLANET.
I AM AWARE OF THIS.
ONCE, THIS PLANET HAD THREE FACTIONS THAT RESISTED ONE ANOTHER. THAT TENSION WAS MUCH LIKE THE STAKES IN A TENT...EACH PULLING AGAINST THE OTHER...AND EACH ESSENTIAL TO MAINTAINING THE STRUCTURE.
AND NOW...WE BELIEVE THE AZURE SEEK TO COMPLETELY ERADICATE US AND CONSOLIDATE THEIR KINGDOM. WITHOUT THE CADMIUM TO KEEP THEM IN CHECK, THEY HAVE BECOME TOO POWERFUL.
BUT NOW, THE CADMIUM HAVE BEEN DESTROYED. THE BALANCE IS COLLAPSING.
I AM IN A DIFFICULT POSITION, KING...
YOU ARE IN THE POSITION TO HELP US.
IF YOU ARE STRONG ENOUGH TO DO SO.
WHY ARE YOU SEEKING REFUGE WITH AZURIAN CITIES? WHAT EXACTLY IS DESTROYING YOUR VILLAGES? SHOW ME.

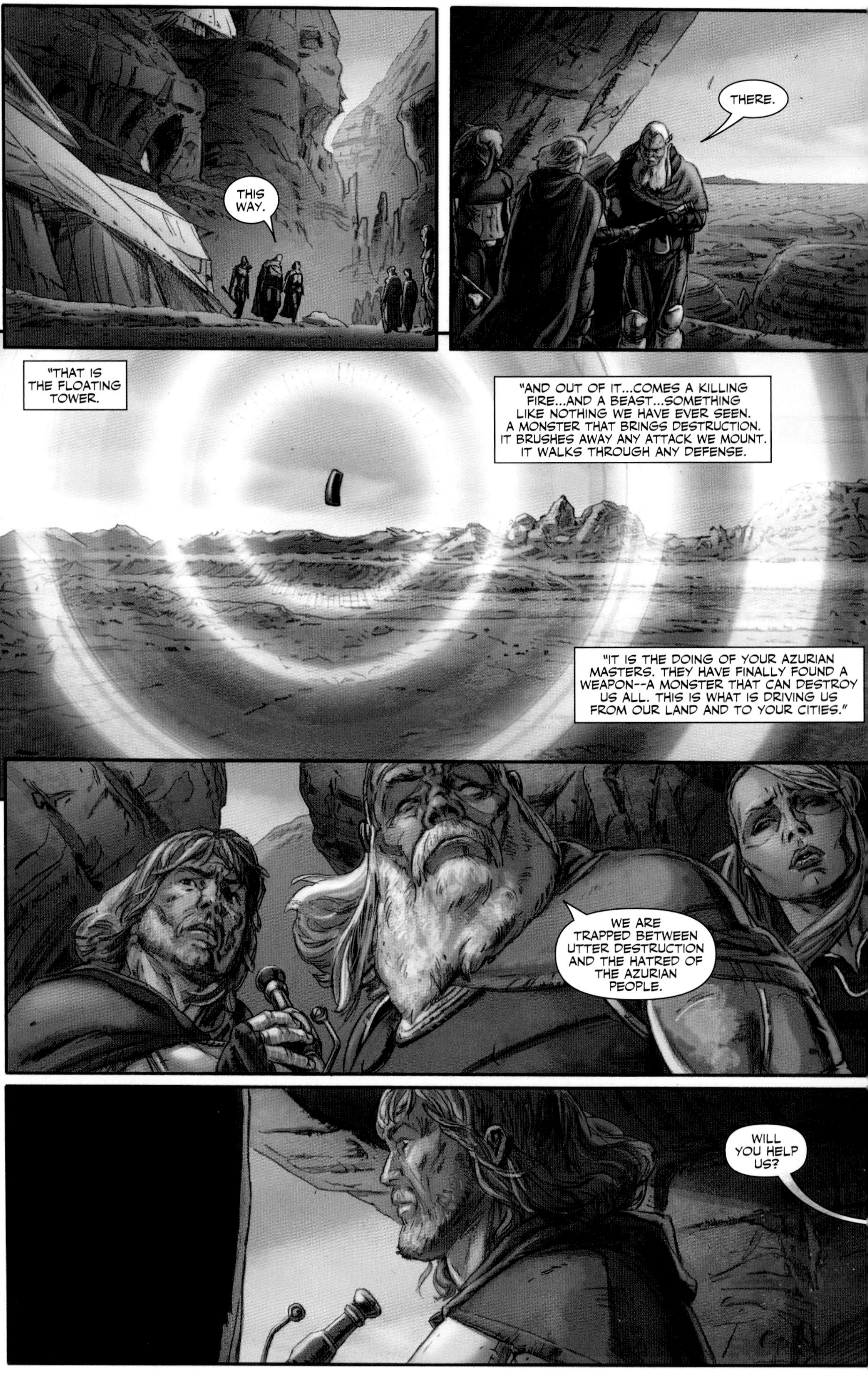
THIS WAY.
THERE.
"THAT IS THE FLOATING TOWER.
"AND OUT OF IT...COMES A KILLING FIRE...AND A BEAST...SOMETHING LIKE NOTHING WE HAVE EVER SEEN. A MONSTER THAT BRINGS DESTRUCTION. IT BRUSHES AWAY ANY ATTACK WE MOUNT. IT WALKS THROUGH ANY DEFENSE.
"IT IS THE DOING OF YOUR AZURIAN MASTERS. THEY HAVE FINALLY FOUND A WEAPON--A MONSTER THAT CAN DESTROY US ALL. THIS IS WHAT IS DRIVING US FROM OUR LAND AND TO YOUR CITIES."
WE ARE TRAPPED BETWEEN UTTER DESTRUCTION AND THE HATRED OF THE AZURIAN PEOPLE.
WILL YOU HELP US?

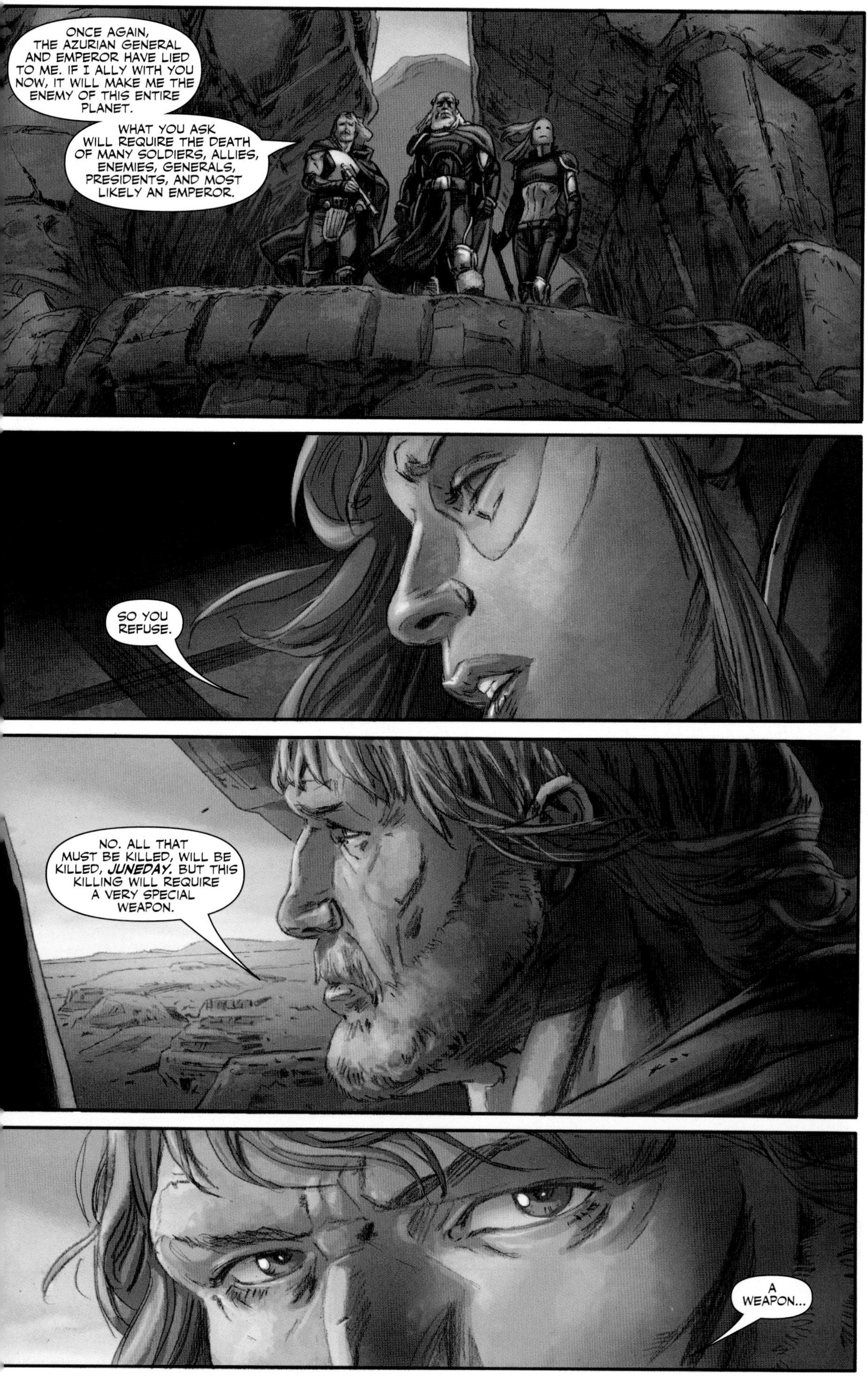
ONCE AGAIN, THE AZURIAN GENERAL AND EMPEROR HAVE LIED TO ME. IF I ALLY WITH YOU NOW, IT WILL MAKE ME THE ENEMY OF THIS ENTIRE PLANET.
WHAT YOU ASK WILL REQUIRE THE DEATH OF MANY SOLDIERS, ALLIES, ENEMIES, GENERALS, PRESIDENTS, AND MOST LIKELY AN EMPEROR.
SO YOU REFUSE.
NO. ALL THAT MUST BE KILLED, WILL BE KILLED, ***JUNEDAY.*** BUT THIS KILLING WILL REQUIRE A VERY SPECIAL WEAPON.
A WEAPON...

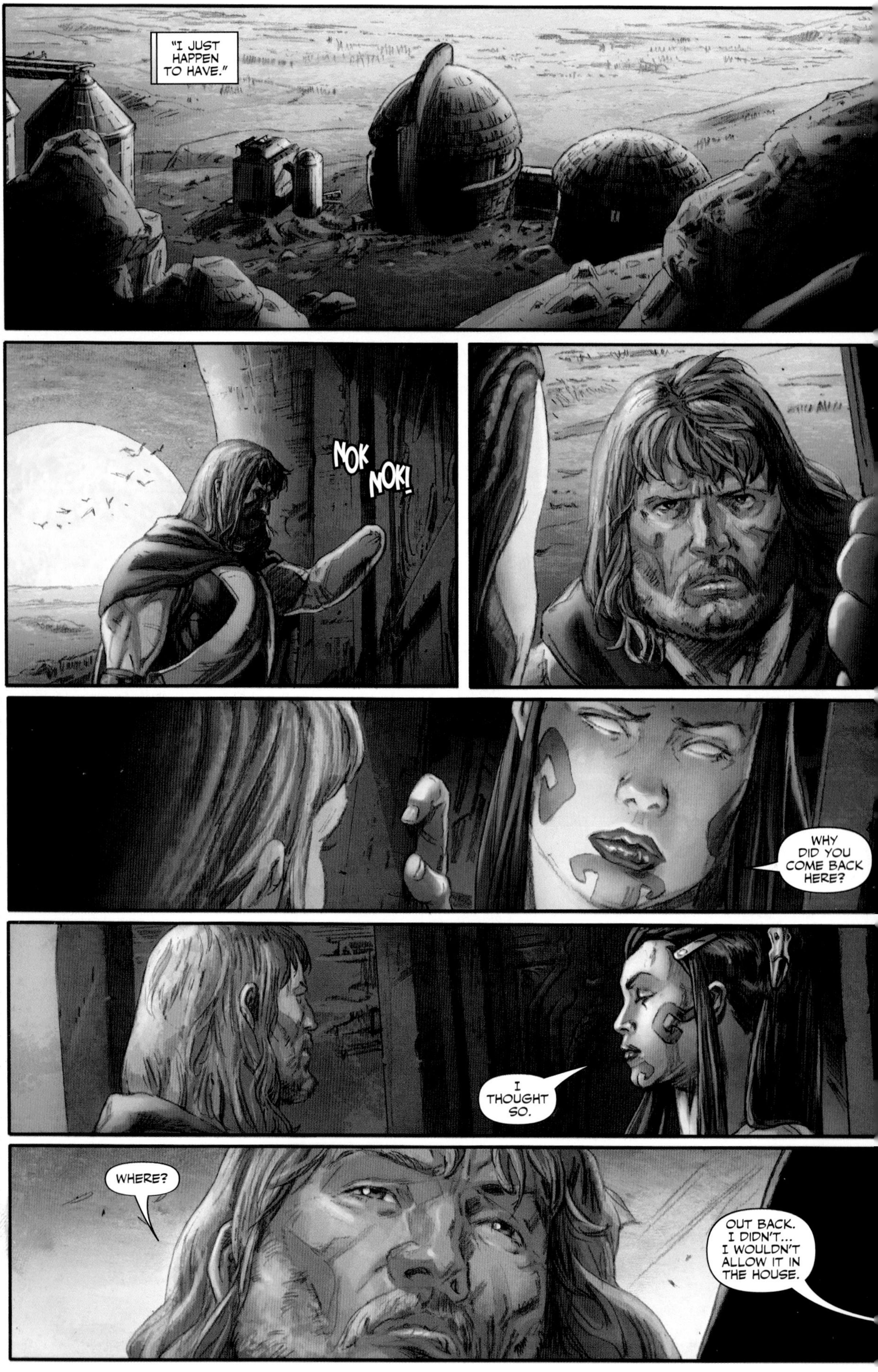
"I JUST HAPPEN TO HAVE."
NOK NOK!
WHY DID YOU COME BACK HERE?
I THOUGHT SO.
WHERE?
OUT BACK. I DIDN'T... I WOULDN'T ALLOW IT IN THE HOUSE.

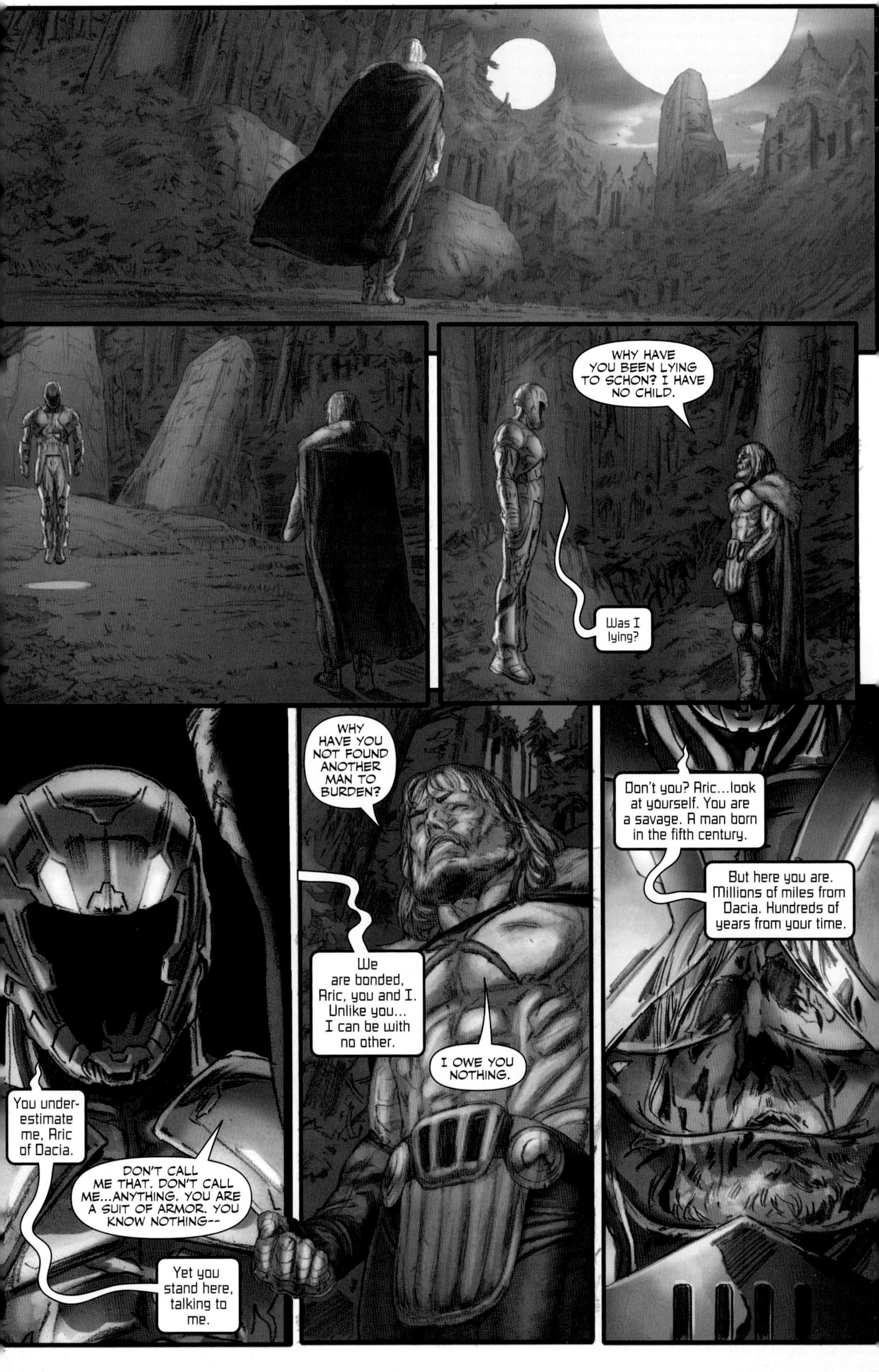
WHY HAVE YOU BEEN LYING TO SCHON? I HAVE NO CHILD.
Was I lying?
You under-estimate me, Aric of Dacia.
DON'T CALL ME THAT. DON'T CALL ME...ANYTHING. YOU ARE A SUIT OF ARMOR. YOU KNOW NOTHING--
Yet you stand here, talking to me.
WHY HAVE YOU NOT FOUND ANOTHER MAN TO BURDEN?
We are bonded, Aric, you and I. Unlike you... I can be with no other.
I OWE YOU NOTHING.
Don't you? Aric...look at yourself. You are a savage. A man born in the fifth century.
But here you are. Millions of miles from Dacia. Hundreds of years from your time.

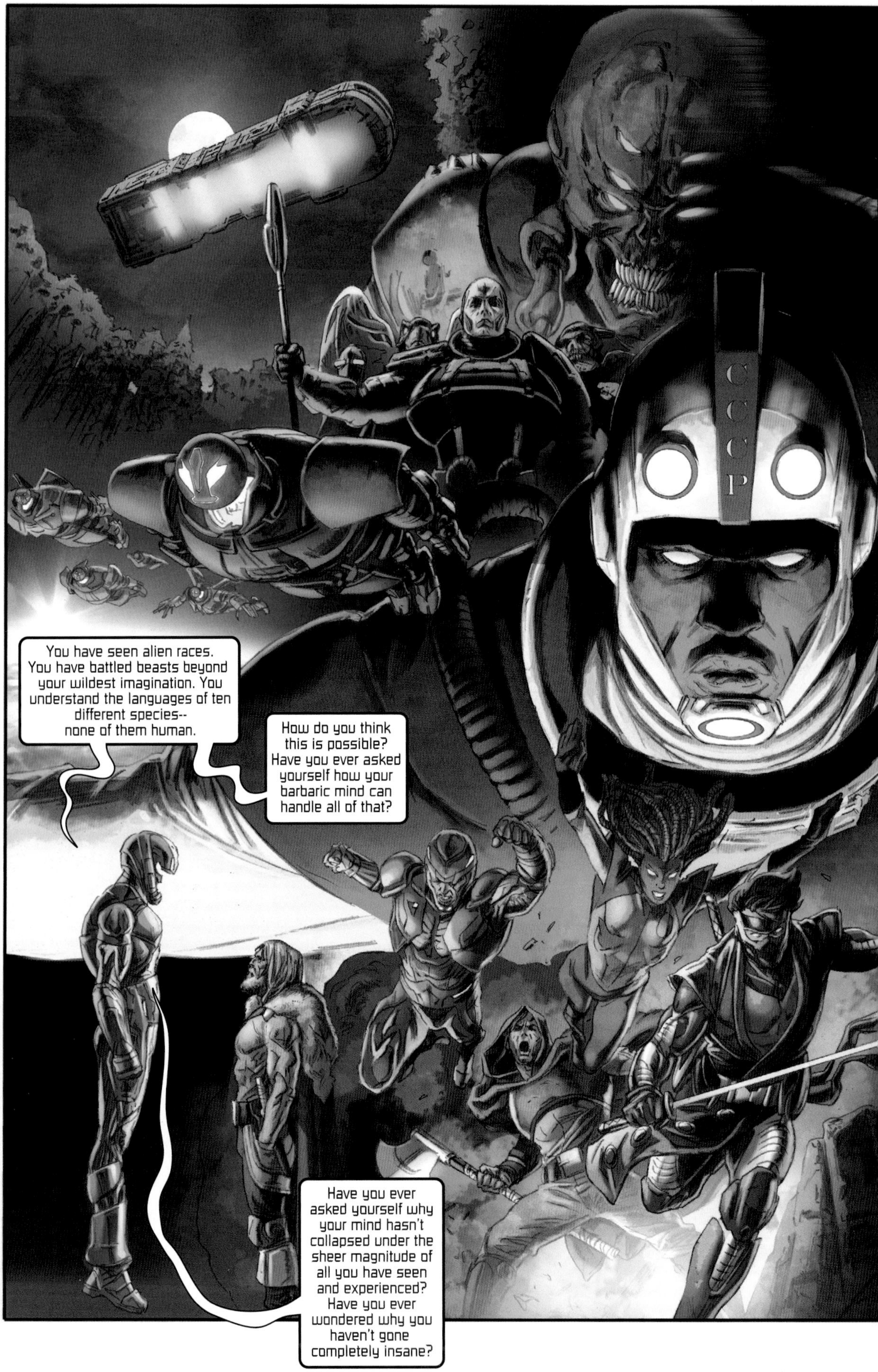
CCCP
You have seen alien races. You have battled beasts beyond your wildest imagination. You understand the languages of ten different species-- none of them human.
How do you think this is possible? Have you ever asked yourself how your barbaric mind can handle all of that?
Have you ever asked yourself why your mind hasn't collapsed under the sheer magnitude of all you have seen and experienced? Have you ever wondered why you haven't gone completely insane?

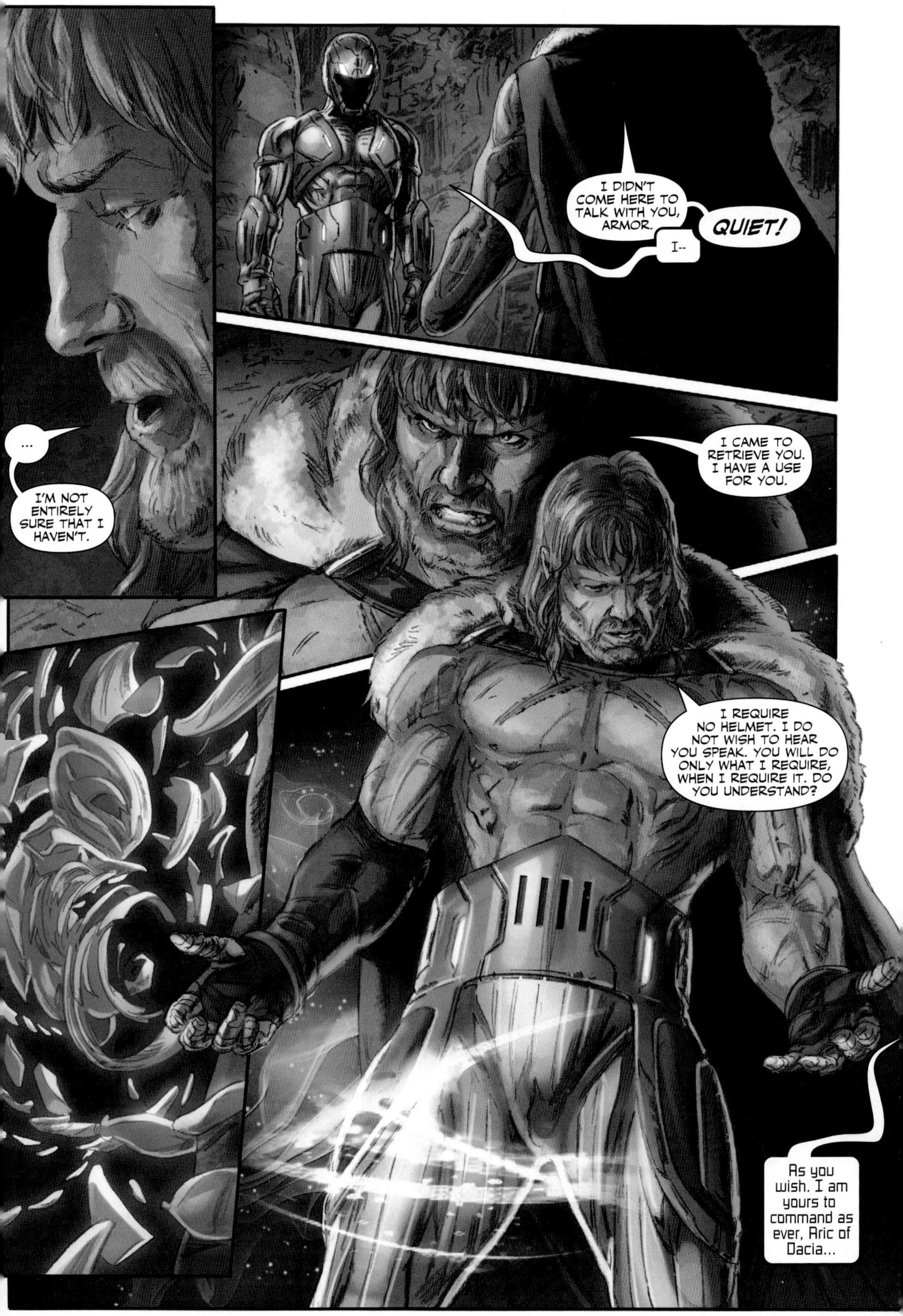
...
I'M NOT ENTIRELY SURE THAT I HAVEN'T.
I DIDN'T COME HERE TO TALK WITH YOU, ARMOR.
I--
QUIET!
I CAME TO RETRIEVE YOU. I HAVE A USE FOR YOU.
I REQUIRE NO HELMET. I DO NOT WISH TO HEAR YOU SPEAK. YOU WILL DO ONLY WHAT I REQUIRE, WHEN I REQUIRE IT. DO YOU UNDERSTAND?
As you wish. I am yours to command as ever, Aric of Dacia...

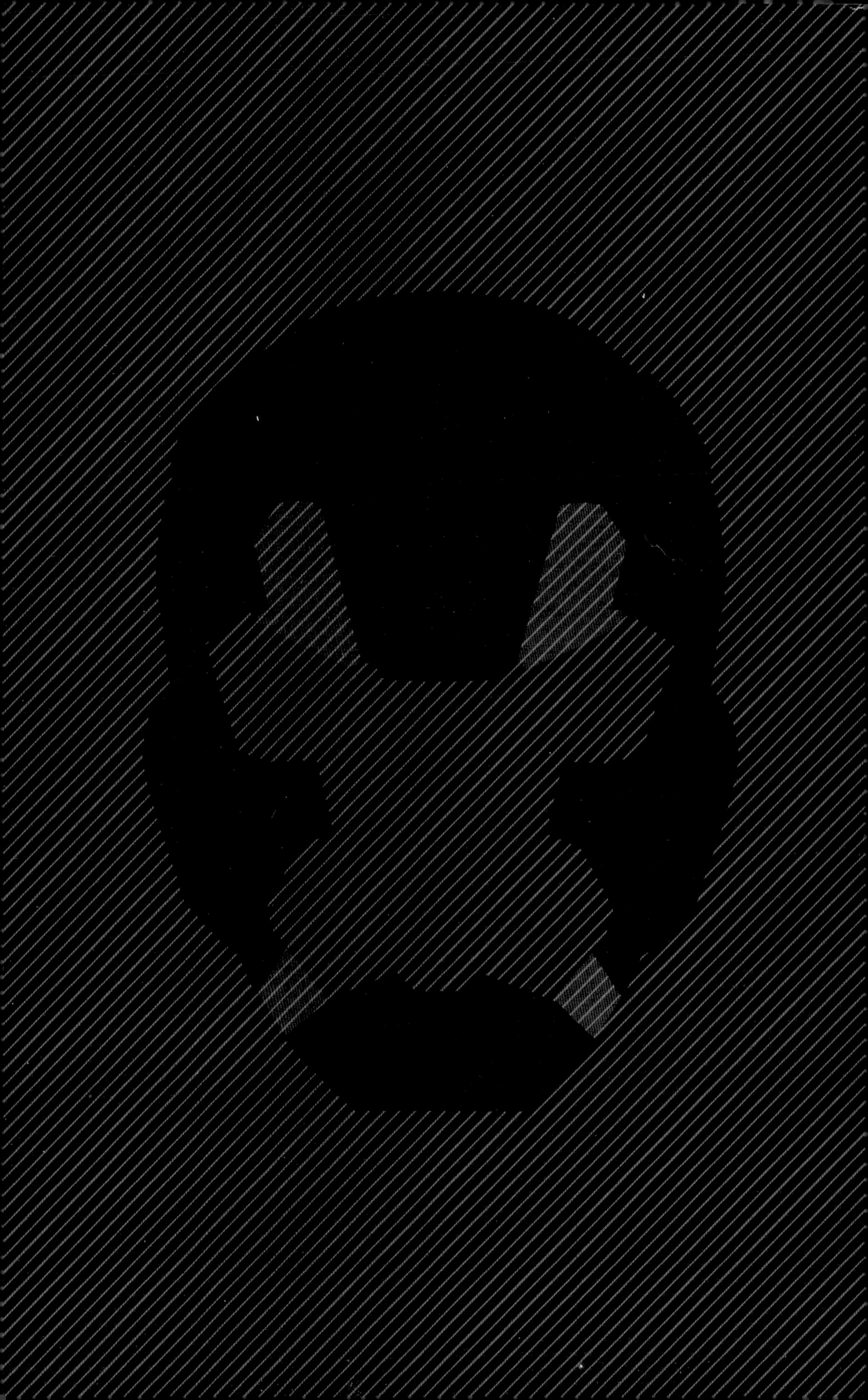

X-O MANOWAR

ISSUE 06

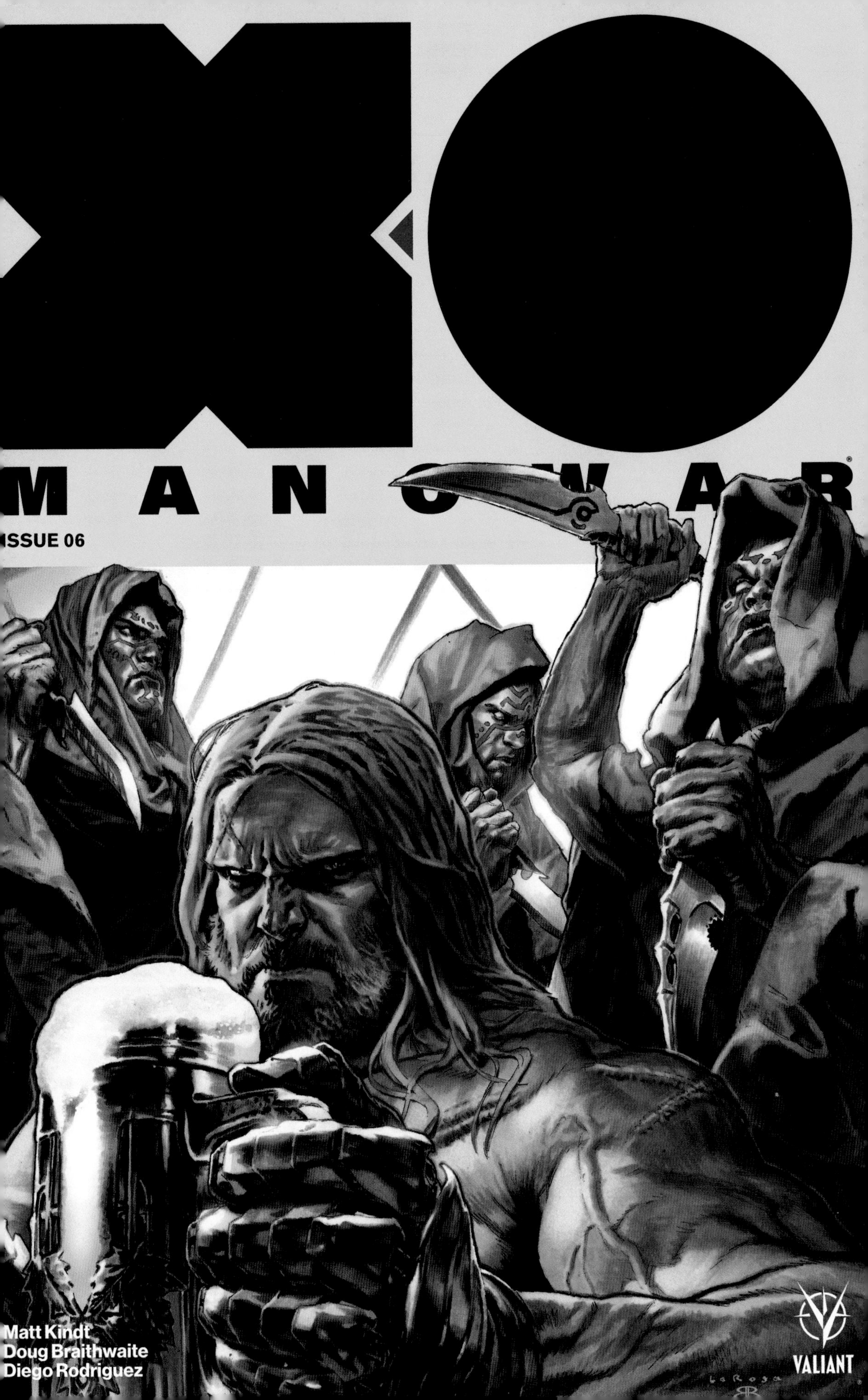

Matt Kindt
Doug Braithwaite
Diego Rodriguez

VALIANT

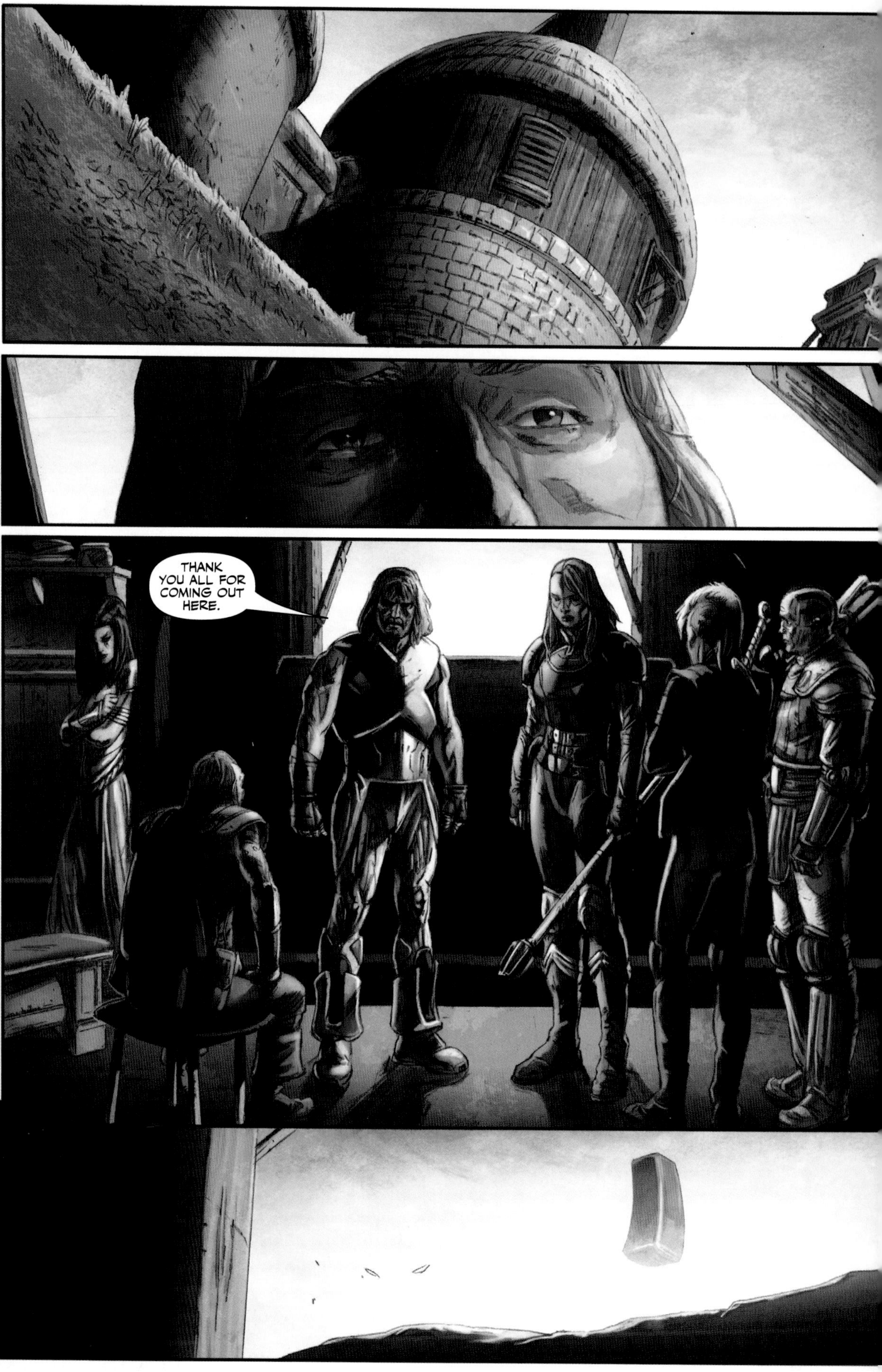
THANK YOU ALL FOR COMING OUT HERE.

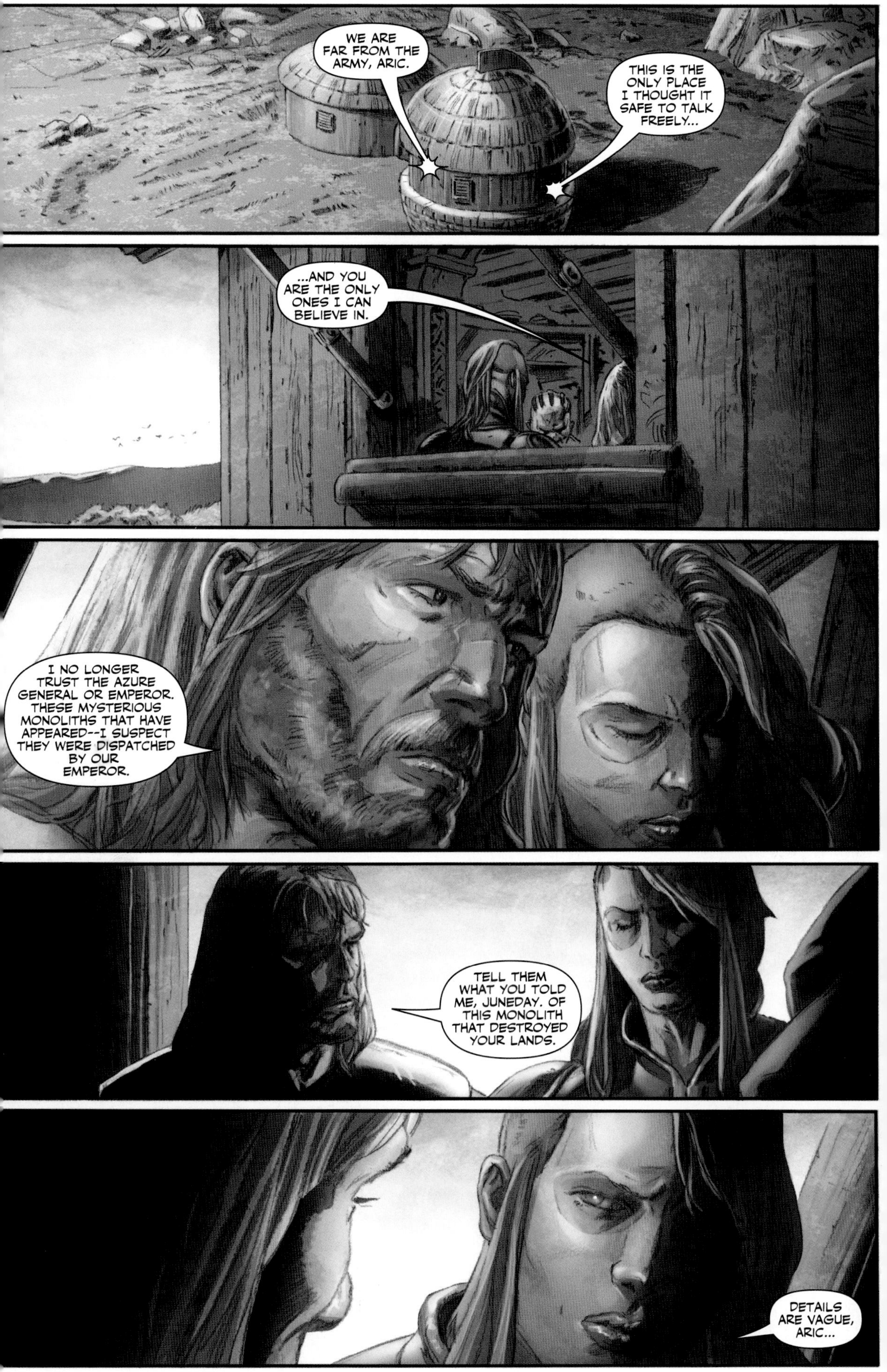
WE ARE FAR FROM THE ARMY, ARIC.
THIS IS THE ONLY PLACE I THOUGHT IT SAFE TO TALK FREELY...
...AND YOU ARE THE ONLY ONES I CAN BELIEVE IN.
I NO LONGER TRUST THE AZURE GENERAL OR EMPEROR. THESE MYSTERIOUS MONOLITHS THAT HAVE APPEARED--I SUSPECT THEY WERE DISPATCHED BY OUR EMPEROR.
TELL THEM WHAT YOU TOLD ME, JUNEDAY. OF THIS MONOLITH THAT DESTROYED YOUR LANDS.
DETAILS ARE VAGUE, ARIC...

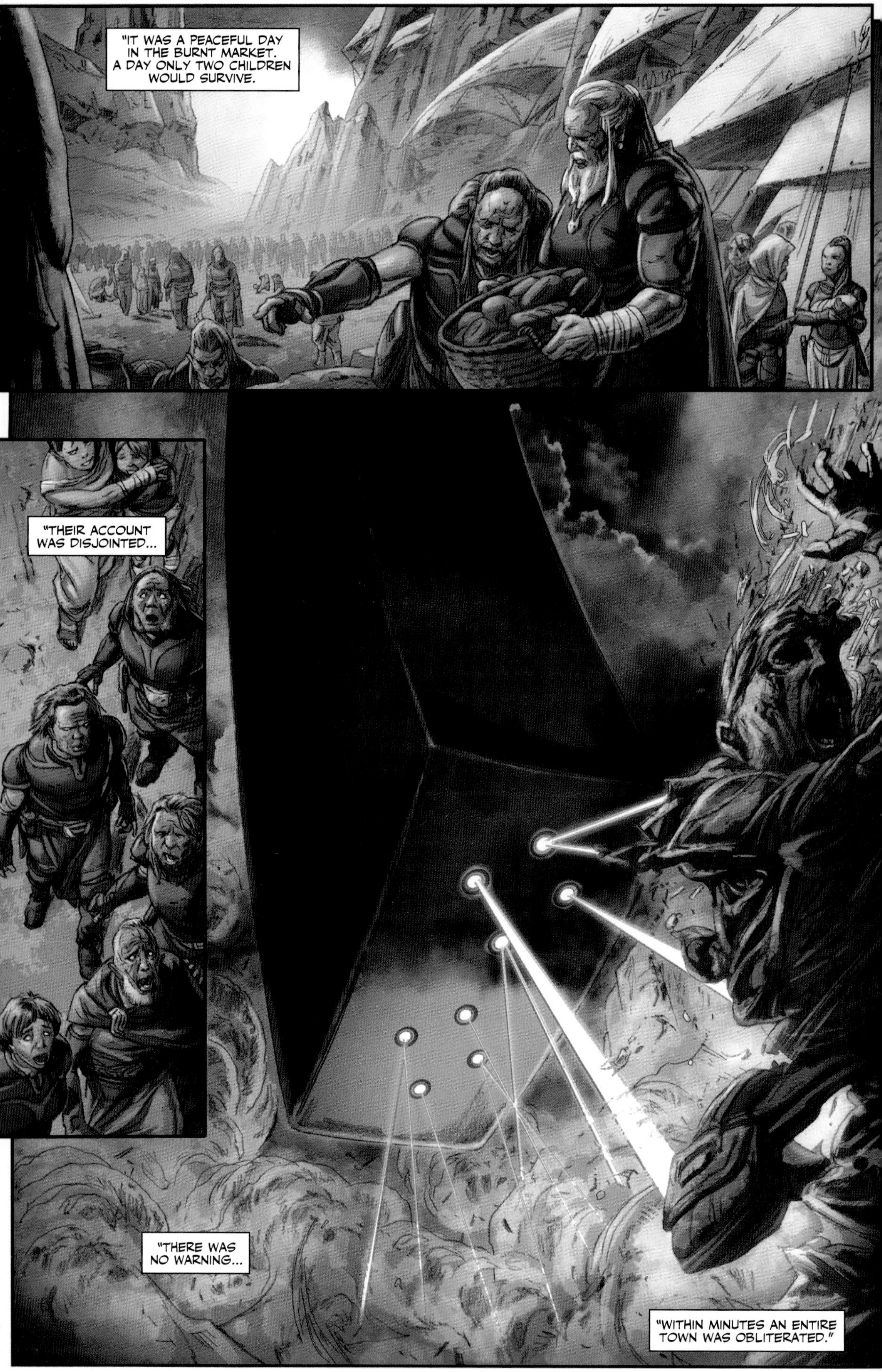
"IT WAS A PEACEFUL DAY IN THE BURNT MARKET. A DAY ONLY TWO CHILDREN WOULD SURVIVE.
"THEIR ACCOUNT WAS DISJOINTED...
"THERE WAS NO WARNING...
"WITHIN MINUTES AN ENTIRE TOWN WAS OBLITERATED."

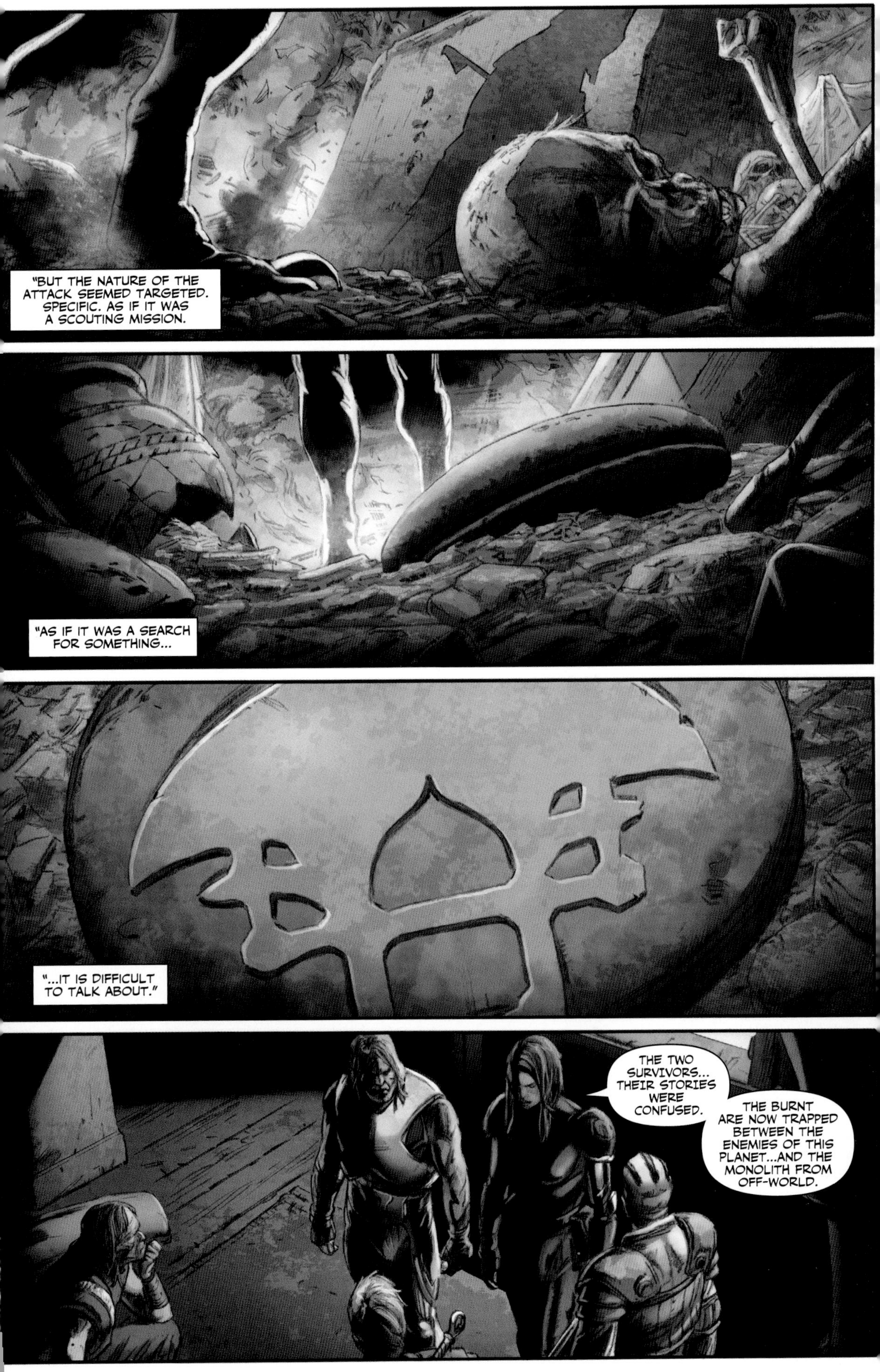
"BUT THE NATURE OF THE ATTACK SEEMED TARGETED. SPECIFIC. AS IF IT WAS A SCOUTING MISSION.
"AS IF IT WAS A SEARCH FOR SOMETHING...
"...IT IS DIFFICULT TO TALK ABOUT."
THE TWO SURVIVORS... THEIR STORIES WERE CONFUSED.
THE BURNT ARE NOW TRAPPED BETWEEN THE ENEMIES OF THIS PLANET...AND THE MONOLITH FROM OFF-WORLD.

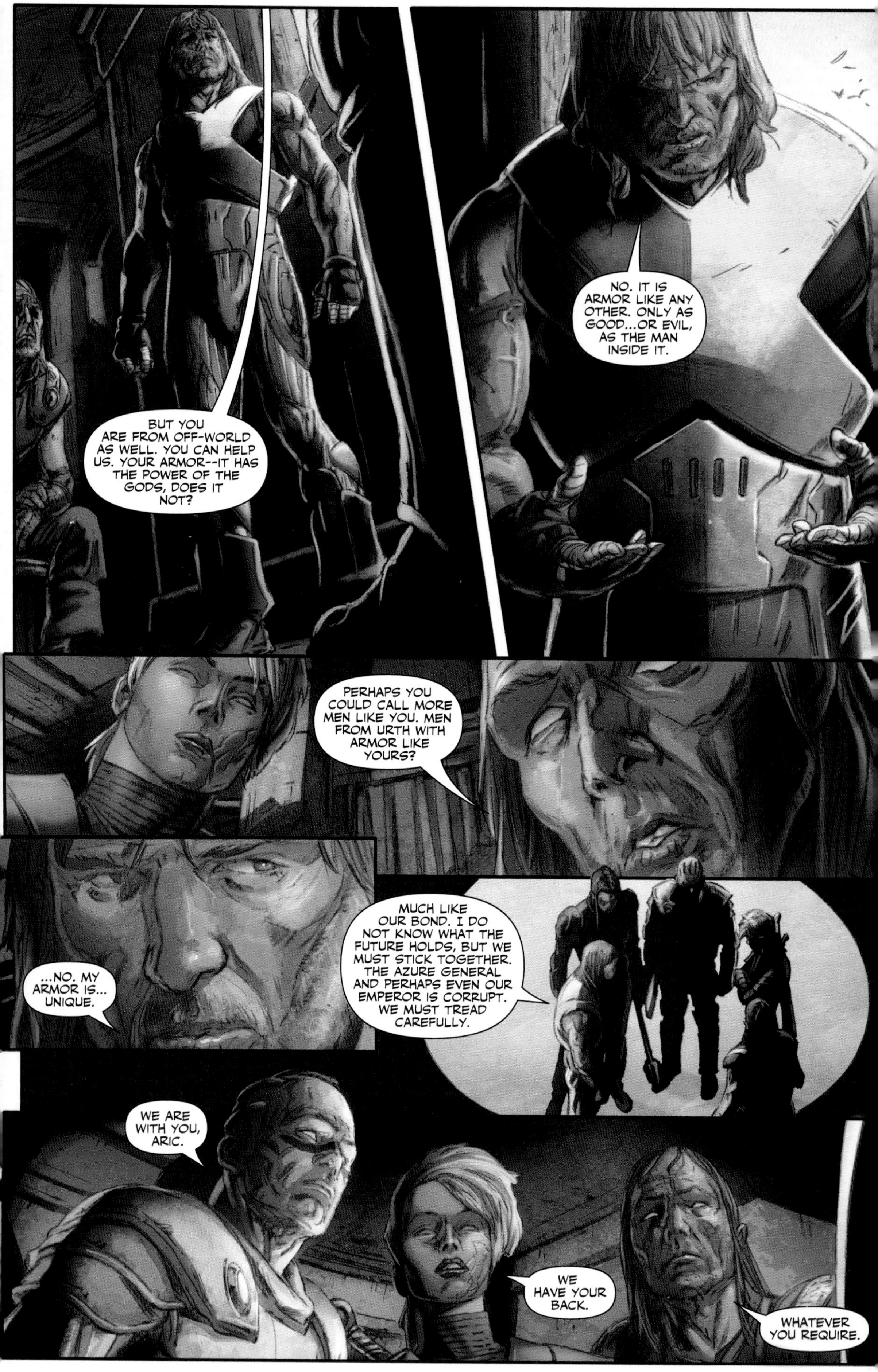
BUT YOU ARE FROM OFF-WORLD AS WELL. YOU CAN HELP US. YOUR ARMOR--IT HAS THE POWER OF THE GODS, DOES IT NOT?
NO. IT IS ARMOR LIKE ANY OTHER. ONLY AS GOOD...OR EVIL, AS THE MAN INSIDE IT.
PERHAPS YOU COULD CALL MORE MEN LIKE YOU. MEN FROM URTH WITH ARMOR LIKE YOURS?
...NO. MY ARMOR IS... UNIQUE.
MUCH LIKE OUR BOND. I DO NOT KNOW WHAT THE FUTURE HOLDS, BUT WE MUST STICK TOGETHER. THE AZURE GENERAL AND PERHAPS EVEN OUR EMPEROR IS CORRUPT. WE MUST TREAD CAREFULLY.
WE ARE WITH YOU, ARIC.
WE HAVE YOUR BACK.
WHATEVER YOU REQUIRE.

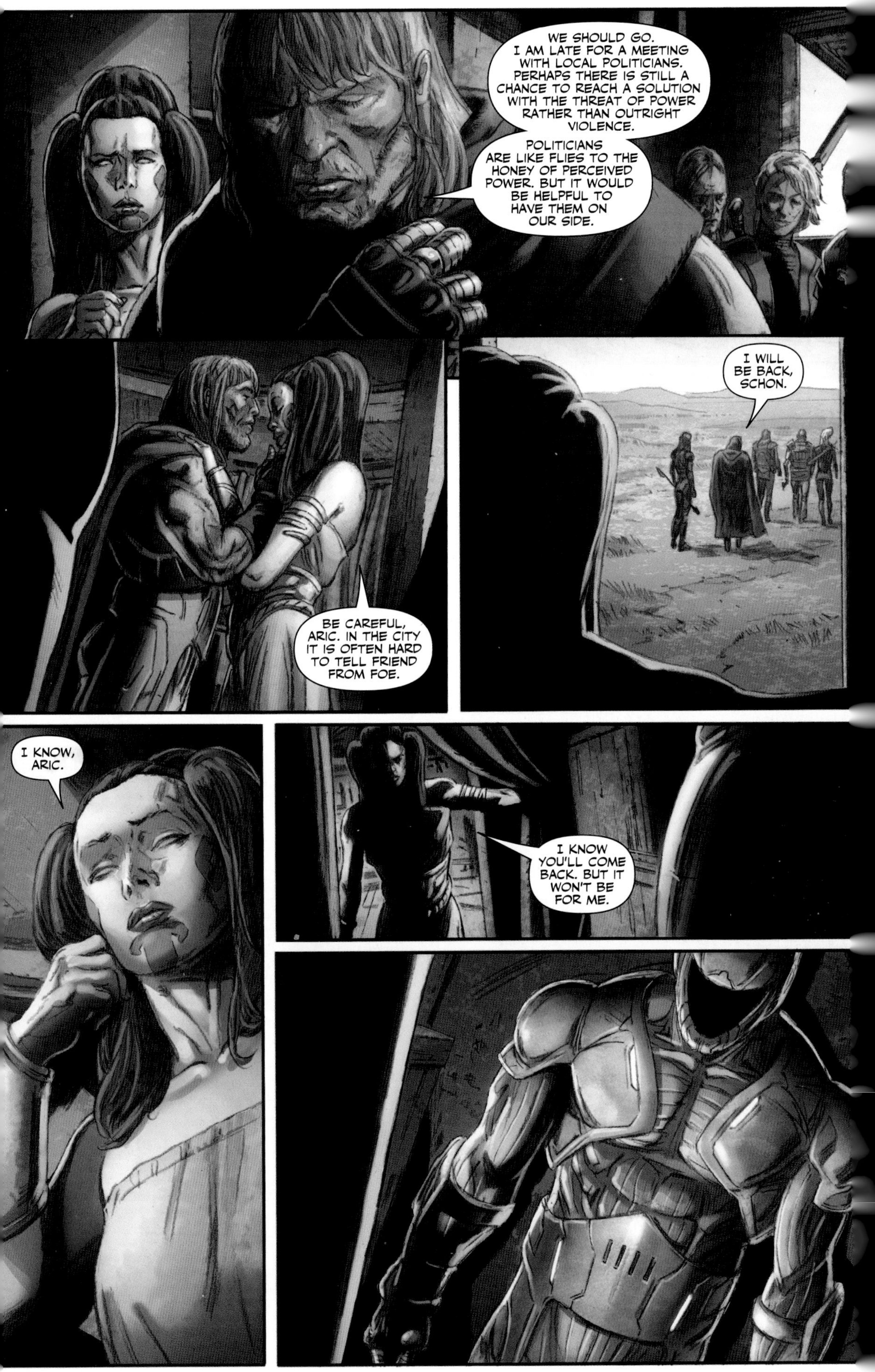
WE SHOULD GO. I AM LATE FOR A MEETING WITH LOCAL POLITICIANS. PERHAPS THERE IS STILL A CHANCE TO REACH A SOLUTION WITH THE THREAT OF POWER RATHER THAN OUTRIGHT VIOLENCE.
POLITICIANS ARE LIKE FLIES TO THE HONEY OF PERCEIVED POWER. BUT IT WOULD BE HELPFUL TO HAVE THEM ON OUR SIDE.
BE CAREFUL, ARIC. IN THE CITY IT IS OFTEN HARD TO TELL FRIEND FROM FOE.
I WILL BE BACK, SCHON.
I KNOW, ARIC.
I KNOW YOU'LL COME BACK. BUT IT WON'T BE FOR ME.

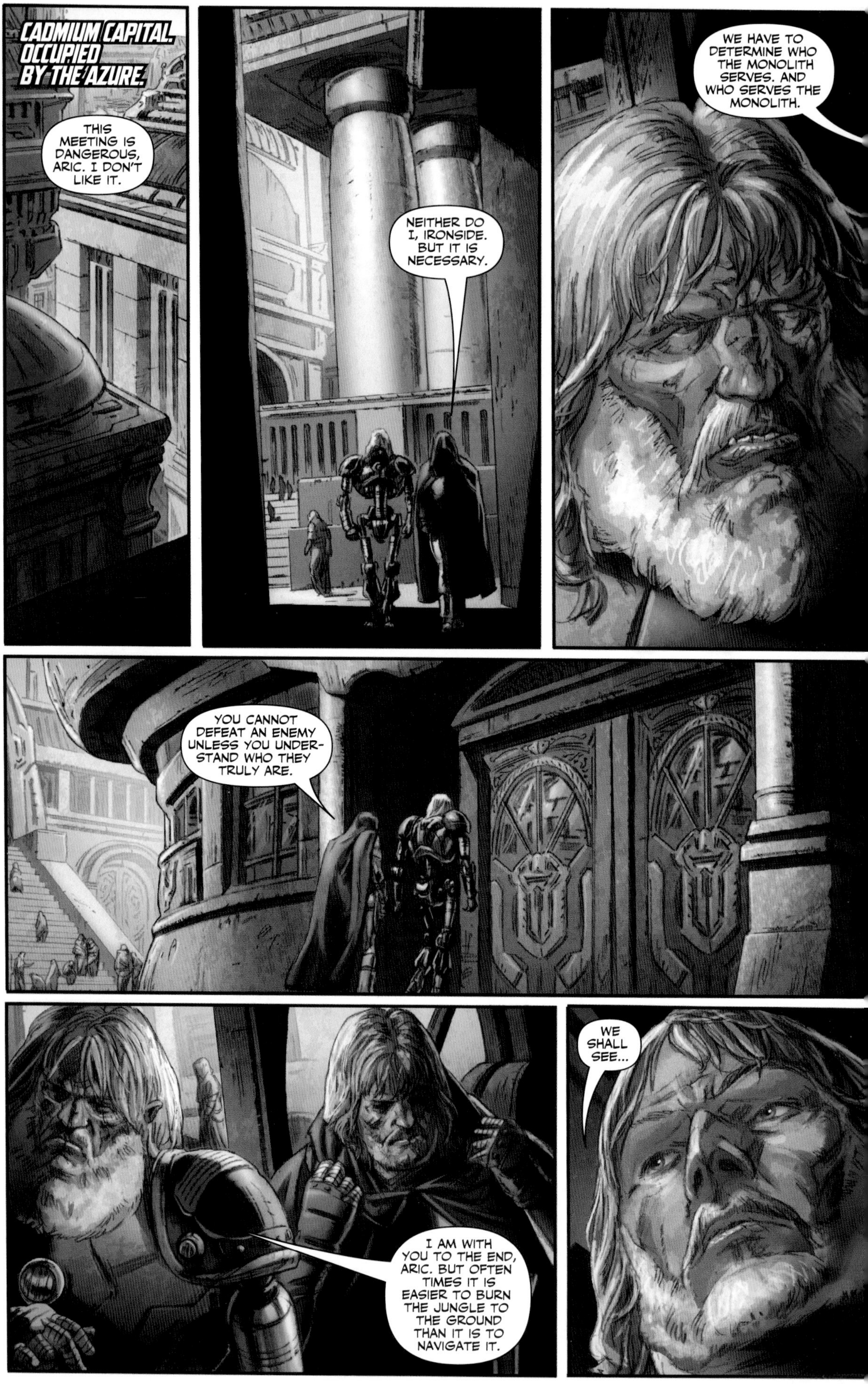
CADMIUM CAPITAL. OCCUPIED BY THE AZURE.
THIS MEETING IS DANGEROUS, ARIC. I DON'T LIKE IT.
NEITHER DO I, IRONSIDE. BUT IT IS NECESSARY.
WE HAVE TO DETERMINE WHO THE MONOLITH SERVES. AND WHO SERVES THE MONOLITH.
YOU CANNOT DEFEAT AN ENEMY UNLESS YOU UNDER-STAND WHO THEY TRULY ARE.
I AM WITH YOU TO THE END, ARIC. BUT OFTEN TIMES IT IS EASIER TO BURN THE JUNGLE TO THE GROUND THAN IT IS TO NAVIGATE IT.
WE SHALL SEE...

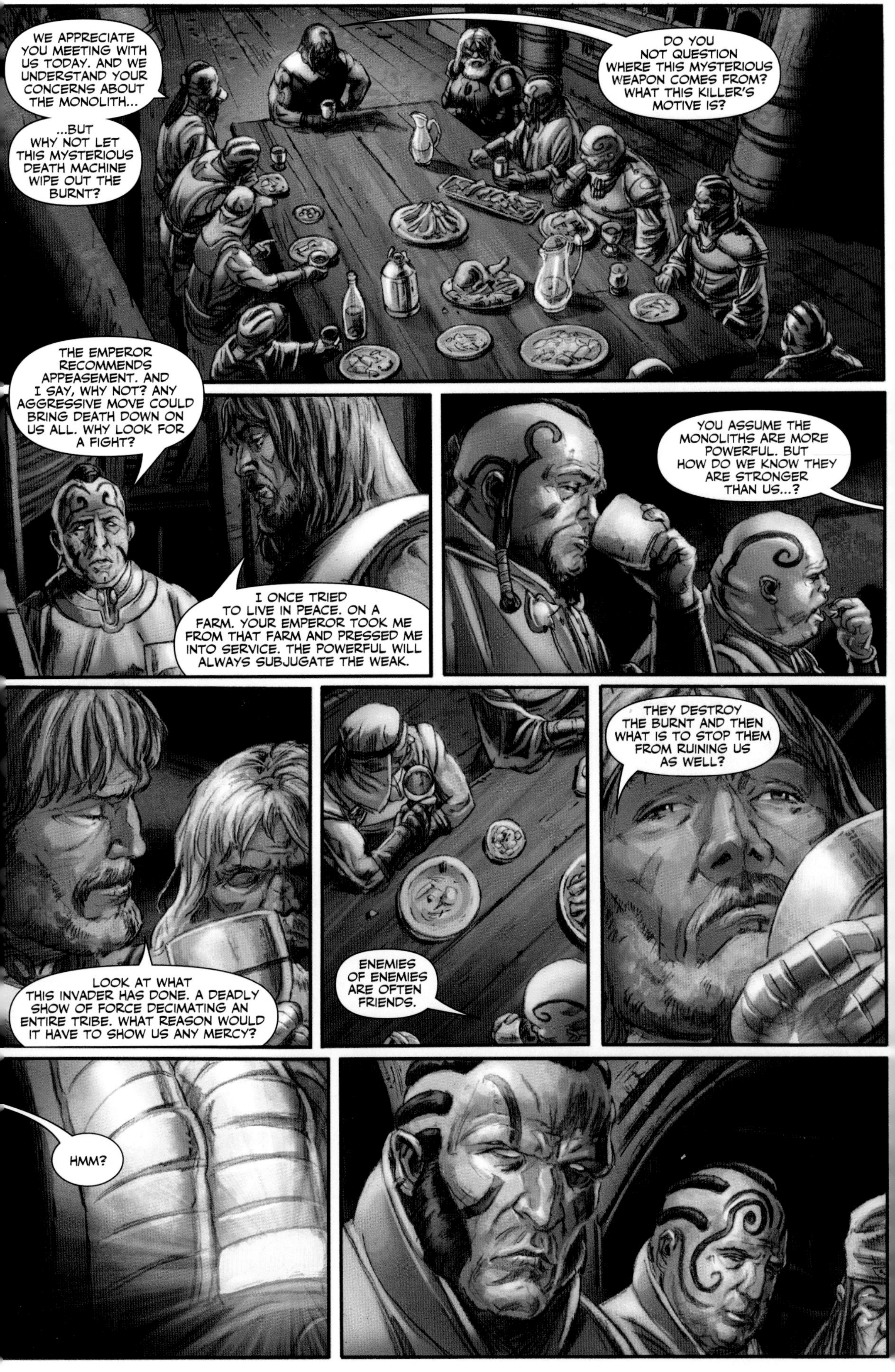
WE APPRECIATE YOU MEETING WITH US TODAY. AND WE UNDERSTAND YOUR CONCERNS ABOUT THE MONOLITH...
...BUT WHY NOT LET THIS MYSTERIOUS DEATH MACHINE WIPE OUT THE BURNT?
DO YOU NOT QUESTION WHERE THIS MYSTERIOUS WEAPON COMES FROM? WHAT THIS KILLER'S MOTIVE IS?
THE EMPEROR RECOMMENDS APPEASEMENT. AND I SAY, WHY NOT? ANY AGGRESSIVE MOVE COULD BRING DEATH DOWN ON US ALL. WHY LOOK FOR A FIGHT?
I ONCE TRIED TO LIVE IN PEACE. ON A FARM. YOUR EMPEROR TOOK ME FROM THAT FARM AND PRESSED ME INTO SERVICE. THE POWERFUL WILL ALWAYS SUBJUGATE THE WEAK.
YOU ASSUME THE MONOLITHS ARE MORE POWERFUL. BUT HOW DO WE KNOW THEY ARE STRONGER THAN US...?
LOOK AT WHAT THIS INVADER HAS DONE. A DEADLY SHOW OF FORCE DECIMATING AN ENTIRE TRIBE. WHAT REASON WOULD IT HAVE TO SHOW US ANY MERCY?
ENEMIES OF ENEMIES ARE OFTEN FRIENDS.
THEY DESTROY THE BURNT AND THEN WHAT IS TO STOP THEM FROM RUINING US AS WELL?
HMM?

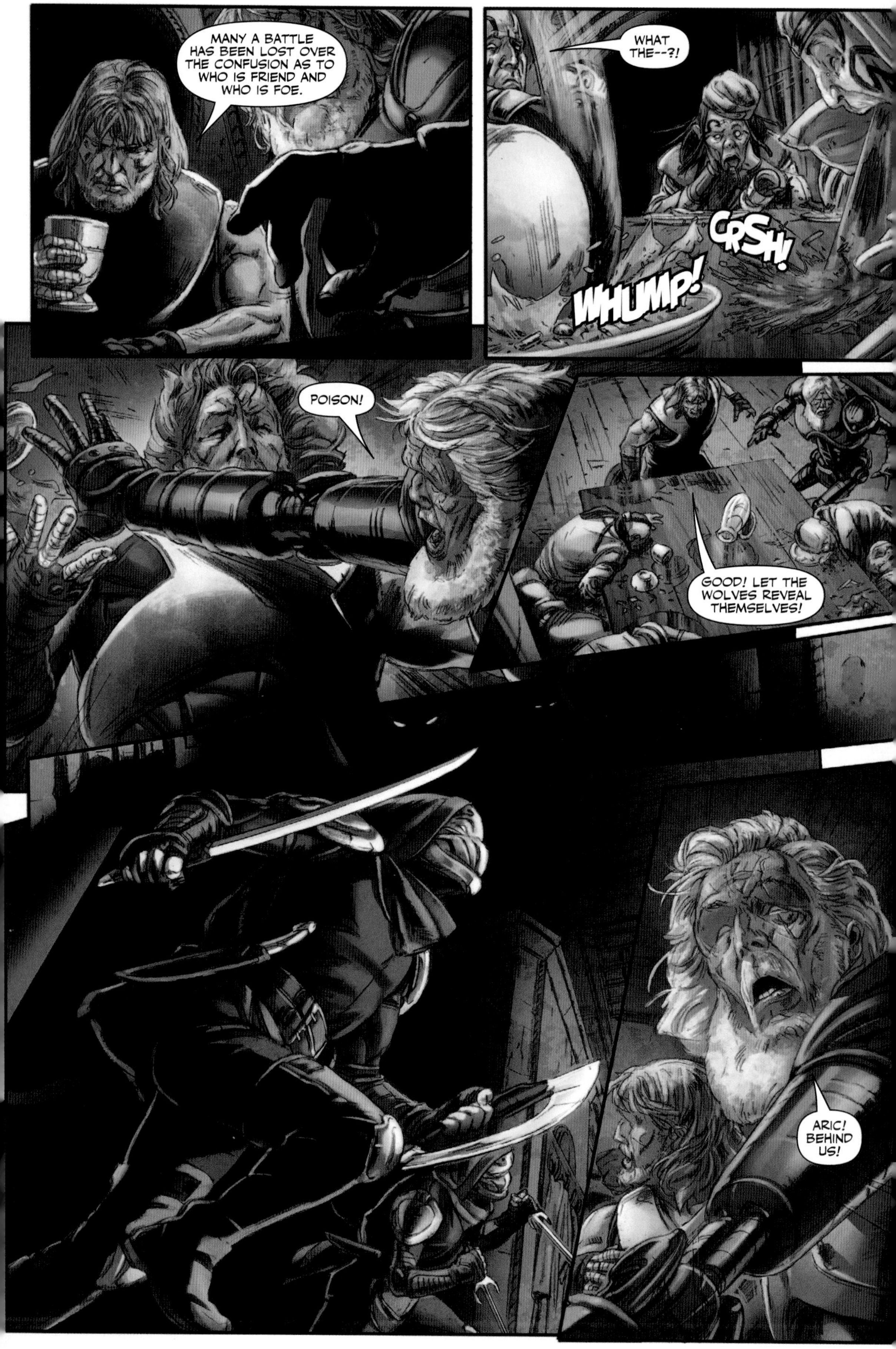
MANY A BATTLE HAS BEEN LOST OVER THE CONFUSION AS TO WHO IS FRIEND AND WHO IS FOE.
WHAT THE--?!
CRSH!
WHUMP!
POISON!
GOOD! LET THE WOLVES REVEAL THEMSELVES!
ARIC! BEHIND US!

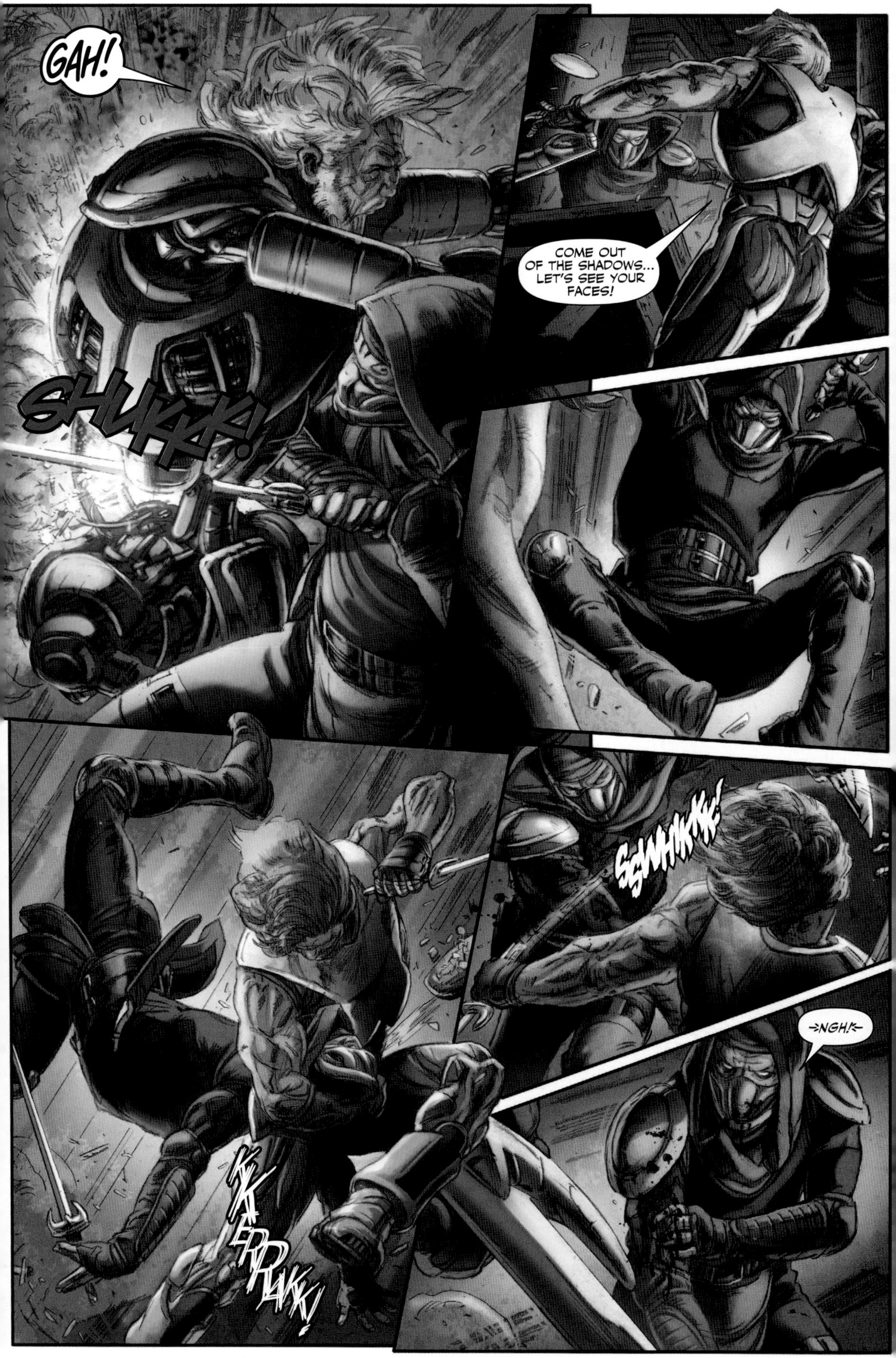
GAH!
SHUKKK!
COME OUT OF THE SHADOWS... LET'S SEE YOUR FACES!
SSNHKKK!
KKKERRAKK!
NGH!

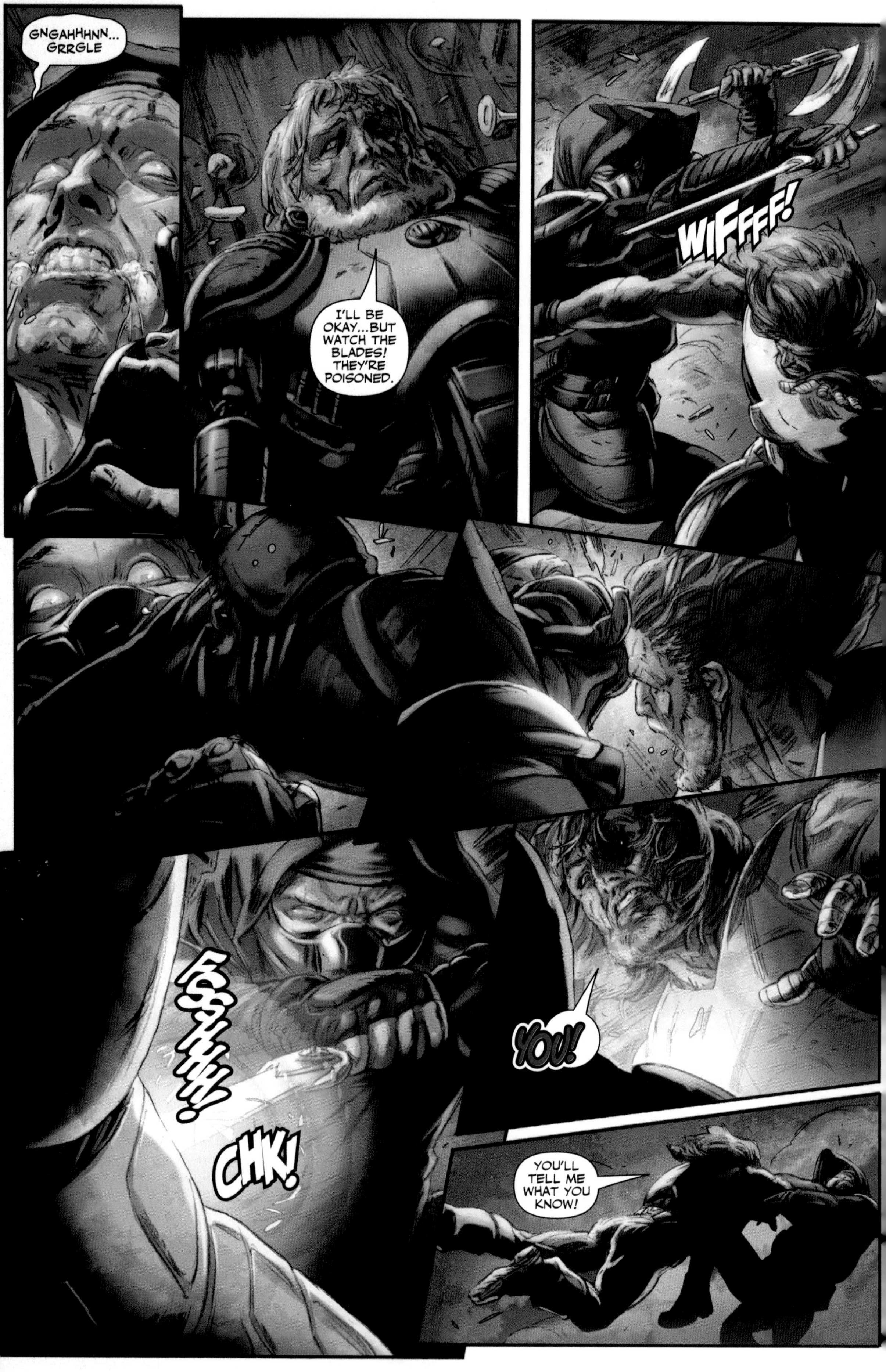
GNGAHHHNN... GRRGLE
I'LL BE OKAY...BUT WATCH THE BLADES! THEY'RE POISONED.
WIFFFF!
FSSHHH!
CHK!
YOU!
YOU'LL TELL ME WHAT YOU KNOW!

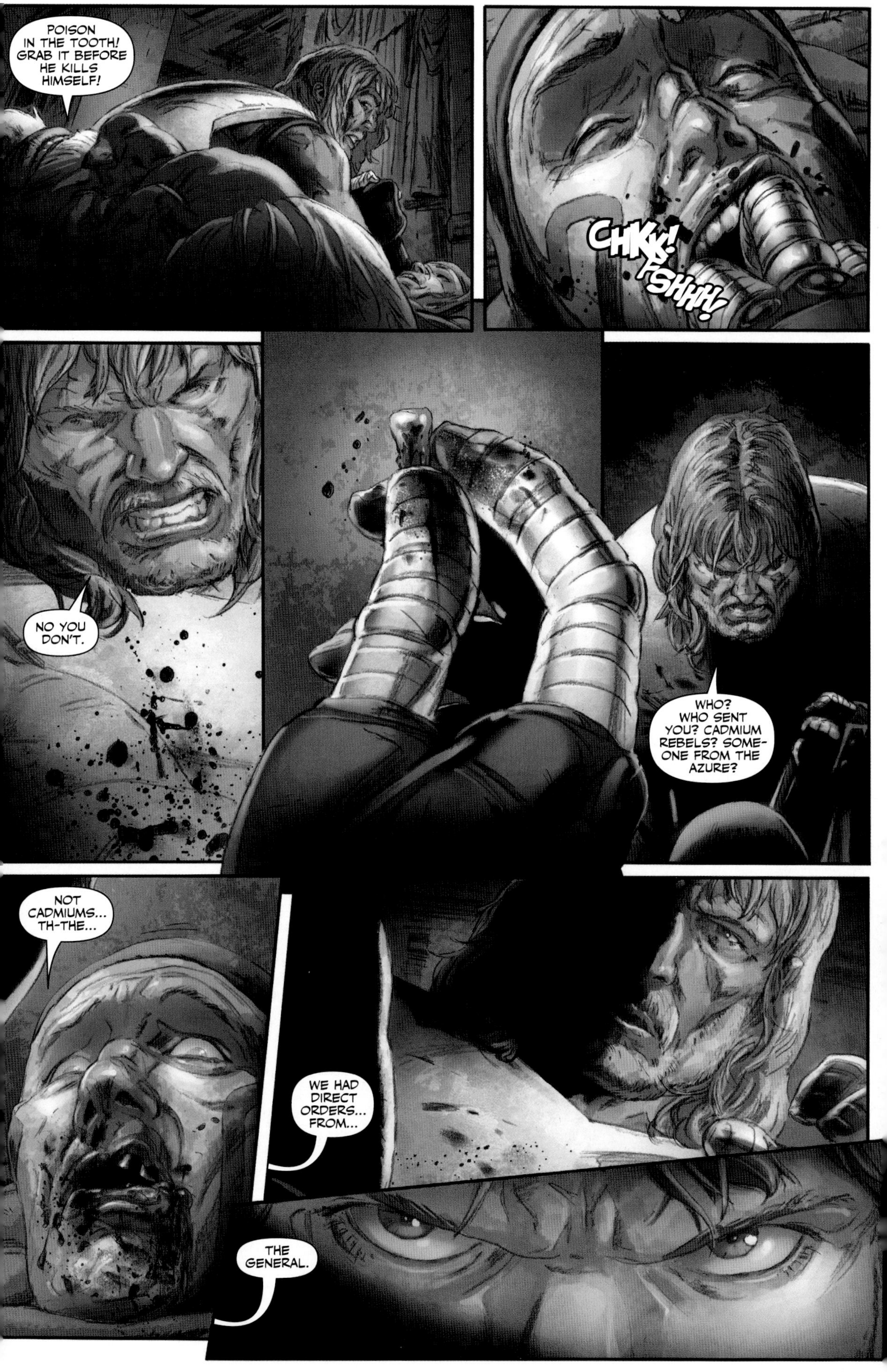
POISON IN THE TOOTH! GRAB IT BEFORE HE KILLS HIMSELF!
CHKK!
FSHHH!
NO YOU DON'T.
WHO? WHO SENT YOU? CADMIUM REBELS? SOME-ONE FROM THE AZURE?
NOT CADMIUMS... TH-THE...
WE HAD DIRECT ORDERS... FROM...
THE GENERAL.

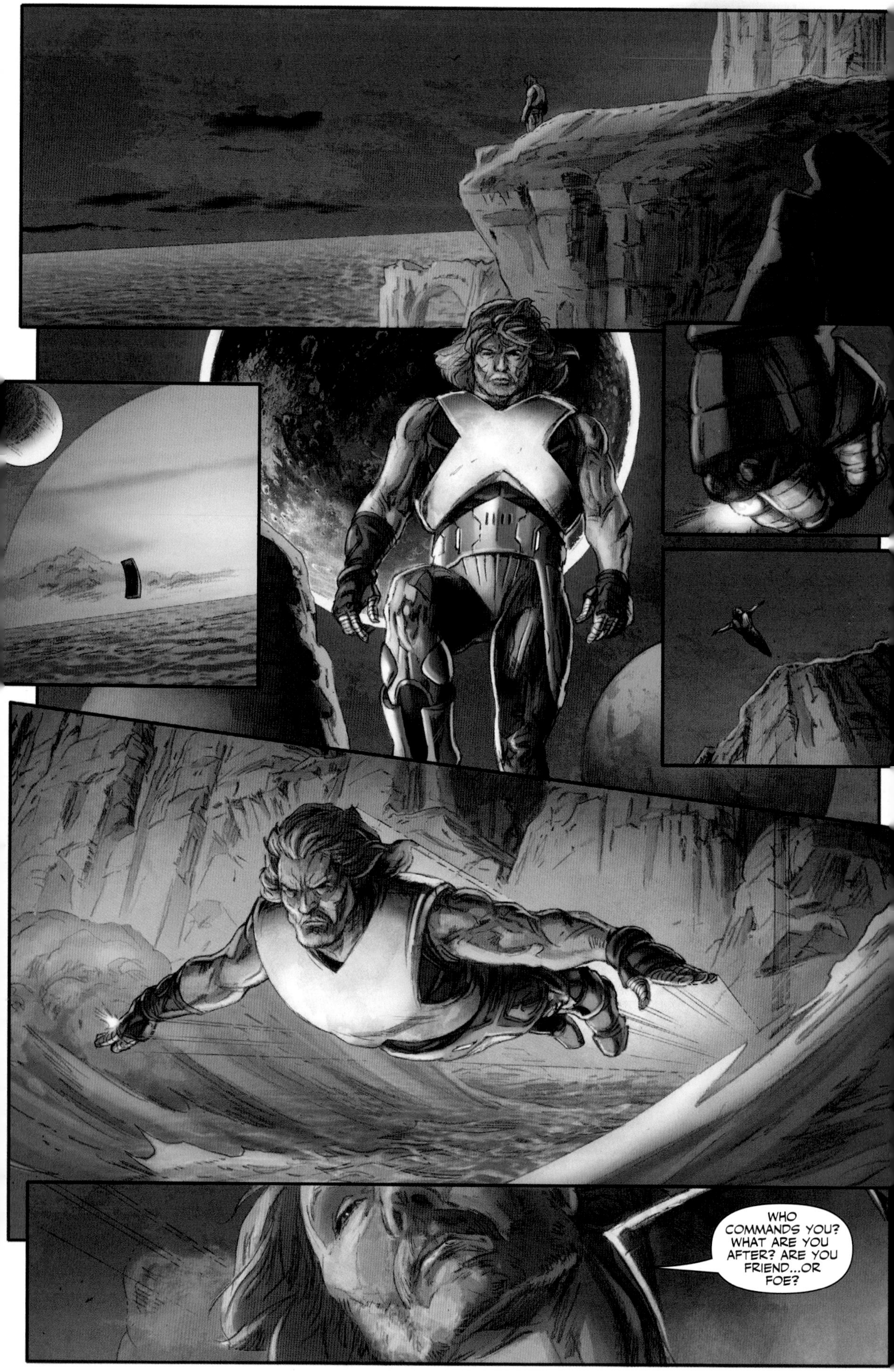
WHO COMMANDS YOU? WHAT ARE YOU AFTER? ARE YOU FRIEND...OR FOE?

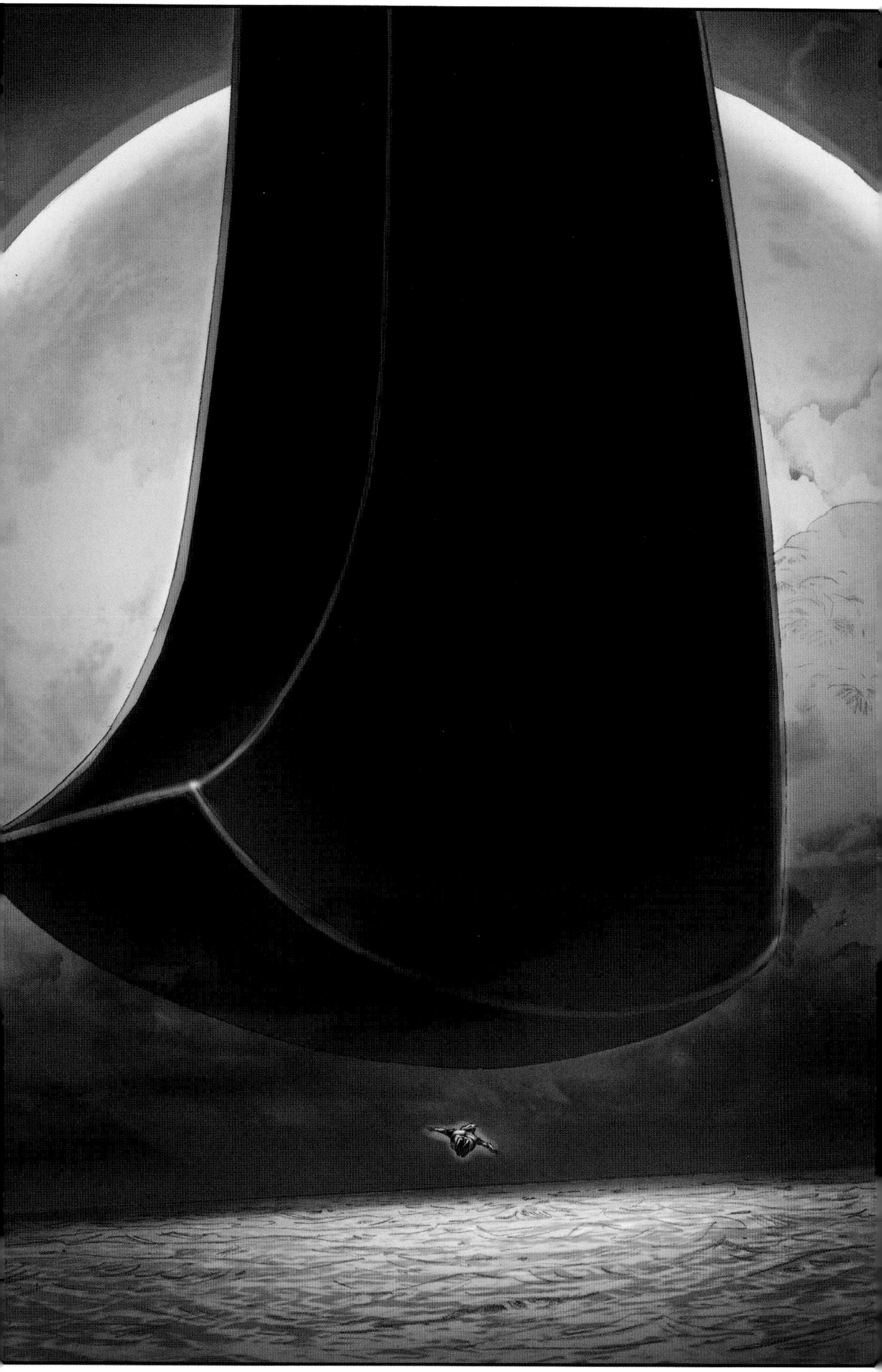

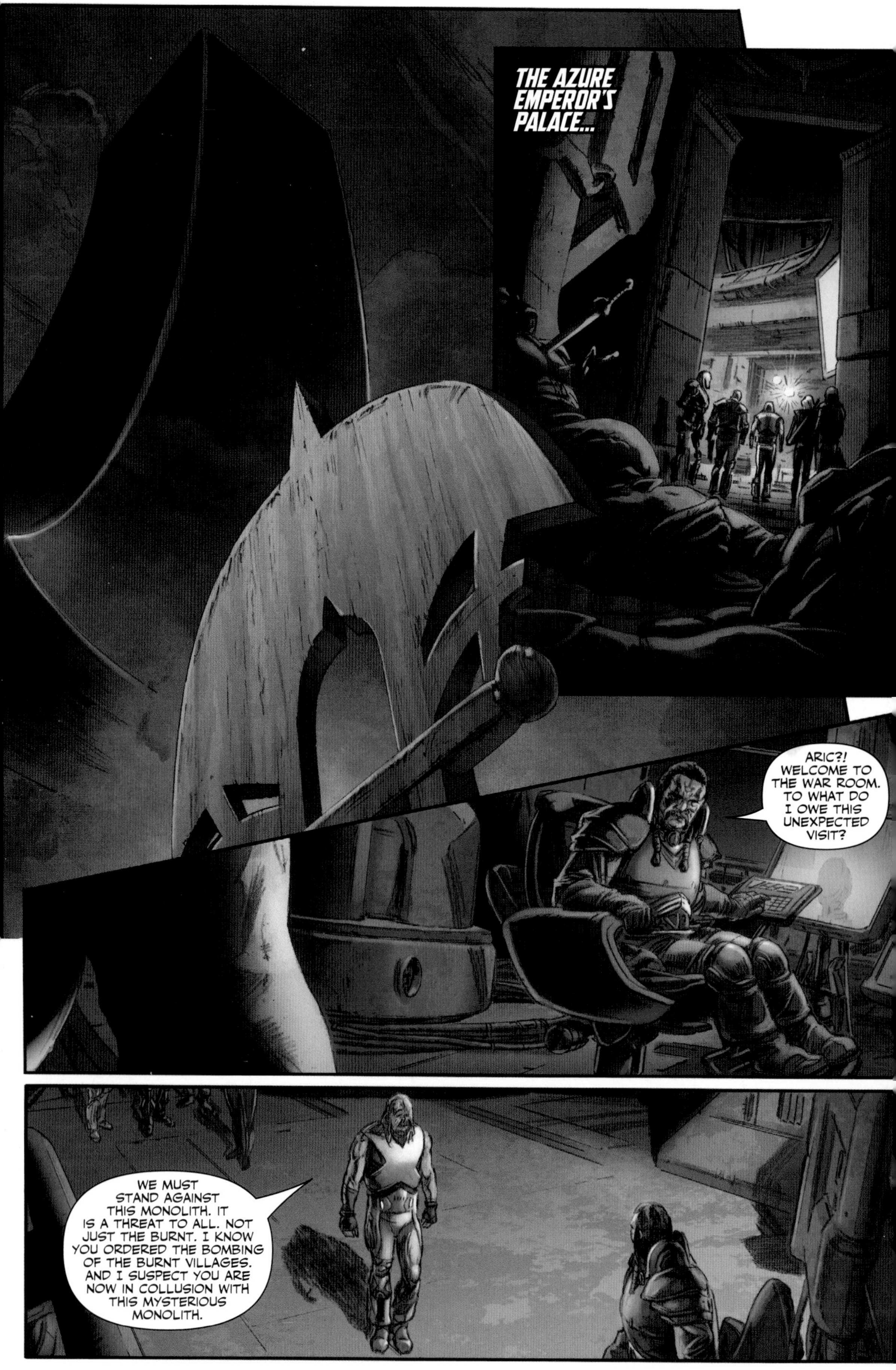
THE AZURE EMPEROR'S PALACE...
ARIC?! WELCOME TO THE WAR ROOM. TO WHAT DO I OWE THIS UNEXPECTED VISIT?
WE MUST STAND AGAINST THIS MONOLITH. IT IS A THREAT TO ALL. NOT JUST THE BURNT. I KNOW YOU ORDERED THE BOMBING OF THE BURNT VILLAGES. AND I SUSPECT YOU ARE NOW IN COLLUSION WITH THIS MYSTERIOUS MONOLITH.

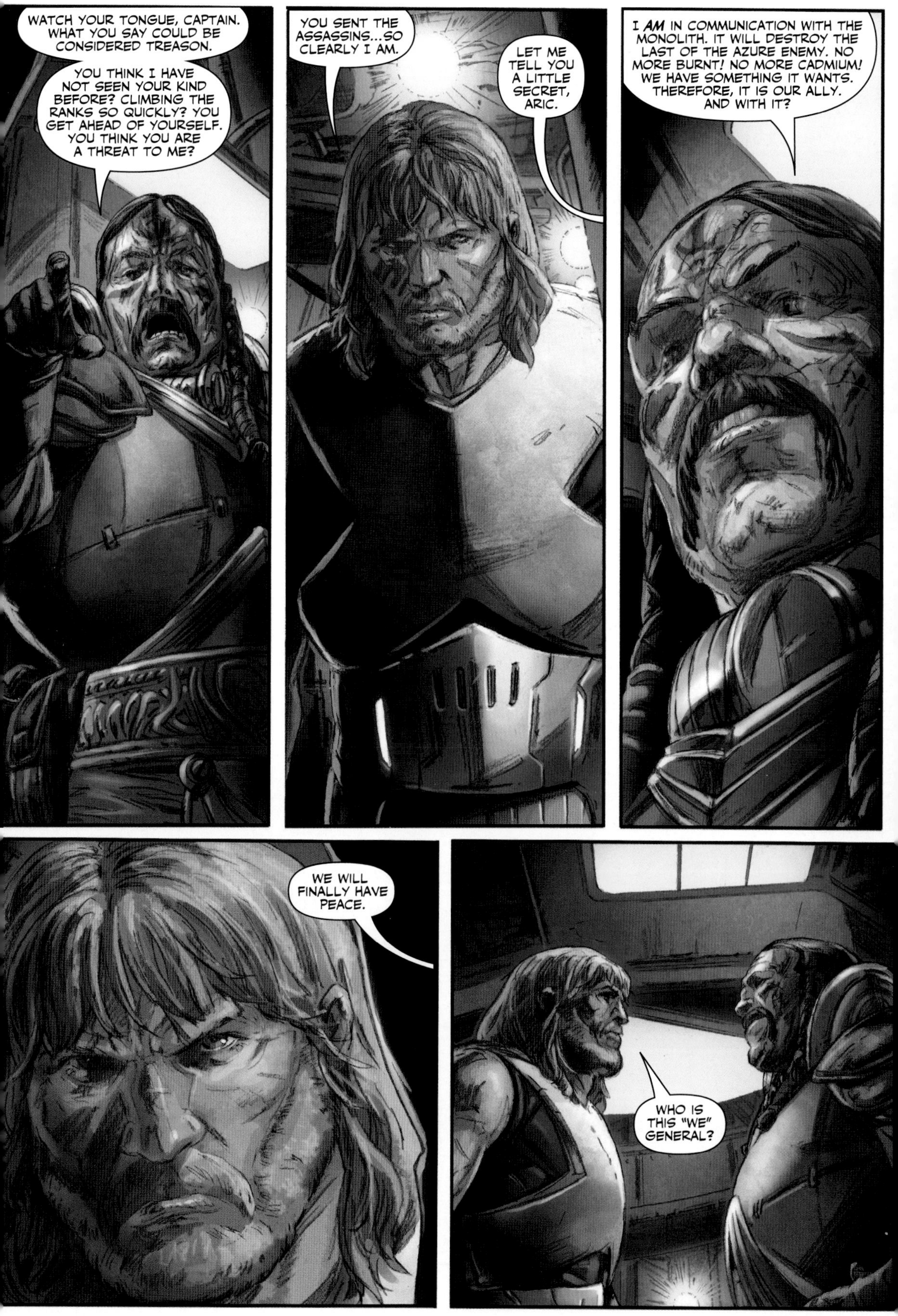
WATCH YOUR TONGUE, CAPTAIN. WHAT YOU SAY COULD BE CONSIDERED TREASON.
YOU THINK I HAVE NOT SEEN YOUR KIND BEFORE? CLIMBING THE RANKS SO QUICKLY? YOU GET AHEAD OF YOURSELF. YOU THINK YOU ARE A THREAT TO ME?
YOU SENT THE ASSASSINS...SO CLEARLY I AM.
LET ME TELL YOU A LITTLE SECRET, ARIC.
I AM IN COMMUNICATION WITH THE MONOLITH. IT WILL DESTROY THE LAST OF THE AZURE ENEMY. NO MORE BURNT! NO MORE CADMIUM! WE HAVE SOMETHING IT WANTS. THEREFORE, IT IS OUR ALLY. AND WITH IT?
WE WILL FINALLY HAVE PEACE.
WHO IS THIS "WE" GENERAL?

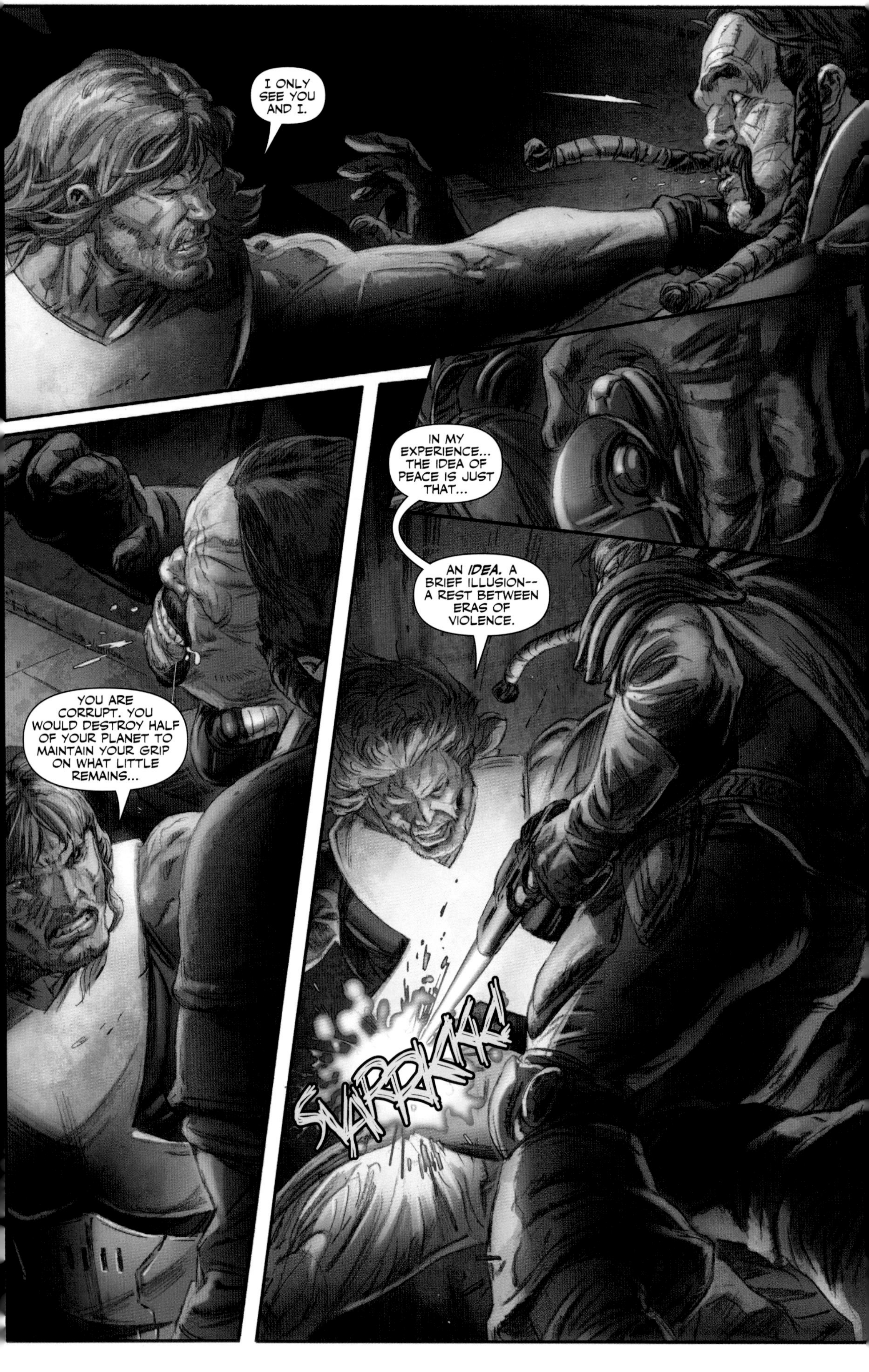
I ONLY SEE YOU AND I.
IN MY EXPERIENCE... THE IDEA OF PEACE IS JUST THAT...
AN *IDEA.* A BRIEF ILLUSION-- A REST BETWEEN ERAS OF VIOLENCE.
YOU ARE CORRUPT. YOU WOULD DESTROY HALF OF YOUR PLANET TO MAINTAIN YOUR GRIP ON WHAT LITTLE REMAINS...

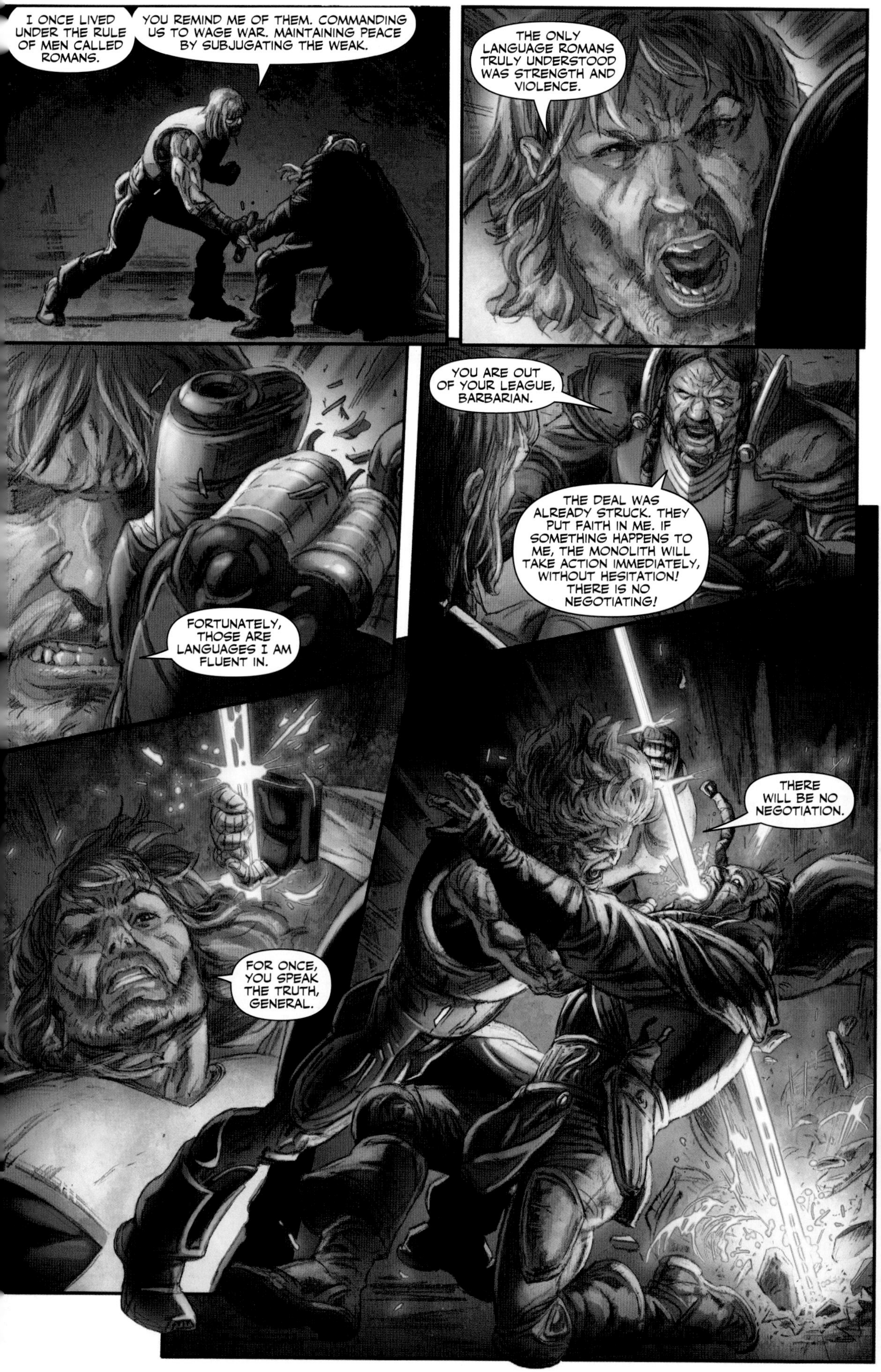
I ONCE LIVED UNDER THE RULE OF MEN CALLED ROMANS.
YOU REMIND ME OF THEM. COMMANDING US TO WAGE WAR. MAINTAINING PEACE BY SUBJUGATING THE WEAK.
THE ONLY LANGUAGE ROMANS TRULY UNDERSTOOD WAS STRENGTH AND VIOLENCE.
FORTUNATELY, THOSE ARE LANGUAGES I AM FLUENT IN.
YOU ARE OUT OF YOUR LEAGUE, BARBARIAN.
THE DEAL WAS ALREADY STRUCK. THEY PUT FAITH IN ME. IF SOMETHING HAPPENS TO ME, THE MONOLITH WILL TAKE ACTION IMMEDIATELY, WITHOUT HESITATION! THERE IS NO NEGOTIATING!
FOR ONCE, YOU SPEAK THE TRUTH, GENERAL.
THERE WILL BE NO NEGOTIATION.

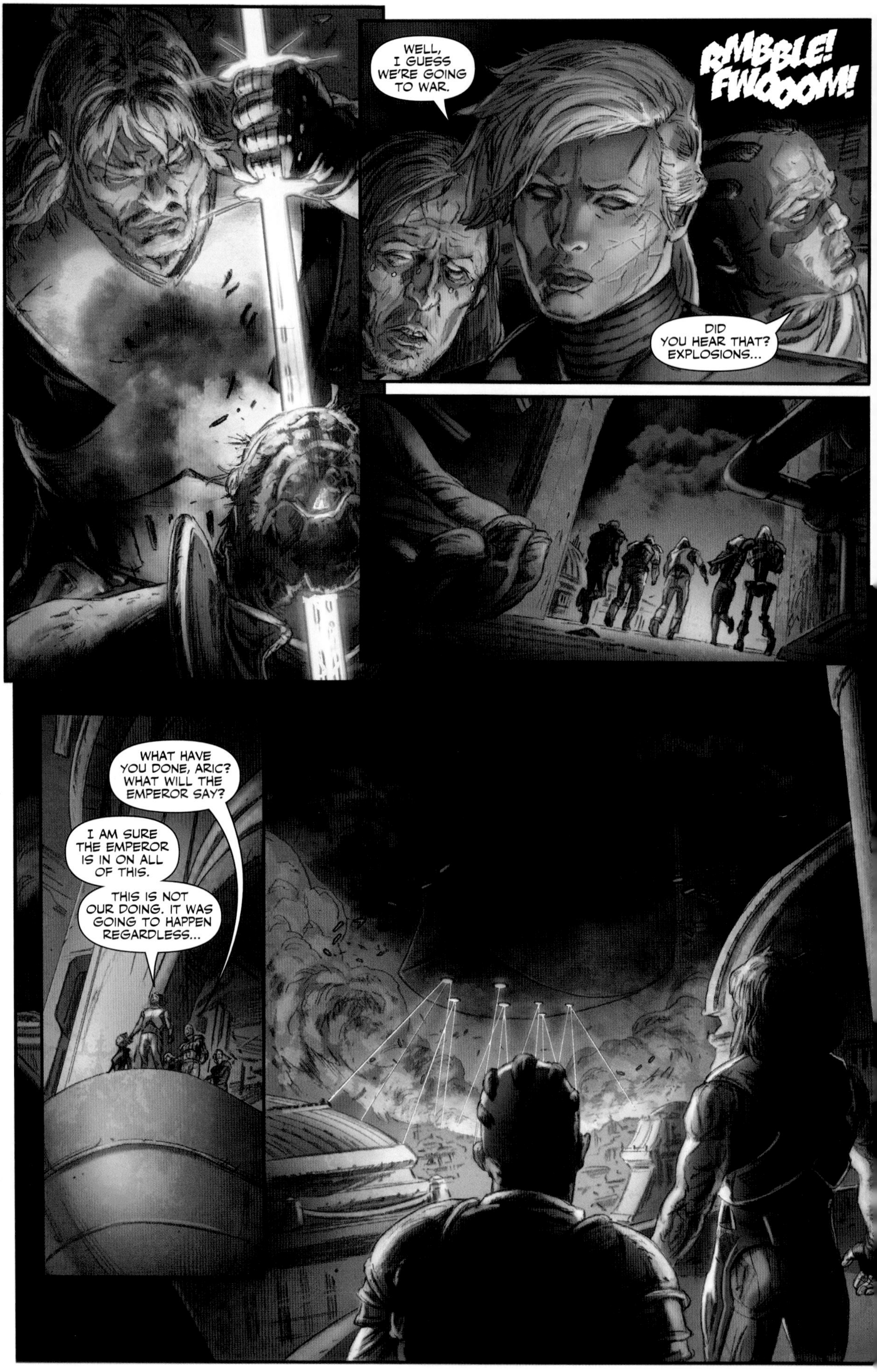
WELL, I GUESS WE'RE GOING TO WAR.
RMBBLE! FWOOOM!
DID YOU HEAR THAT? EXPLOSIONS...
WHAT HAVE YOU DONE, ARIC? WHAT WILL THE EMPEROR SAY?
I AM SURE THE EMPEROR IS IN ON ALL OF THIS.
THIS IS NOT OUR DOING. IT WAS GOING TO HAPPEN REGARDLESS...

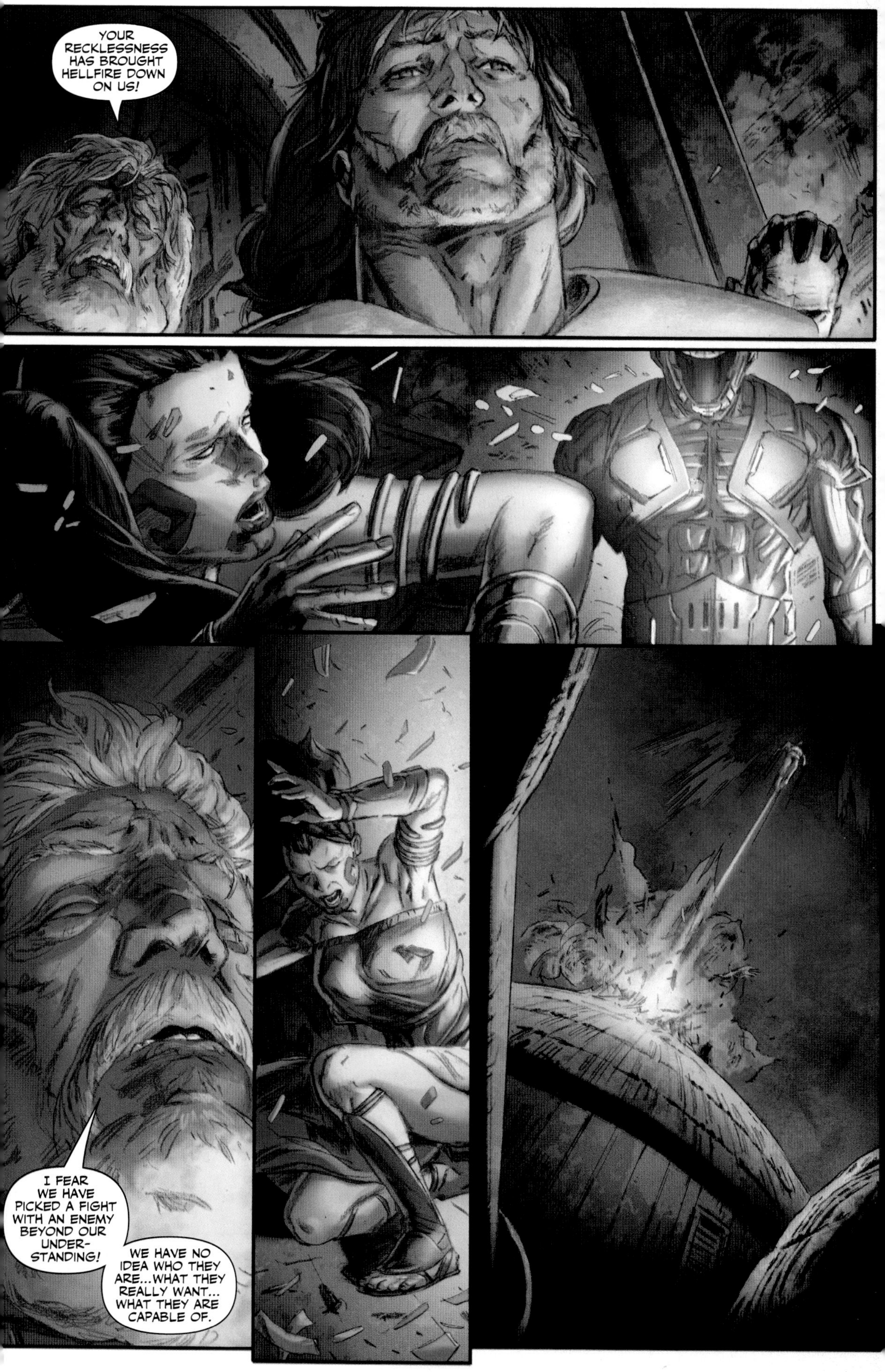
YOUR RECKLESSNESS HAS BROUGHT HELLFIRE DOWN ON US!
I FEAR WE HAVE PICKED A FIGHT WITH AN ENEMY BEYOND OUR UNDER-STANDING!
WE HAVE NO IDEA WHO THEY ARE...WHAT THEY REALLY WANT... WHAT THEY ARE CAPABLE OF.

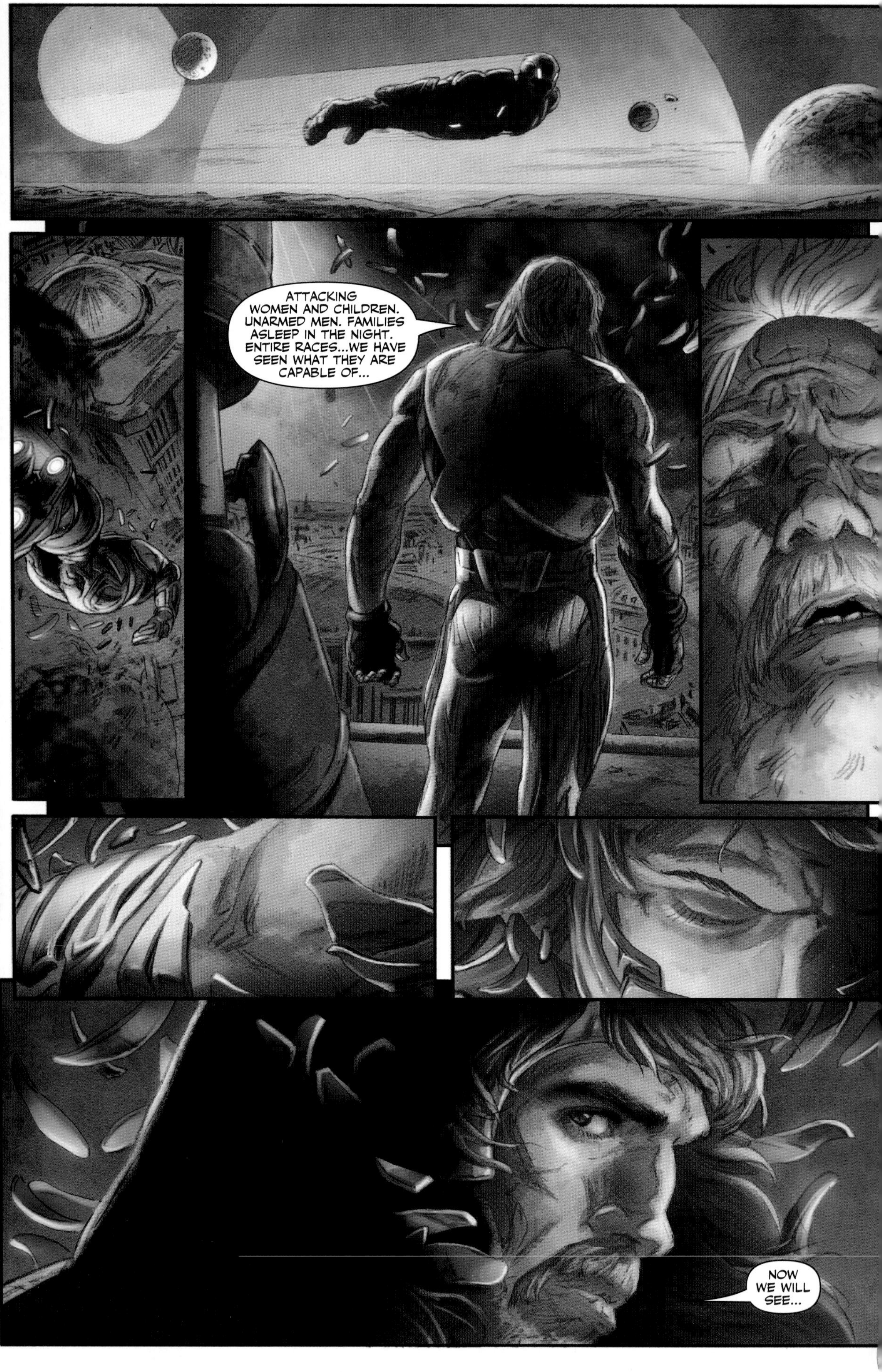
ATTACKING WOMEN AND CHILDREN. UNARMED MEN. FAMILIES ASLEEP IN THE NIGHT. ENTIRE RACES...WE HAVE SEEN WHAT THEY ARE CAPABLE OF...
NOW WE WILL SEE...

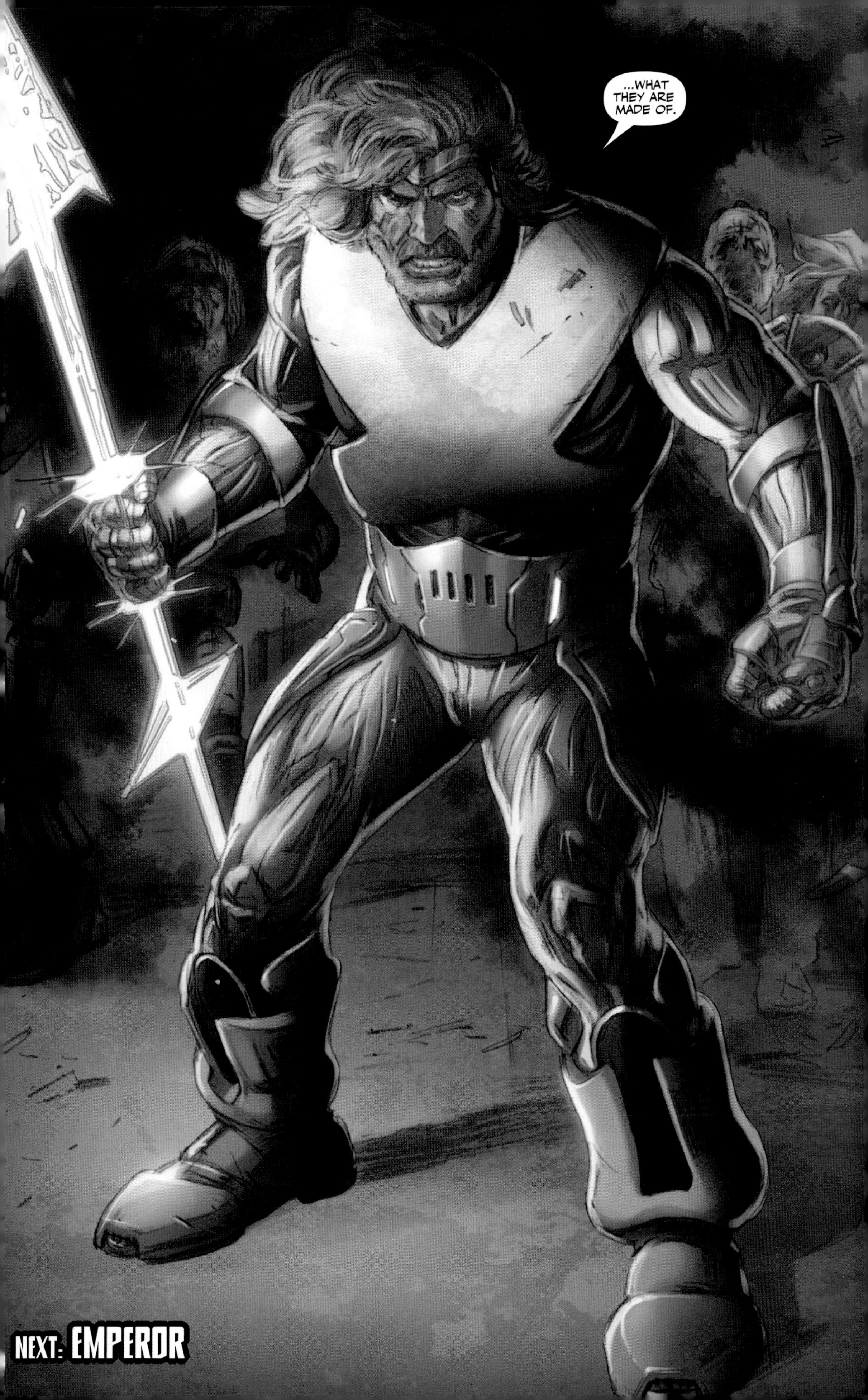
...WHAT THEY ARE MADE OF.
NEXT: EMPEROR

X-O
MANOWAR
SOLDIER
ISSUE 01
Matt Kindt
Tomás Giorello
Diego Rodriguez
VALIANT

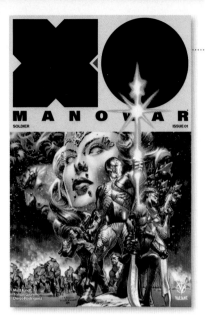

X-O MANOWAR #1

LL: When Warren Simons told me to "think Star Wars" for the first cover, I knew exactly what I'd do. I'd been wanting to do an homage to the famous Hildebrandt cover for years, so I could see this cover pretty clearly before I even put pencil to paper. I thought it was a great way to immediately give a sense of the scale of Kindt's story and X-O's cast -- right up my alley.

X-O
MANOWAR
SOLDIER
ISSUE 02
Matt Kindt
Tomás Giorello
Diego Rodriguez
VALIANT

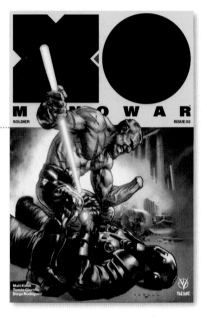

X-O MANOWAR #2

LL: The main thing I was going for here was some dynamic tension in Aric's anatomy, with a lot of fleshy striations and vascularity. I also think it worked as a nice contrast to his enemy's polished armor. I'm rarely pleased with my work, but I was fairly happy with the intensity in Aric's eyes here.

X-O
MANOWAR
SOLDIER
ISSUE 03
Matt Kindt
Tomás Giorello
David Mack
Diego Rodriguez
VALIANT

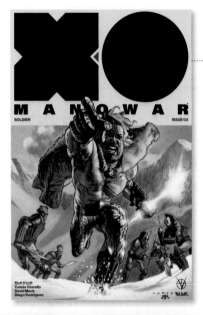

X-O MANOWAR #3

LL: I had a lot of fun with Aric here, his metal hand, the figure work, and the intricate armor on his legs, but the snowy background was difficult for me to pull off in black and white. Thankfully I had Brian Reber backing me up, who I asked to reference Frank Frazetta's colors in his amazing Silver Warrior painting.

Originally published in *X-O MANOWAR (2017) #5 PRE-ORDER EDITION*

X-O
MANOWAR
GENERAL
ISSUE 04
Matt Kindt
Doug Braithwaite
Brian Reber
VALIANT

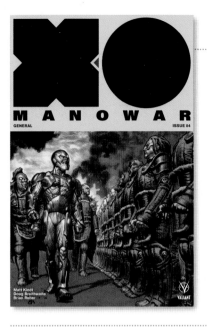

X-O MANOWAR #4

LL: This one was a lot of work! Rendering all the figures and their complicated costumes was time consuming, but it was also important for me to nail X-O's body language here, and finding a mid-walk pose I was happy with took a bit of time. Not only that, but his lieutenants were in mid-walk as well and I wanted them to each have their own build and attitude.

X-O
MANOWAR
GENERAL
ISSUE 05
Matt Kindt
Tomas Giorello
Diego Rodriguez
VALIANT

X-O MANOWAR #5

LL: Warren had suggested the concept for this cover, Aric looking at a map with his lieutenants, for issue 4, but I couldn't immediately come up with a compelling composition at the time. It eventually occurred to me to have a low angle so we can see Aric looking down toward us, connecting with the reader, yet have the horizon high enough so we can still see the map. Holding his knife in the map would give him something to do (I try to avoid just having characters standing there), and his helmet makes for a great paper weight!

X-O
GENERAL
ISSUE 06
Matt Kindt
Doug Braithwaite
Diego Rodriguez
VALIANT

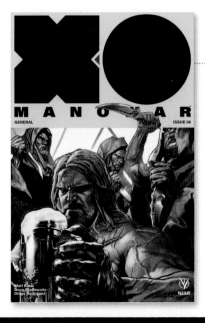

X-O MANOWAR #6

LL: I spent a lot of time differentiating the textures on this piece. At the beginning of my career, the writer of the first book I drew criticized my work, telling me everything I drew looked like it was made of the same stuff, that I really needed to work on textures. Like most great advice, it was hard to hear at the time but eventually proved to be invaluable.

Originally published in *X-O MANOWAR (2017) #4 PRE-ORDER EDITION*

You've worked with Matt Kindt on several Valiant titles before, but what makes this iteration of X-O Manowar unique?

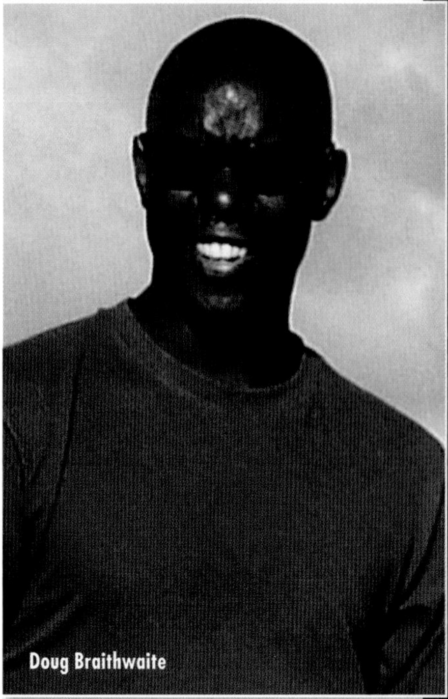
Doug Braithwaite

DB: We have collaborated on a few titles now; Unity, Ninjak and now this re-imagining of X-O. Although each job has been different, one of the things I always enjoy about Matt's writing is his ability to distort "reality," to skew the traditional approaches of comic storytelling to create slightly surreal, sometimes unsettling environments. I love that he always brings me new challenges every time we collaborate and this new version of X-O is no different. The first X-O was mostly based on earth whereas this X-O is set in a far off planet - so anything can happen - and it does!

How is your previous work with the character informing your work on this new series?

DB: Although there are obvious similarities you have to really look at them as two different characters. The Aric I first drew struck me as being slightly overconfident, even arrogant. This Aric is far more reserved, a deep thinker who holds his cards close to his chest. He has a sense of "burden" about him and I find that more fascinating to draw.

What is it like to have the freedom to build a completely new, science fiction-world on Planet Gorin?

DB: I have done this science-fiction, world-building thing several times, but it's always different every time I'm able to do it. Everything about the world is described in the script, the fun part is pulling the visual components together to create a world that is, at first glance fantastical, but at the same time recognizable to the reader and grounded in its own sense of reality. Matt has also brought a lot of his own wonderfully eccentric designs to the table, which we artists have been given free-reign to flesh out and rework to fit the story we want to tell. And the brutal Barbarian environments and futuristic steam-punk machinery are a great combination to play with!

What character do you enjoy drawing the most, and what has drawn you towards them?

DB: I find most of the characters I draw visually interesting and, from a technical point of view, have enjoyed playing around with the looks and various components on some of the costumes.

Of the characters I have drawn in the last few years, the ones I designed for Imperium were fascinating, with Sunlight on Snow being a particular favourite of mine - and a fan favourite apparently. The challenge there was how could I draw an expressionless character but convincingly portray emotion and empathy through body language. That was great fun to do.

This new incarnation of X-O is a great version to get to grips with too - I love his world-weary look. He's more gritty and down to earth and I love the scenes when he's in a reflective mood. I think he's developing into a favourite too.

Originally published in *X-O MANOWAR (2017) #4 PRE-ORDER EDITION*

DESIGNING THE NEW LOOK OF X-O MANOWAR

Art by Matt Kindt, Doug Braithwaite, and Lewis LaRosa with Brian Reber

DOUG BRAITHWAITE

My intention was to follow Matt's "General" design. It also made sense to tie it in with the covers that had him portrayed with more armor.

I thought Lewis' interpretation was a sensible approach for the next stage of development, i.e. armored girdle, legs, boots, right arm, and left hand.

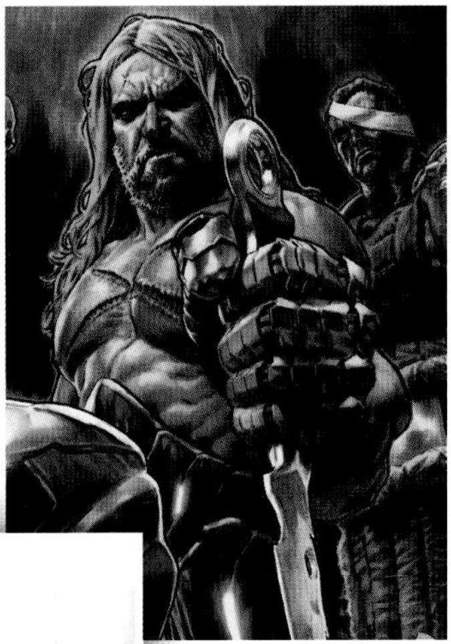

by Lewis LaRosa

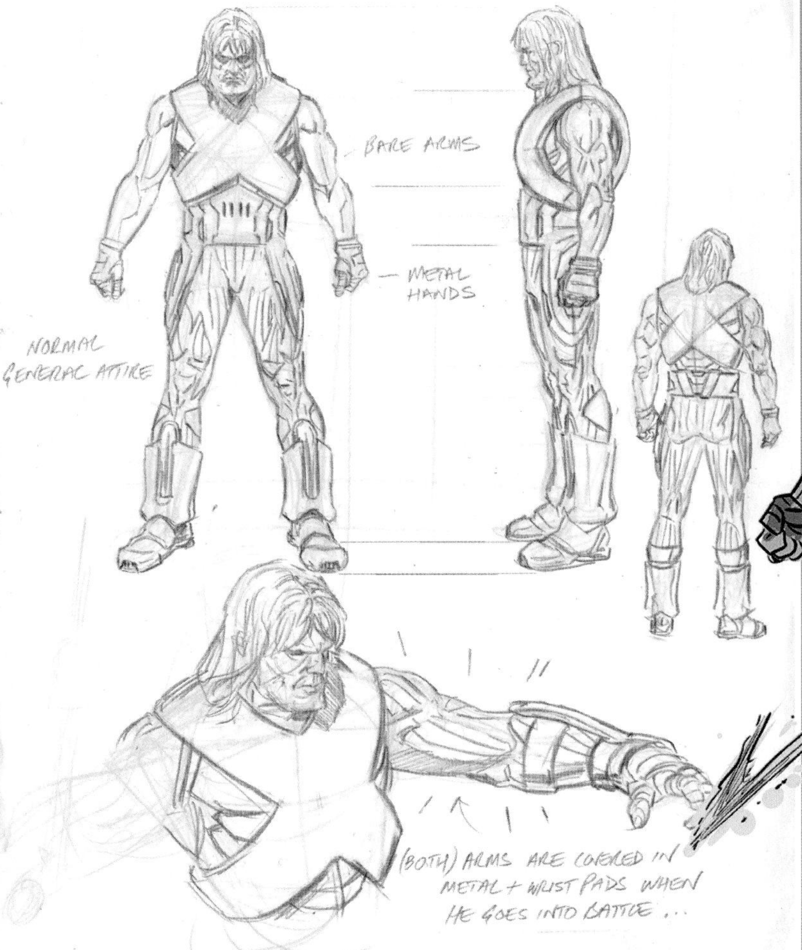
BARE ARMS
METAL HANDS
NORMAL GENERAL ATTIRE
(BOTH) ARMS ARE COVERED IN METAL + WRIST PADS WHEN HE GOES INTO BATTLE ...

by Doug Braithwaite

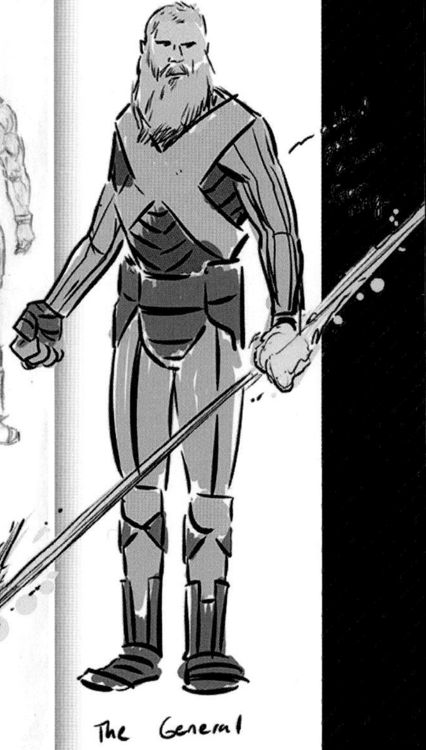
The General

by Matt Kindt

Originally published in *X-O MANOWAR (2017) #5 PRE-ORDER EDITION*

ROBERT MEYERS
MANAGING EDITOR
The poetry of violence brought to life here is visceral. You're gripped with the tension Doug creates with his storytelling, and that feeling is heightened with Diego's color work. Stunning stuff.

CHARLOTTE GREENBAUM
ASSOCIATE EDITOR
Political intrigues abound! I love how Matt is getting into the classic sci-fi trope of the dangers of politics (sometimes they're just as dangerous as a battlefield, or even more so!)

ROBERT MEYERS
MANAGING EDITOR
I love the design for the assassins that Doug came up. This guy is scary.

FRED PIERCE
PUBLISHER
On these pages one can see the visualized process of artistic genius. Rather than the more common double page spread, the bar scene fight is captured in focused images so that the reader feels the chaotic nature of Aric's situation.

WARREN SIMONS
EDITOR-IN-CHIEF
An absolutely wonderful, kinetic action sequence by the brilliant Doug Braithwaite.

Doug always amazes me when it comes to sequences like this. We've got an 8-panel page here, and he's choreographed a violent, brutal fight in close quarters where the action is crisp and clear in every panel.

Aspiring artists, note how Doug's providing enough information in each of these panels – fingers, an arm, an OTS shot – so the action is extraordinarily clear to the reader. All the information is here so we're never wondering, "wait, what just happened?" And just enough information as well so he's not bogging down the action panels with superfluous detail.

Each character is at the apex of his or her motion – the headbutt, the wild miss with the knife, the arm breaking – this is truly a master craftsman at work.

HUNTER GORINSON
VP MARKETING & COMMUNICATIONS
Doug Braithwaite truly is one of the most gifted comics storytellers of his generation. He is the rare artist that can make quiet character moments just as compelling as full-on superhero combat. And here – in one of this series' most violent moments to date – his unique gift for combining intensity and nuance is on full display.

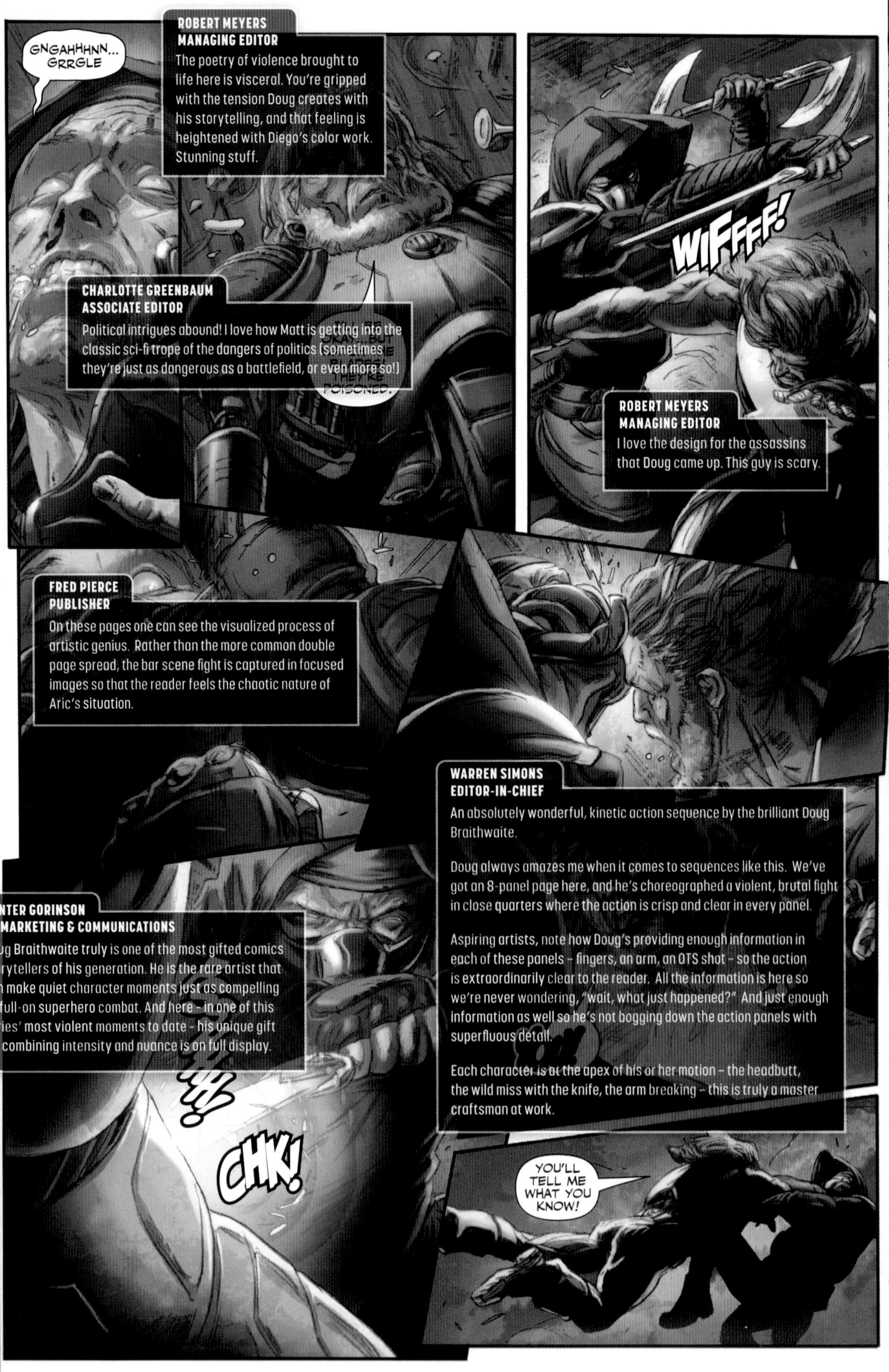
GNGAHHHNN... GRRGLE
WIFFFF!
CHK!
YOU'LL TELL ME WHAT YOU KNOW!

ARTWORK BY DOUG BRAITHWAITE WITH DIEGO RODRIGUEZ

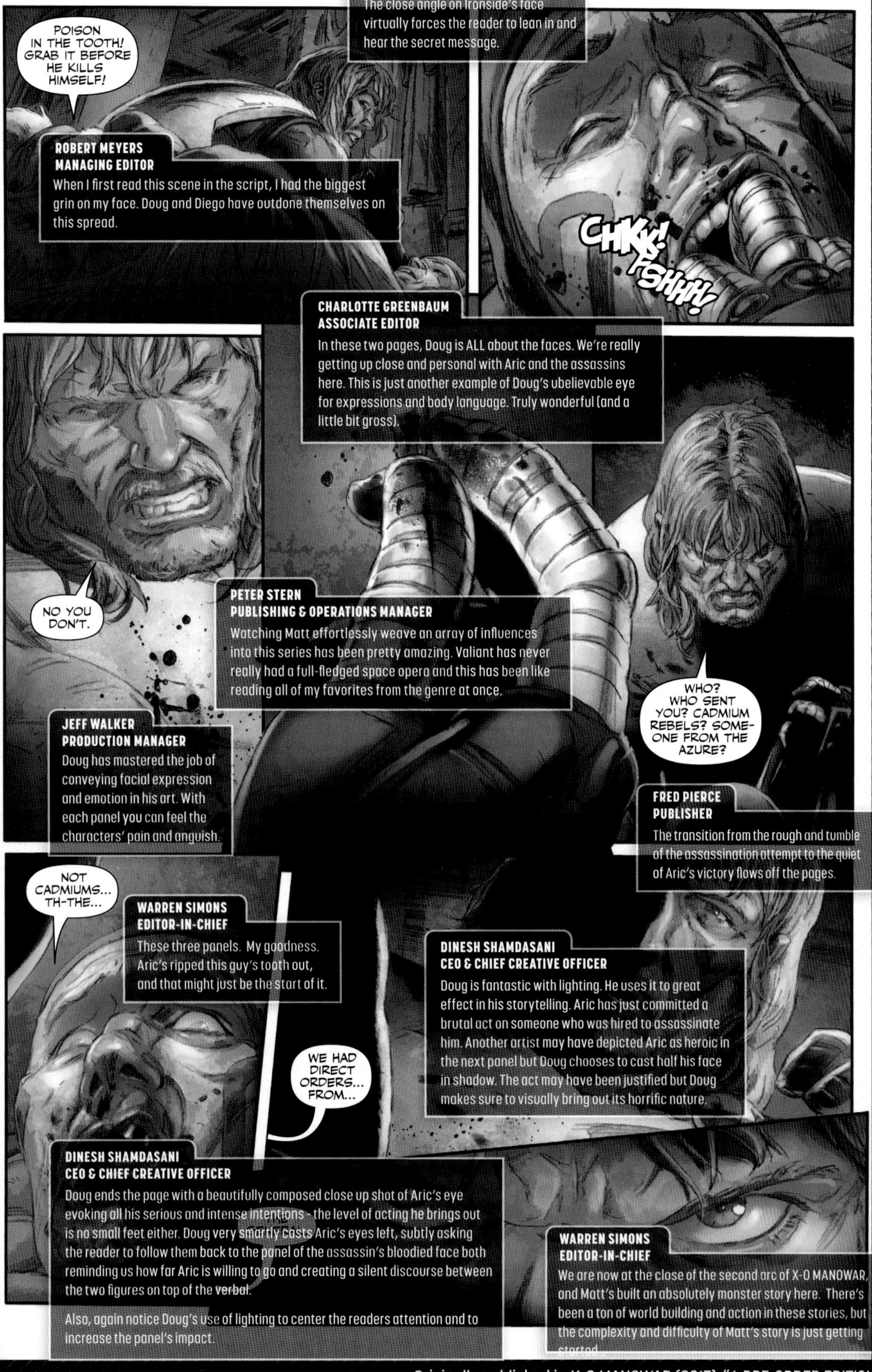
POISON IN THE TOOTH! GRAB IT BEFORE HE KILLS HIMSELF!
CHKK!
FSHHH!
NO YOU DON'T.
WHO? WHO SENT YOU? CADMIUM REBELS? SOME-ONE FROM THE AZURE?
NOT CADMIUMS... TH-THE...
WE HAD DIRECT ORDERS... FROM...

FRED PIERCE
PUBLISHER
The close angle on Ironside's face virtually forces the reader to lean in and hear the secret message.

ROBERT MEYERS
MANAGING EDITOR
When I first read this scene in the script, I had the biggest grin on my face. Doug and Diego have outdone themselves on this spread.

CHARLOTTE GREENBAUM
ASSOCIATE EDITOR
In these two pages, Doug is ALL about the faces. We're really getting up close and personal with Aric and the assassins here. This is just another example of Doug's ubelievable eye for expressions and body language. Truly wonderful (and a little bit gross).

PETER STERN
PUBLISHING & OPERATIONS MANAGER
Watching Matt effortlessly weave an array of influences into this series has been pretty amazing. Valiant has never really had a full-fledged space opera and this has been like reading all of my favorites from the genre at once.

JEFF WALKER
PRODUCTION MANAGER
Doug has mastered the job of conveying facial expression and emotion in his art. With each panel you can feel the characters' pain and anguish.

FRED PIERCE
PUBLISHER
The transition from the rough and tumble of the assassination attempt to the quiet of Aric's victory flows off the pages.

WARREN SIMONS
EDITOR-IN-CHIEF
These three panels. My goodness. Aric's ripped this guy's tooth out, and that might just be the start of it.

DINESH SHAMDASANI
CEO & CHIEF CREATIVE OFFICER
Doug is fantastic with lighting. He uses it to great effect in his storytelling. Aric has just committed a brutal act on someone who was hired to assassinate him. Another artist may have depicted Aric as heroic in the next panel but Doug chooses to cast half his face in shadow. The act may have been justified but Doug makes sure to visually bring out its horrific nature.

DINESH SHAMDASANI
CEO & CHIEF CREATIVE OFFICER
Doug ends the page with a beautifully composed close up shot of Aric's eye evoking all his serious and intense intentions - the level of acting he brings out is no small feet either. Doug very smartly casts Aric's eyes left, subtly asking the reader to follow them back to the panel of the assassin's bloodied face both reminding us how far Aric is willing to go and creating a silent discourse between the two figures on top of the verbal.

Also, again notice Doug's use of lighting to center the readers attention and to increase the panel's impact.

WARREN SIMONS
EDITOR-IN-CHIEF
We are now at the close of the second arc of X-O MANOWAR, and Matt's built an absolutely monster story here. There's been a ton of world building and action in these stories, but the complexity and difficulty of Matt's story is just getting started...

Originally published in *X-O MANOWAR (2017) #6 PRE-ORDER EDITION*

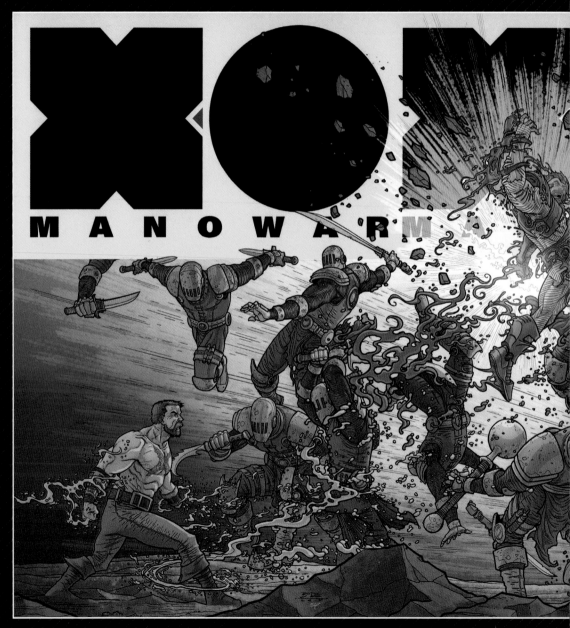

X-O MANOWAR #4-6 INTERLOCKING COVERS

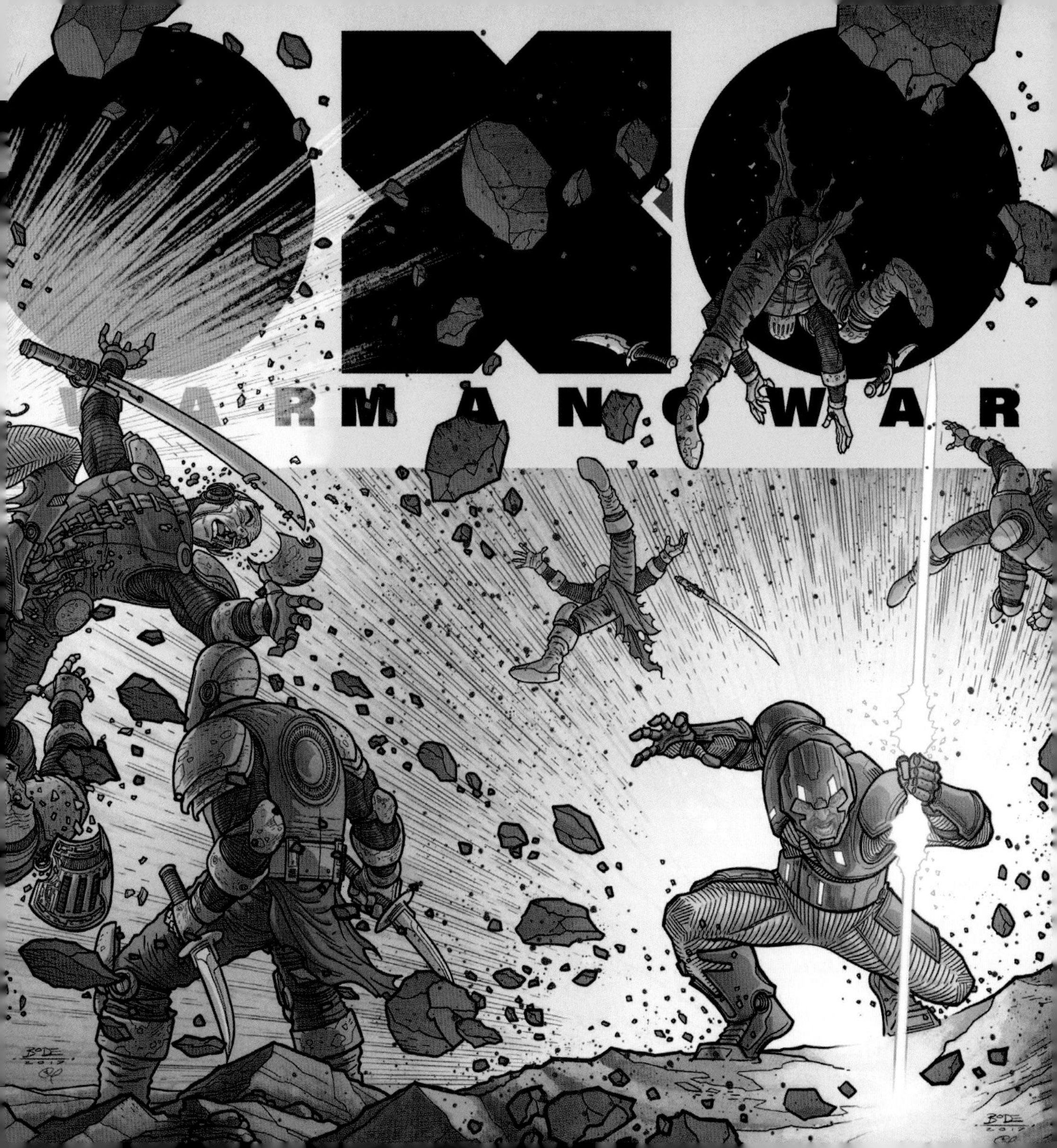
X O
M A N O W A R

X-O MANOWAR #4 COVER B
Art by DAVE JOHNSON

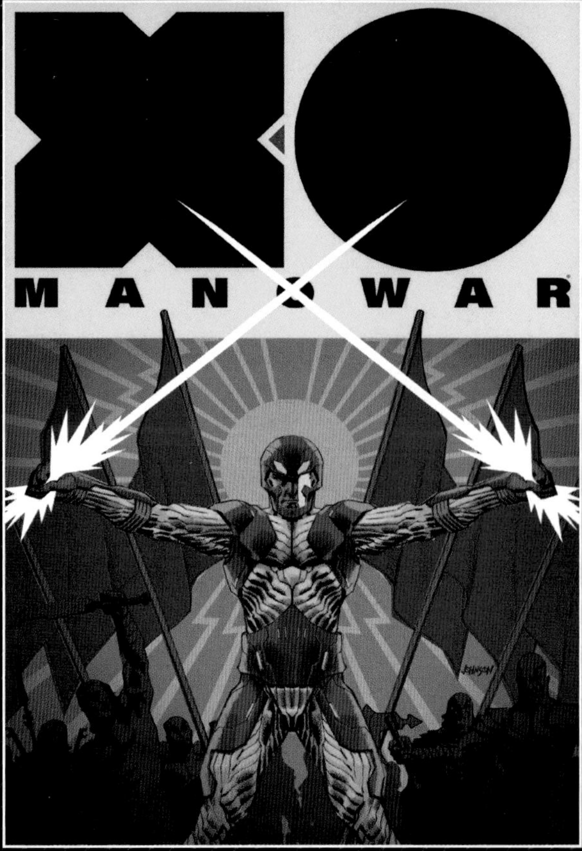
MANOWAR
JOHNSON

X-O MANOWAR #5 COVER B
Art by DAVE JOHNSON

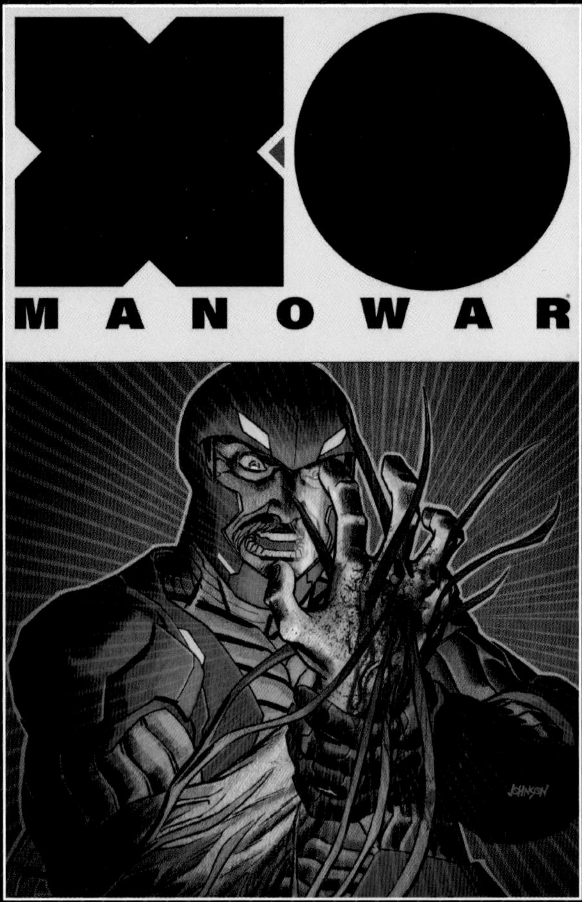
MANOWAR
JOHNSON

X-O MANOWAR #6 COVER B (facing page)
Art by DAVE JOHNSON

X-O MANOWAR®

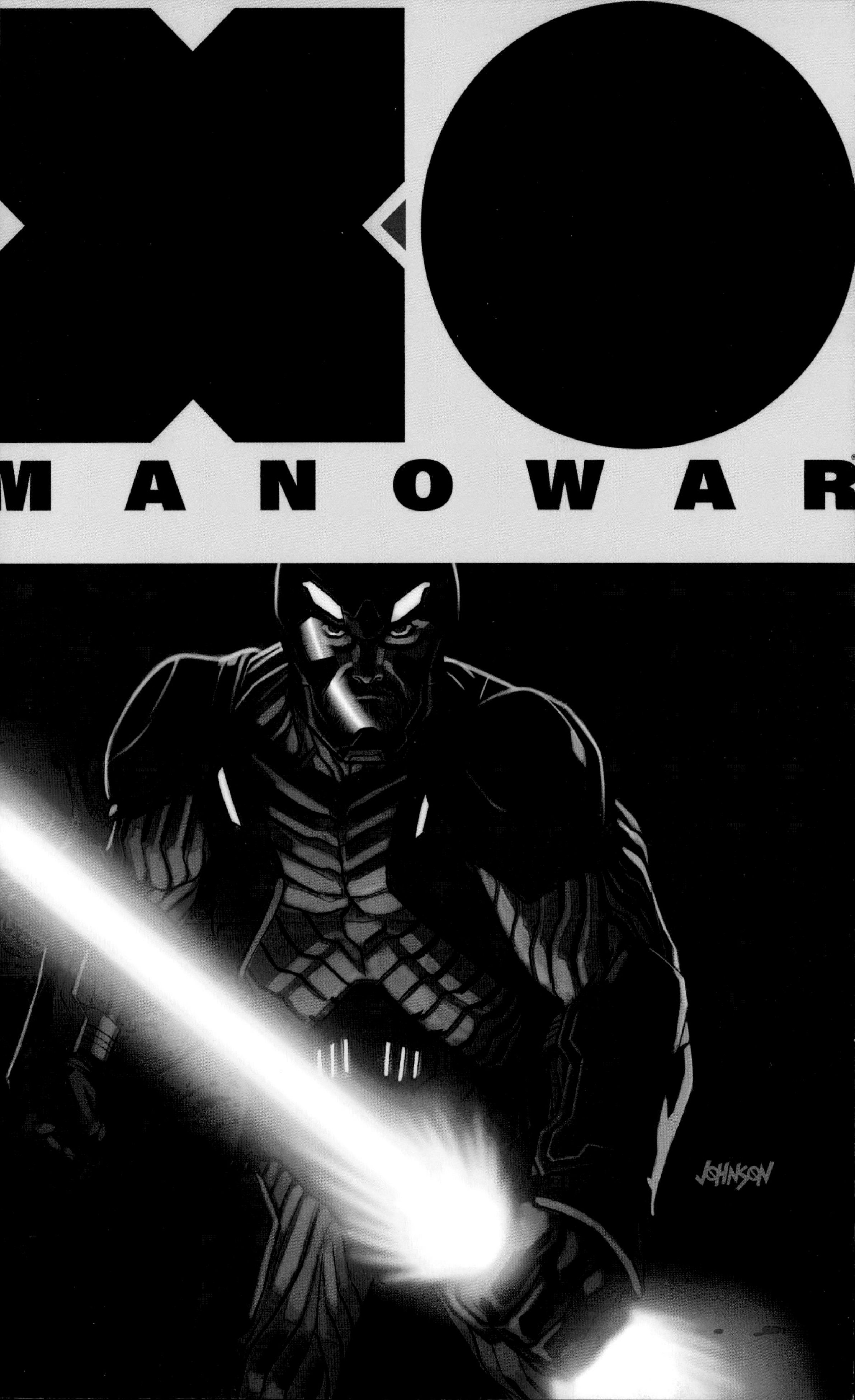
JOHNSON

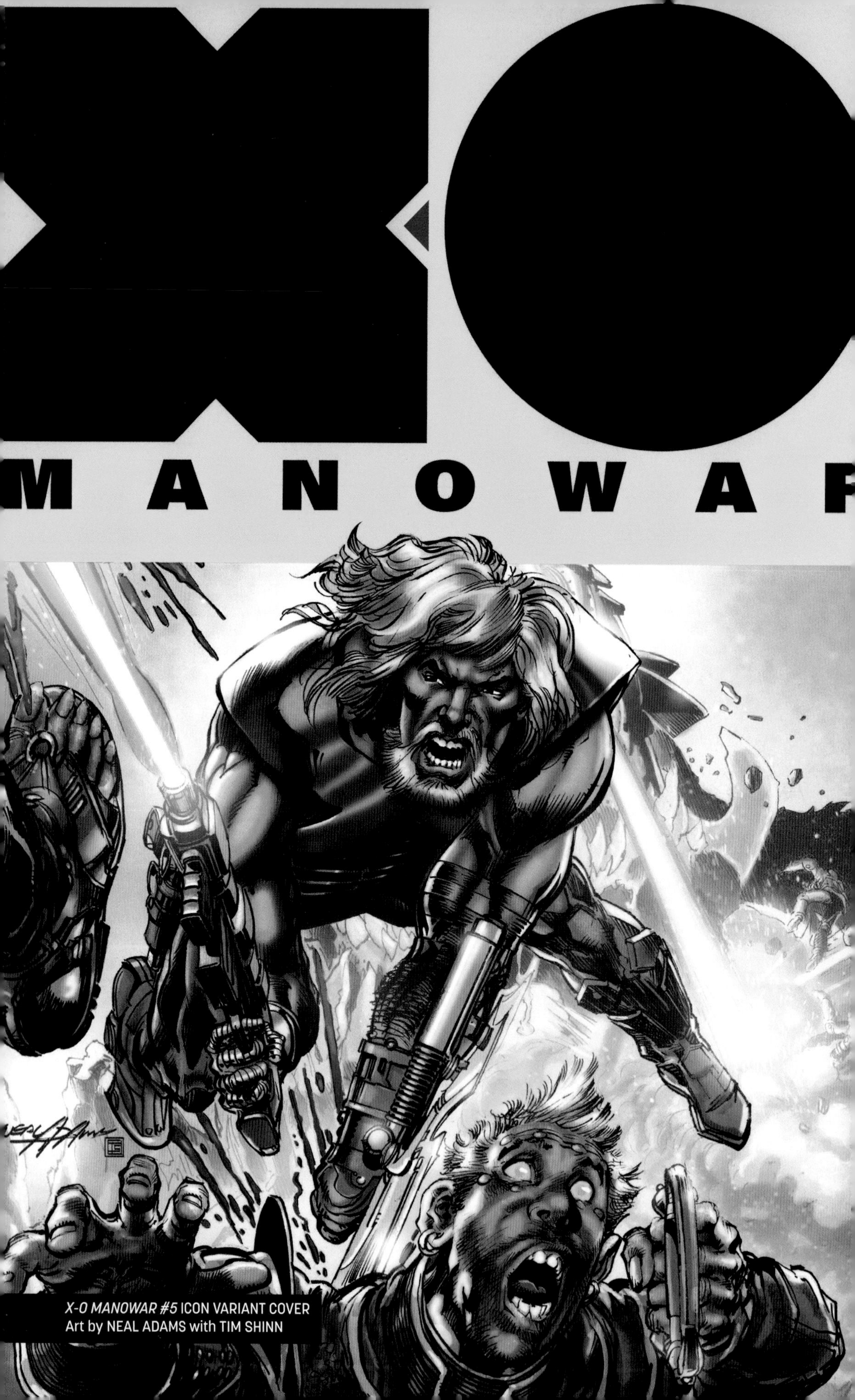
X-O
MANOWAR

X-O MANOWAR #5 ICON VARIANT COVER
Art by NEAL ADAMS with TIM SHINN

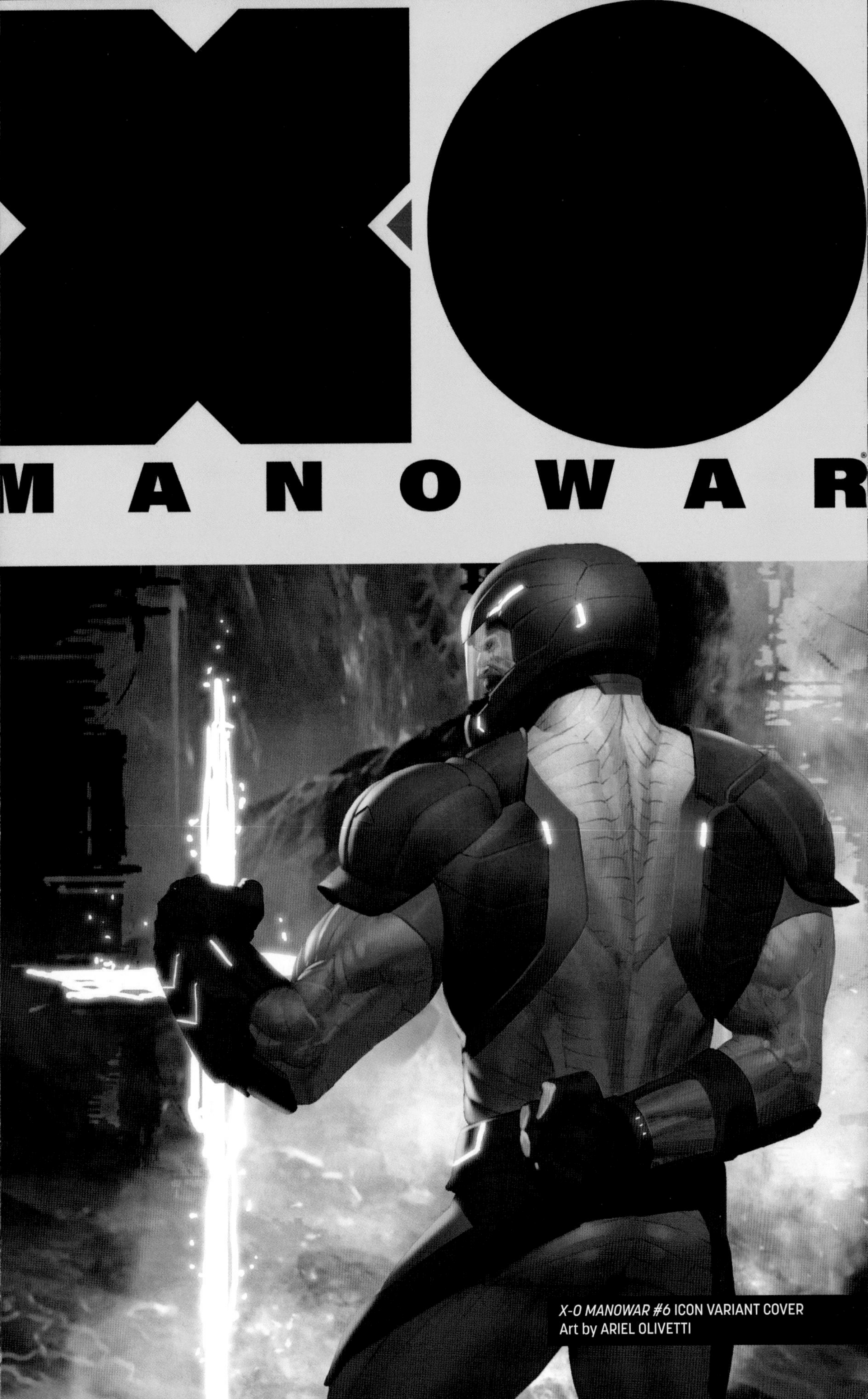
X-O
MANOWAR®

X-O MANOWAR #6 ICON VARIANT COVER
Art by ARIEL OLIVETTI

X-O MANOWAR #4 PRE-ORDER EDITION COVER
Art by DOUG BRAITHWAITE with BRIAN REBER

X-O MANOWAR #5 PRE-ORDER EDITION COVER
Art by DOUG BRAITHWAITE with BRIAN REBER

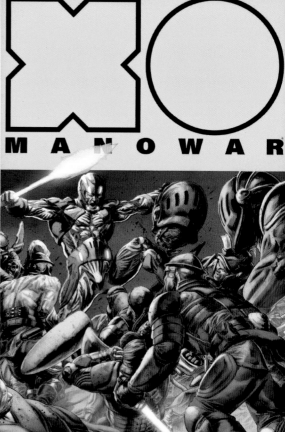

X-O MANOWAR #6 PRE-ORDER EDITION COVER
(facing page)
Art by DOUG BRAITHWAITE with BRIAN REBER

X-O MANOWAR

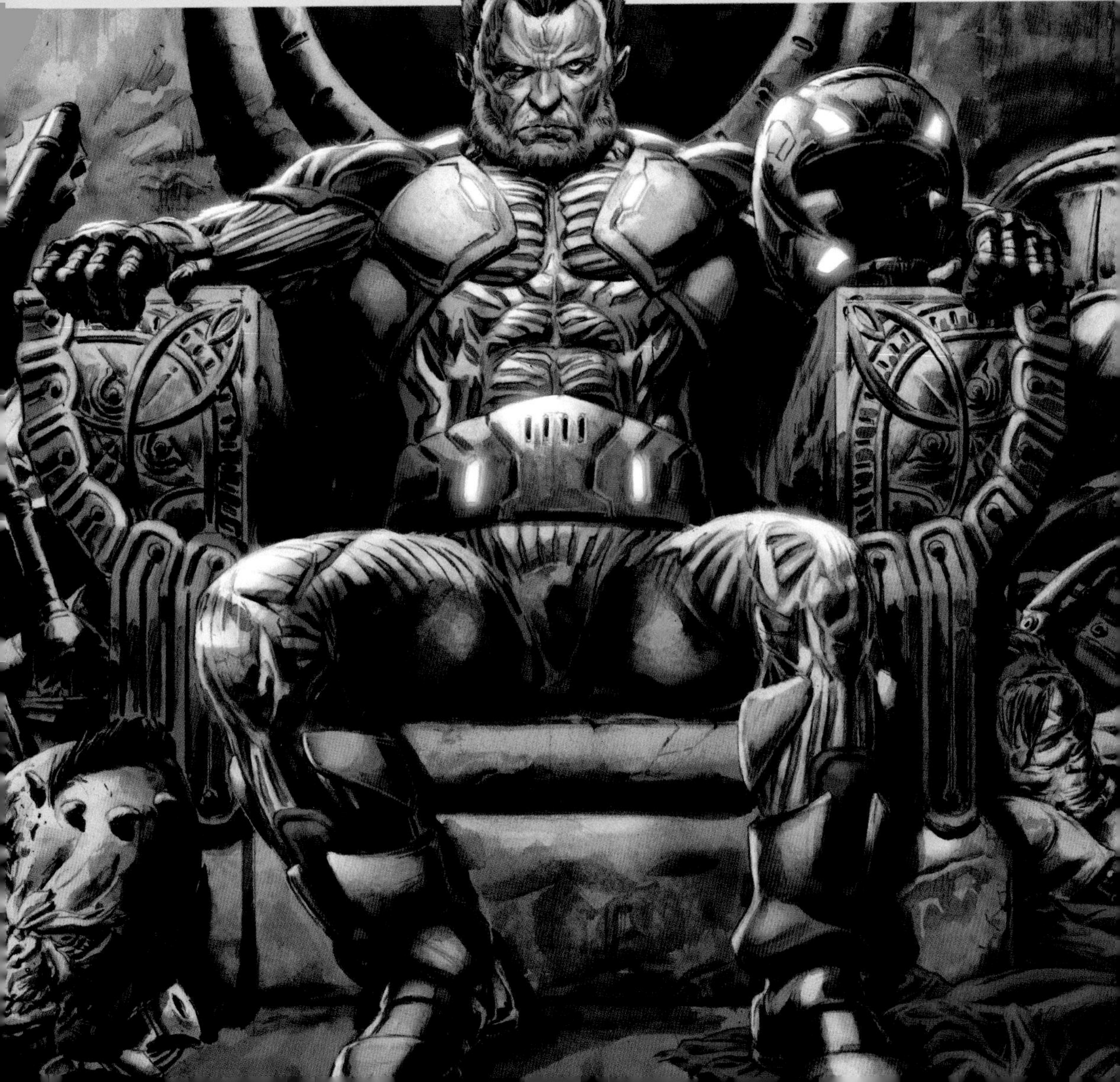

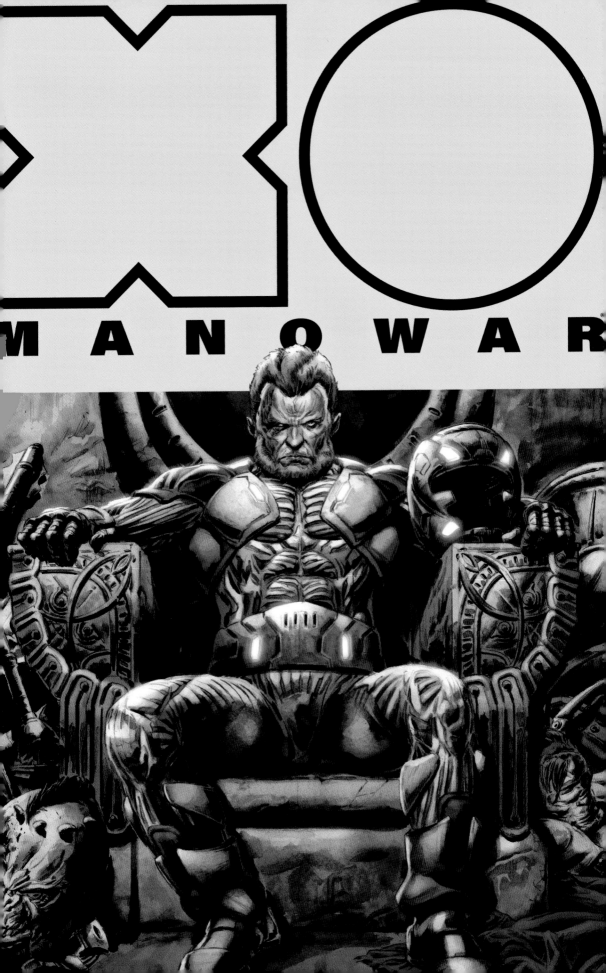

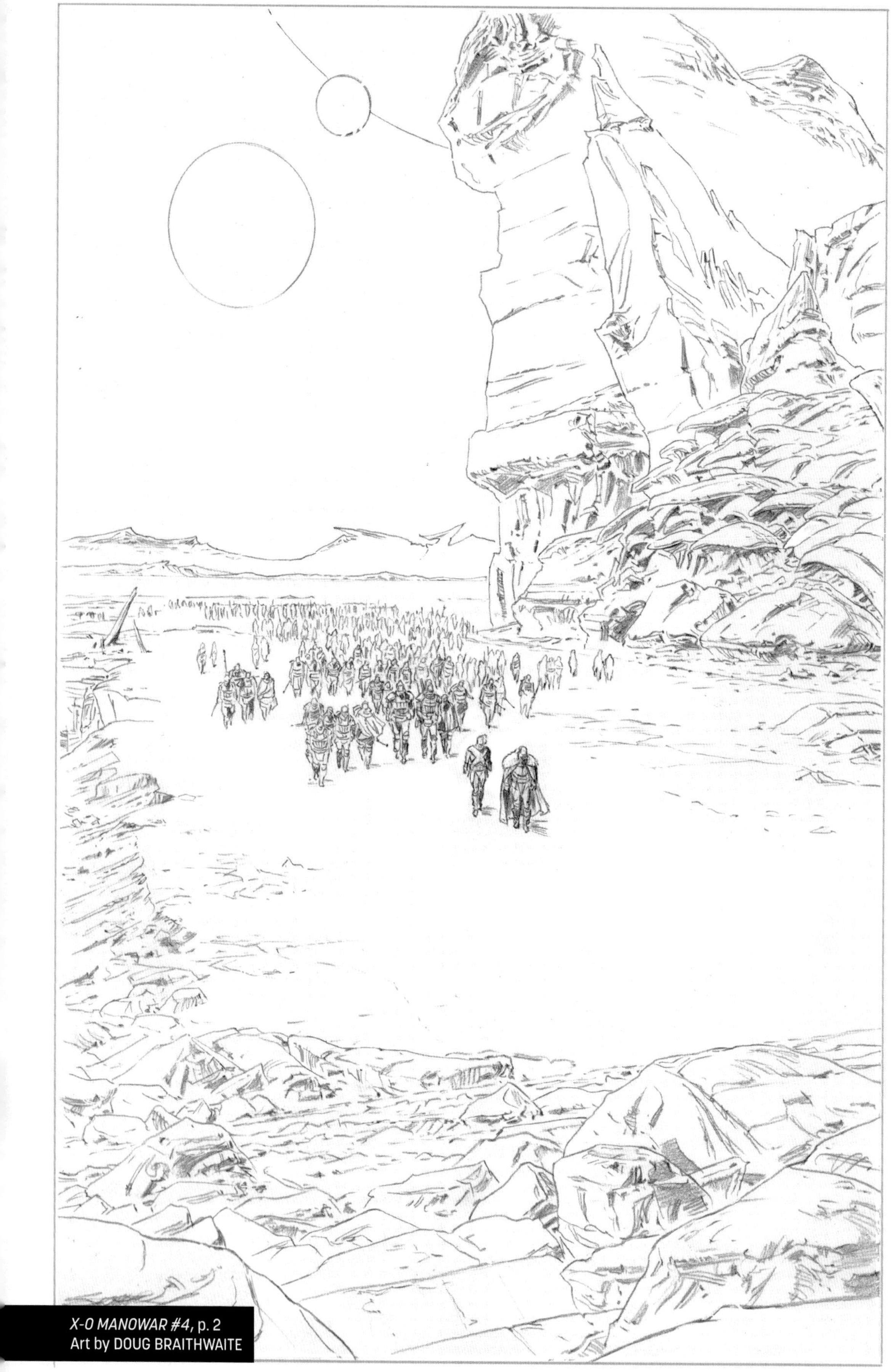
X-O #4 / Pg 1A

X-O MANOWAR #4, p. 2
Art by DOUG BRAITHWAITE

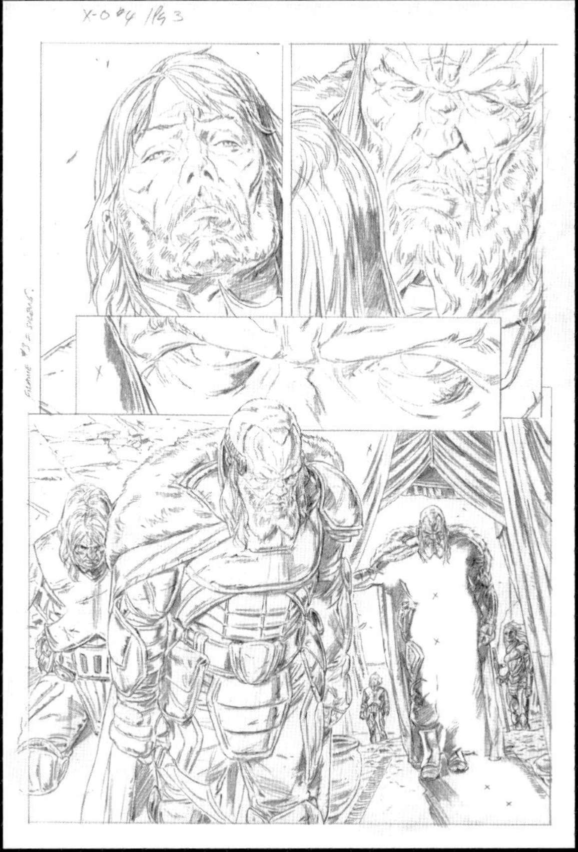

X-O MANOWAR #4, p. 5
Art by DOUG BRAITHWAITE

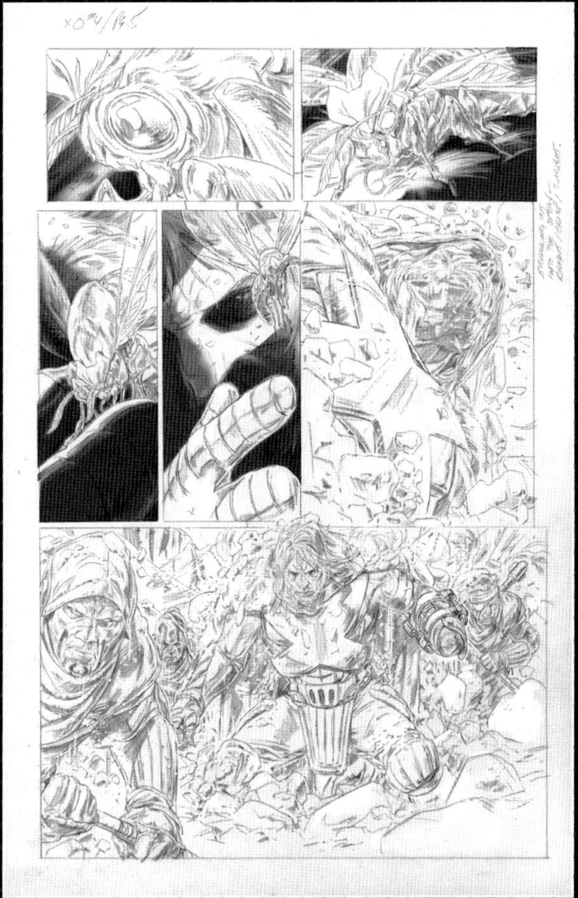

X-O MANOWAR #4, p. 7
Art by DOUG BRAITHWAITE

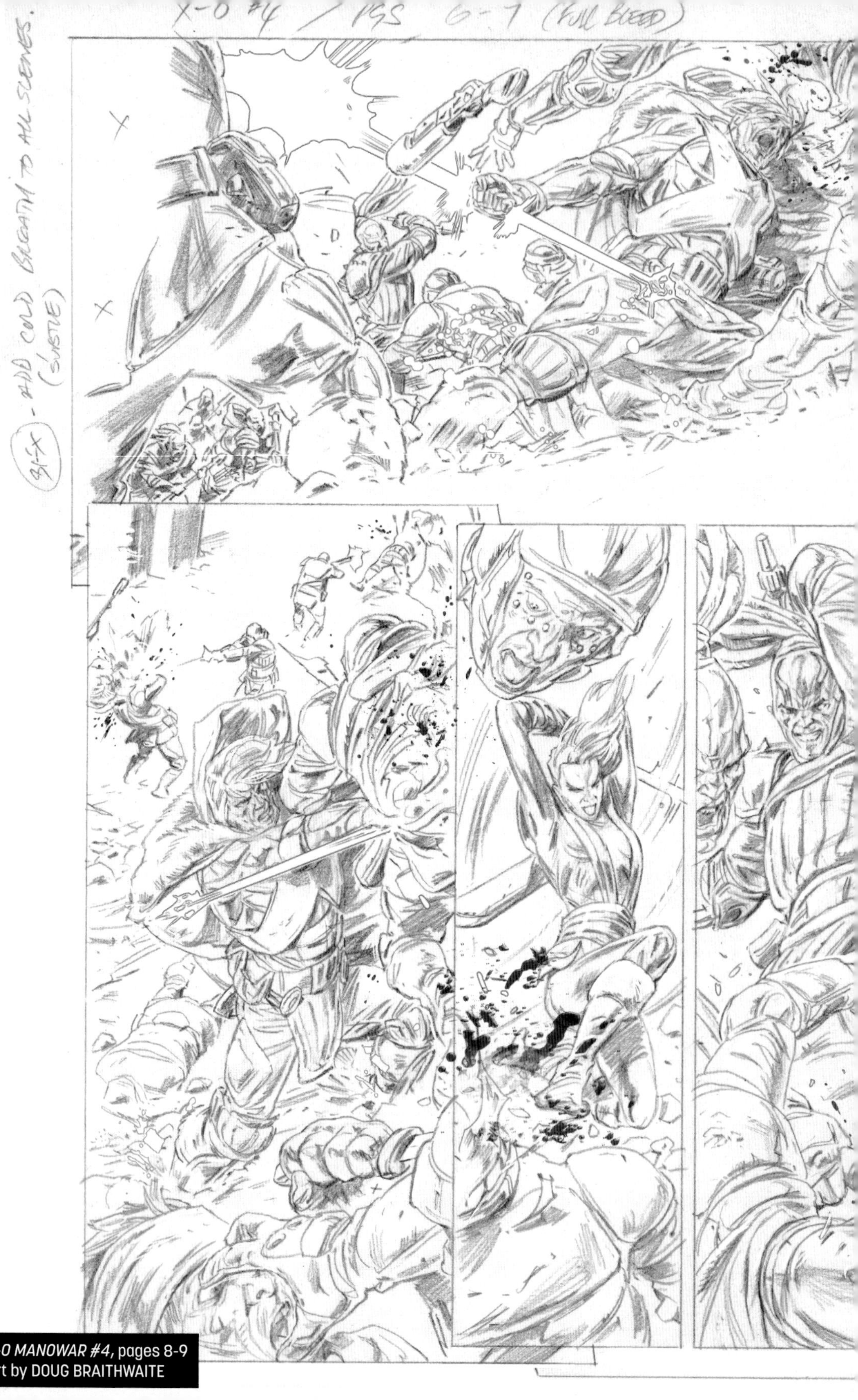
X-O #4 / PGS 6-7 (FULL BLEED)
ADD COLD BREATH TO ALL SCENES (SUBTLE)

X-O MANOWAR #4, pages 8-9
Art by DOUG BRAITHWAITE

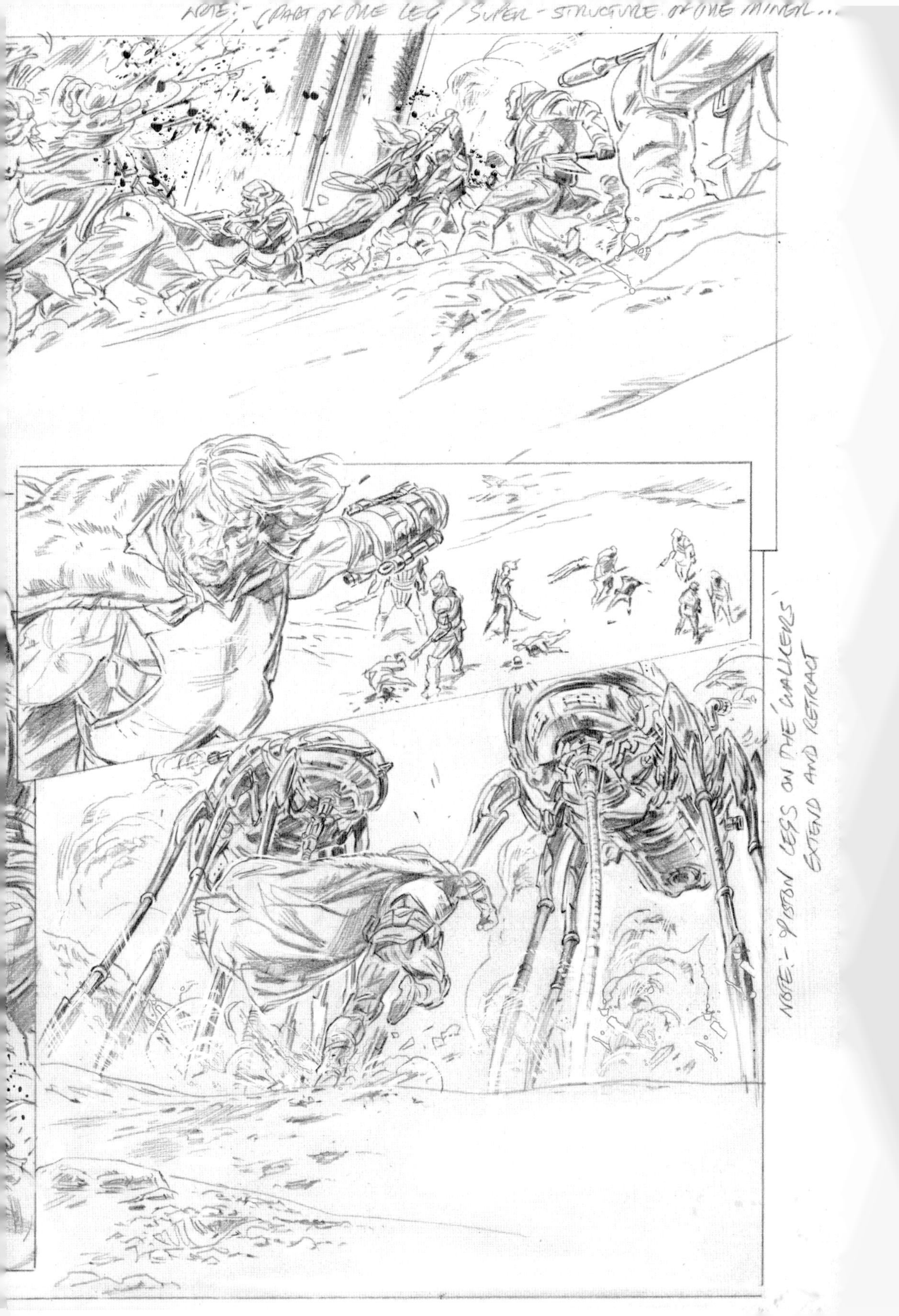
NOTE:- (PART OF ONE LEG / SUPER-STRUCTURE OF ONE MINER...
NOTE:- PISTON LEGS ON THE 'WALKERS' EXTEND AND RETRACT

X-O MANOWAR #4, p. 10
Art by DOUG BRAITHWAITE

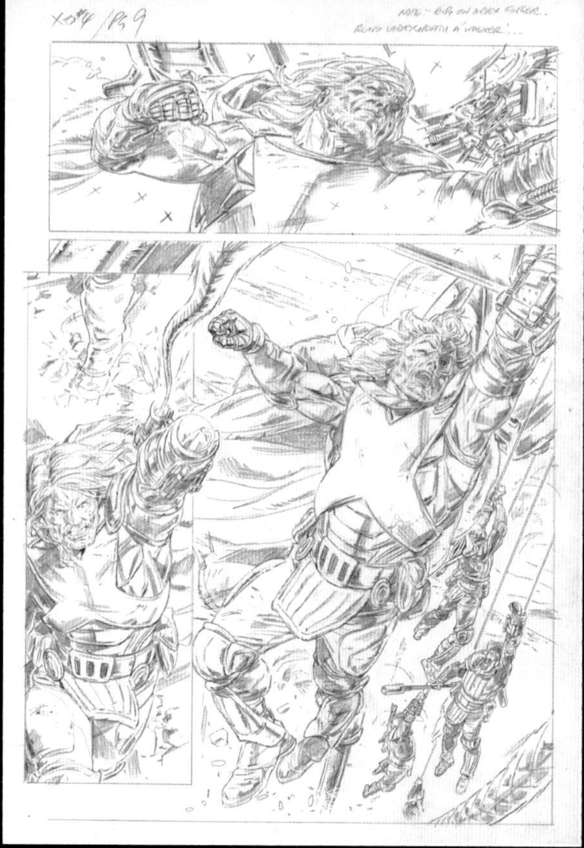
X-O#4/Pg 9

X-O MANOWAR #4, p. 11
Art by DOUG BRAITHWAITE

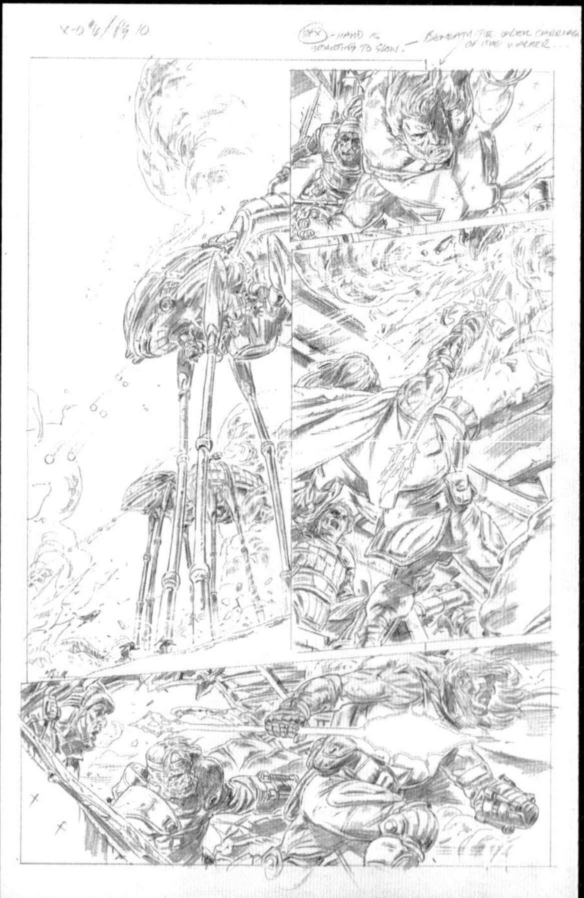
X-O#4/Pg 10
SFX - HAND IS STARTING TO GLOW.
BENEATH THE UNDER CARRIAGE OF THE WALKER...

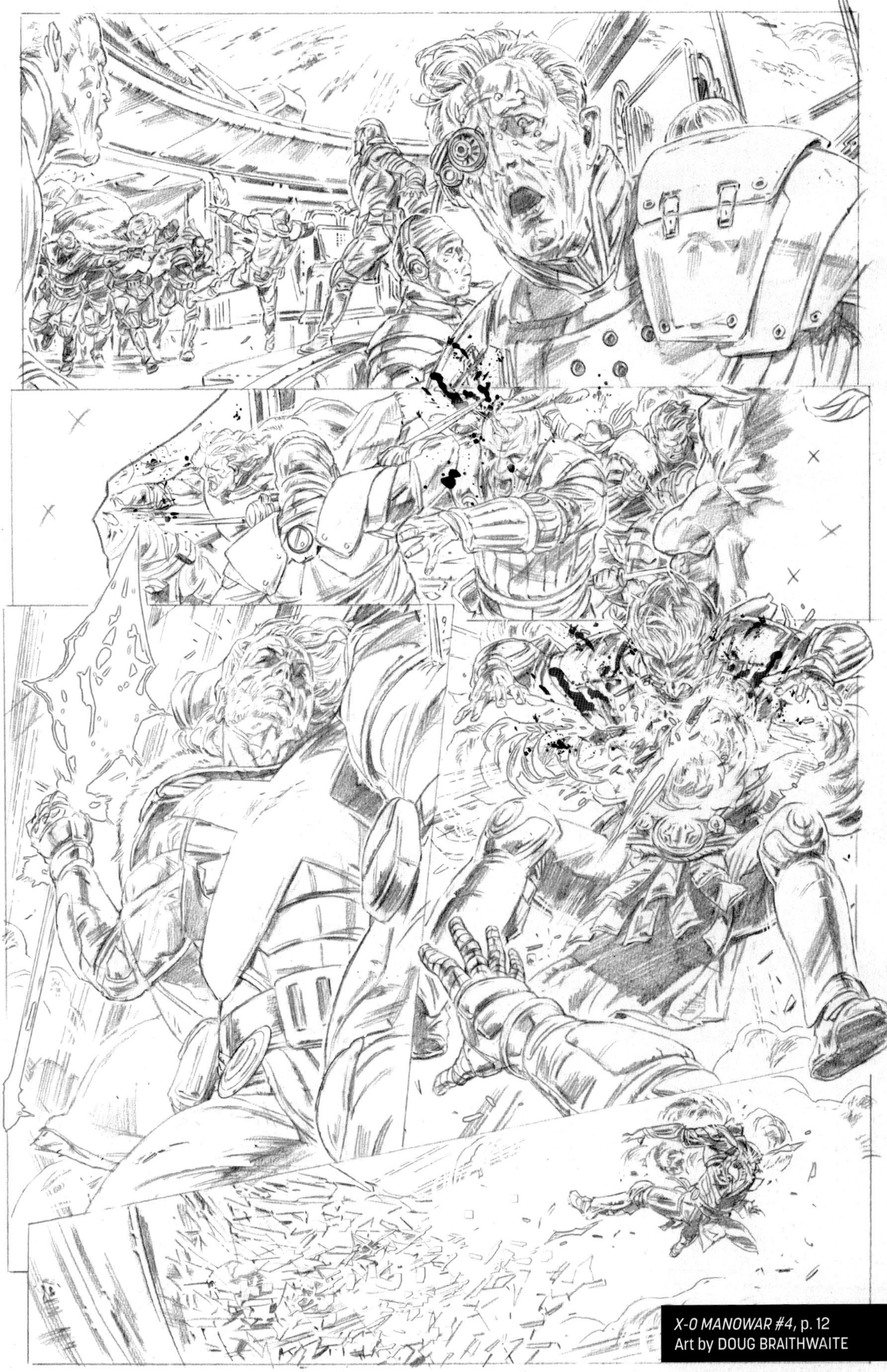
X-O #4 / PG 11

X-O MANOWAR #4, p. 12
Art by DOUG BRAITHWAITE

X-O MANOWAR #4, p. 13
Art by DOUG BRAITHWAITE

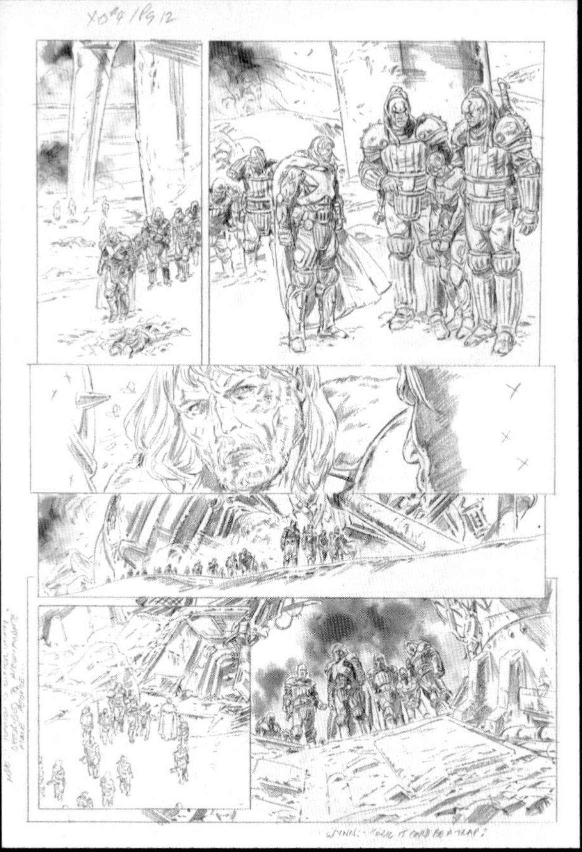
XO#4 / PG 12

X-O MANOWAR #4, p. 14
Art by DOUG BRAITHWAITE

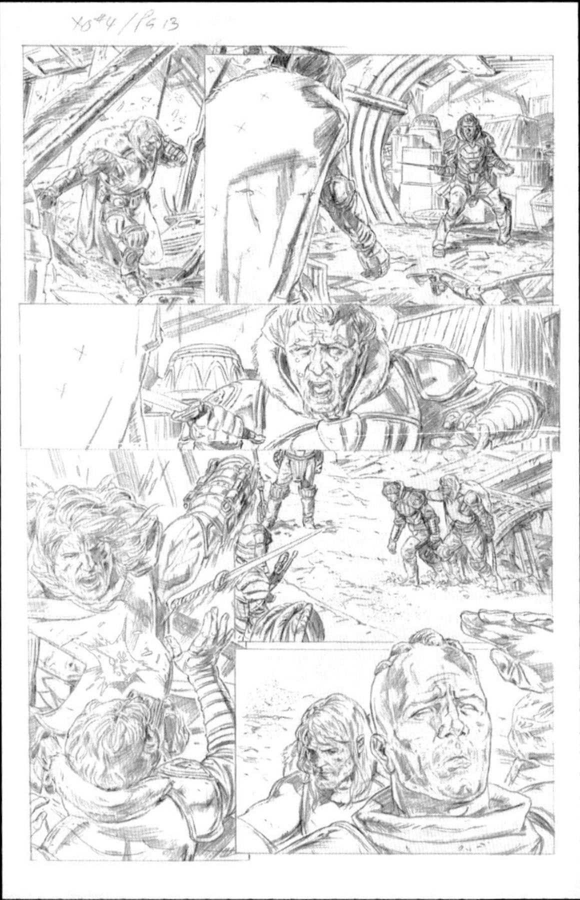
XO#4 / PG 13

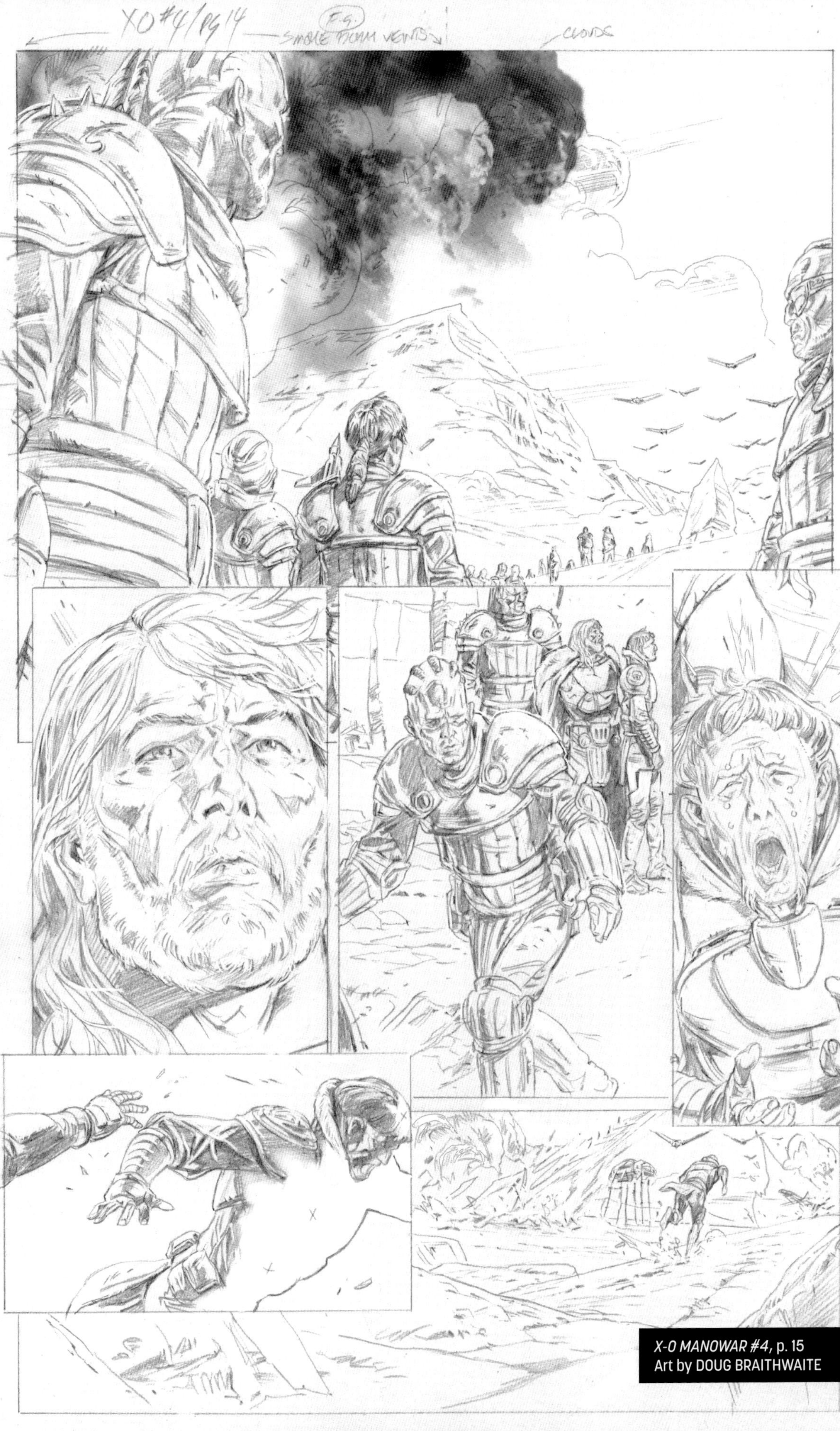
XO #4/Pg 14
SMOKE FROM VENTS
CLOUDS

X-O MANOWAR #4, p. 15
Art by DOUG BRAITHWAITE

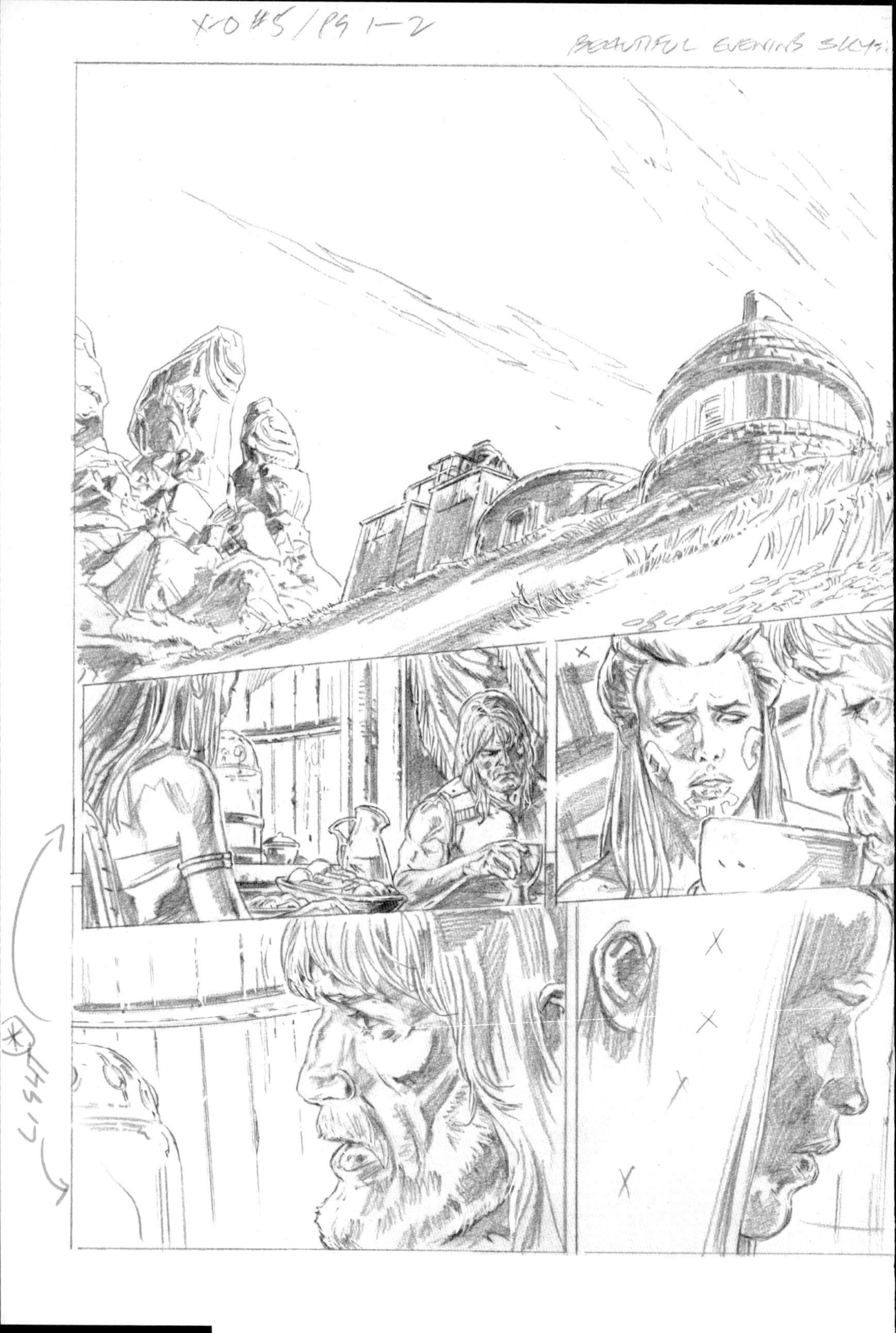
X-O #5 / PG 1–2
BEAUTIFUL EVENING SKY
LIGHT

X-O MANOWAR #5, pages 1-2
Art by DOUG BRAITHWAITE

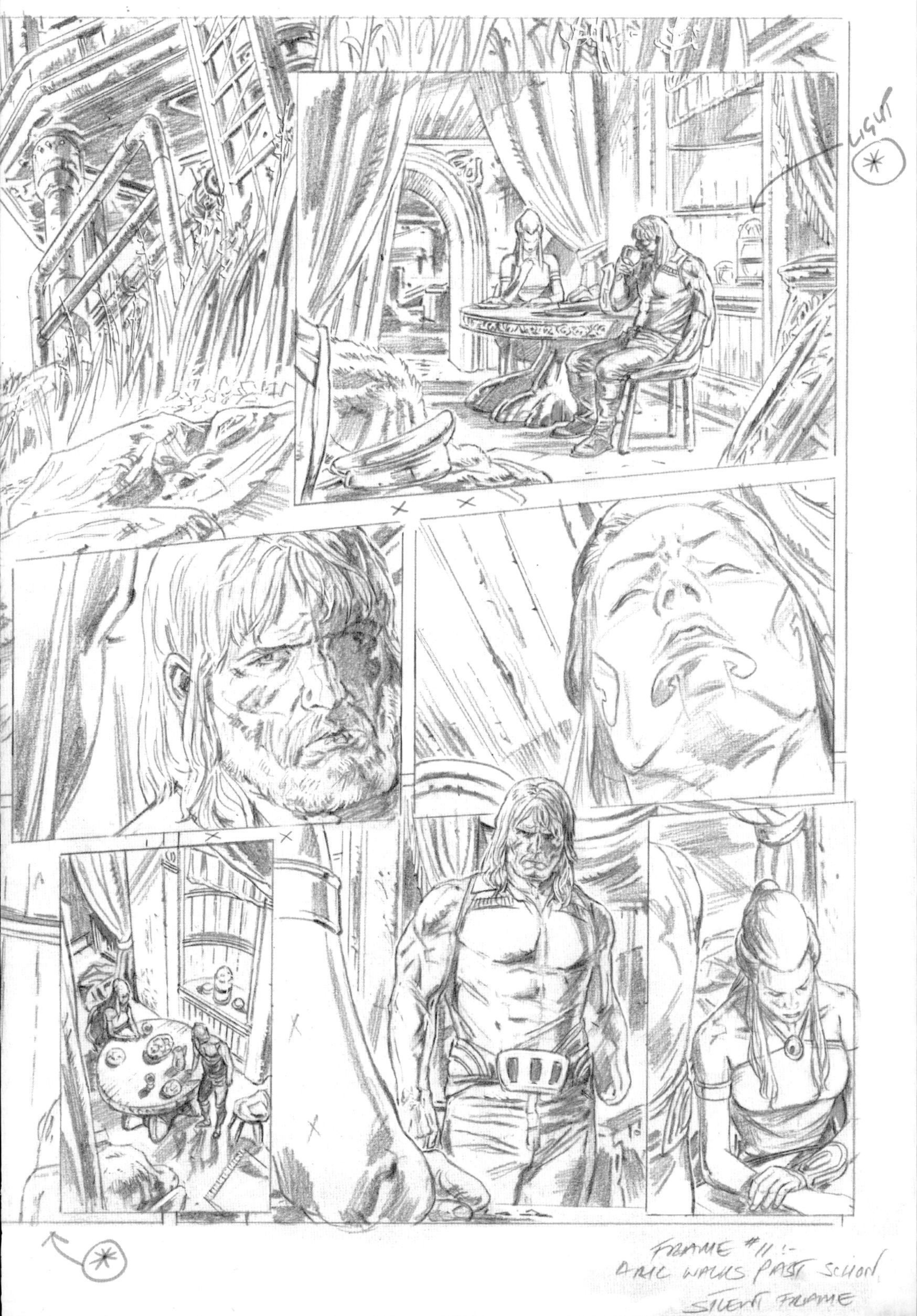
LIGHT
FRAME #11 :-
ARIC WALKS PAST SCHON
SILENT FRAME

X-O MANOWAR #5, p. 3
Art by DOUG BRAITHWAITE

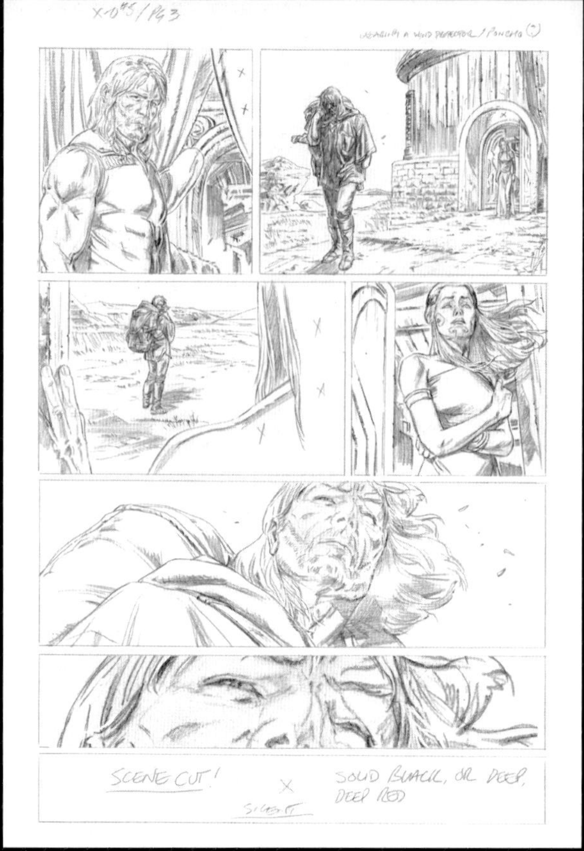
X-O #5 / PG 3
SCENE CUT!
SOLID BLACK, OR DEEP, DEEP RED

X-O MANOWAR #5, p. 4
Art by DOUG BRAITHWAITE

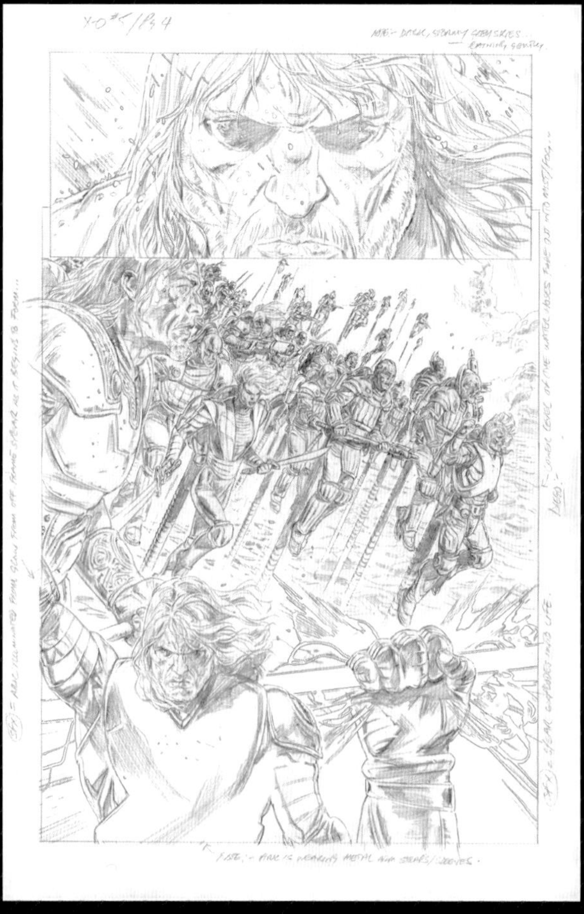
X-O #5 / Pg 4

X-O MANOWAR #5, p. 5 (facing page)
Art by DOUG BRAITHWAITE

X-O #5/PG 5

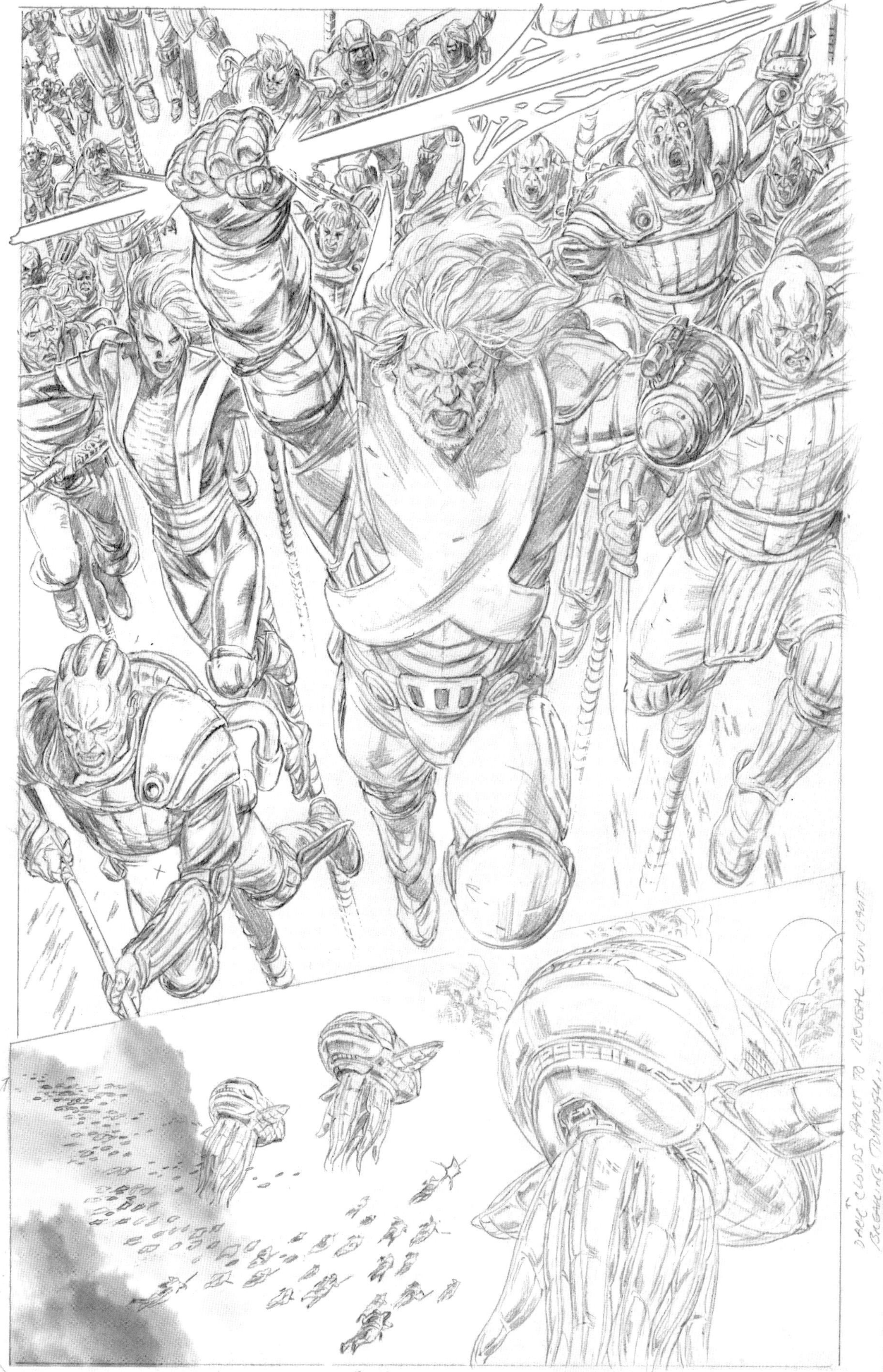

SOLDIERS BREAKING THROUGH FOG
IN LOWER 1/5 OF THE FRAME..

NOTE:- TENTACLES ARE SEMI-TRANSPARENT
HELIUM SACKS...

DARK CLOUDS PART TO REVEAL SUN LIGHT
BREAKING THROUGH...

X-O MANOWAR #6, p. 20
Art by DOUG BRAITHWAITE

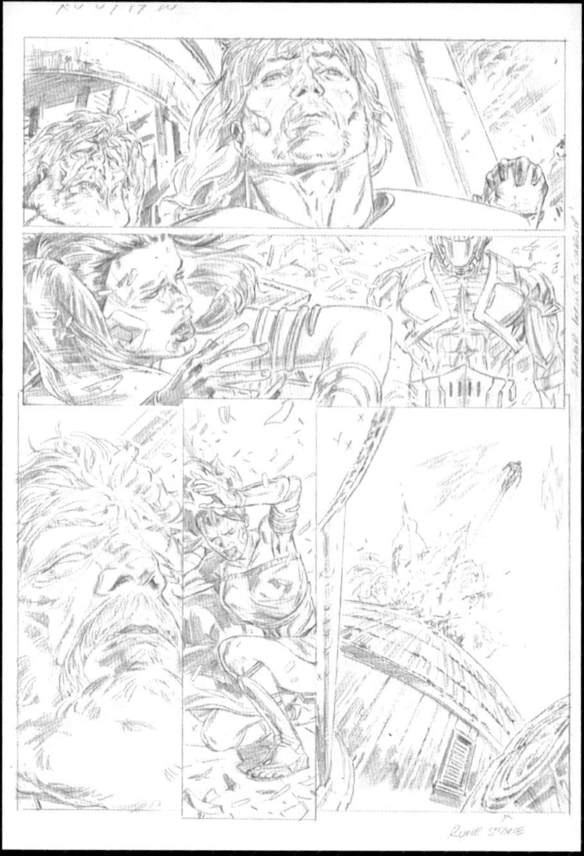
RUNE STONE

X-O MANOWAR #6, p. 21
Art by DOUG BRAITHWAITE

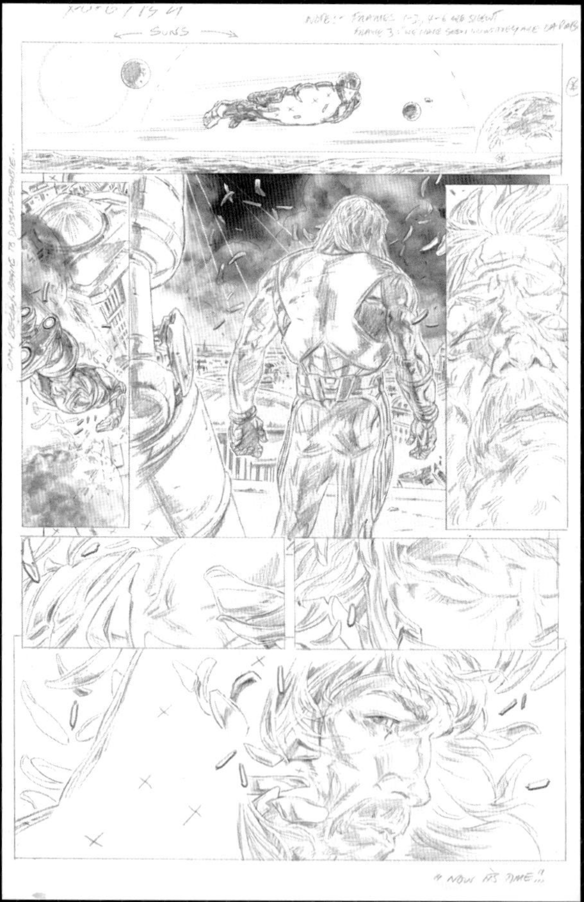
SUNS

X-O MANOWAR #5, p. 22 (facing page)
Art by DOUG BRAITHWAITE

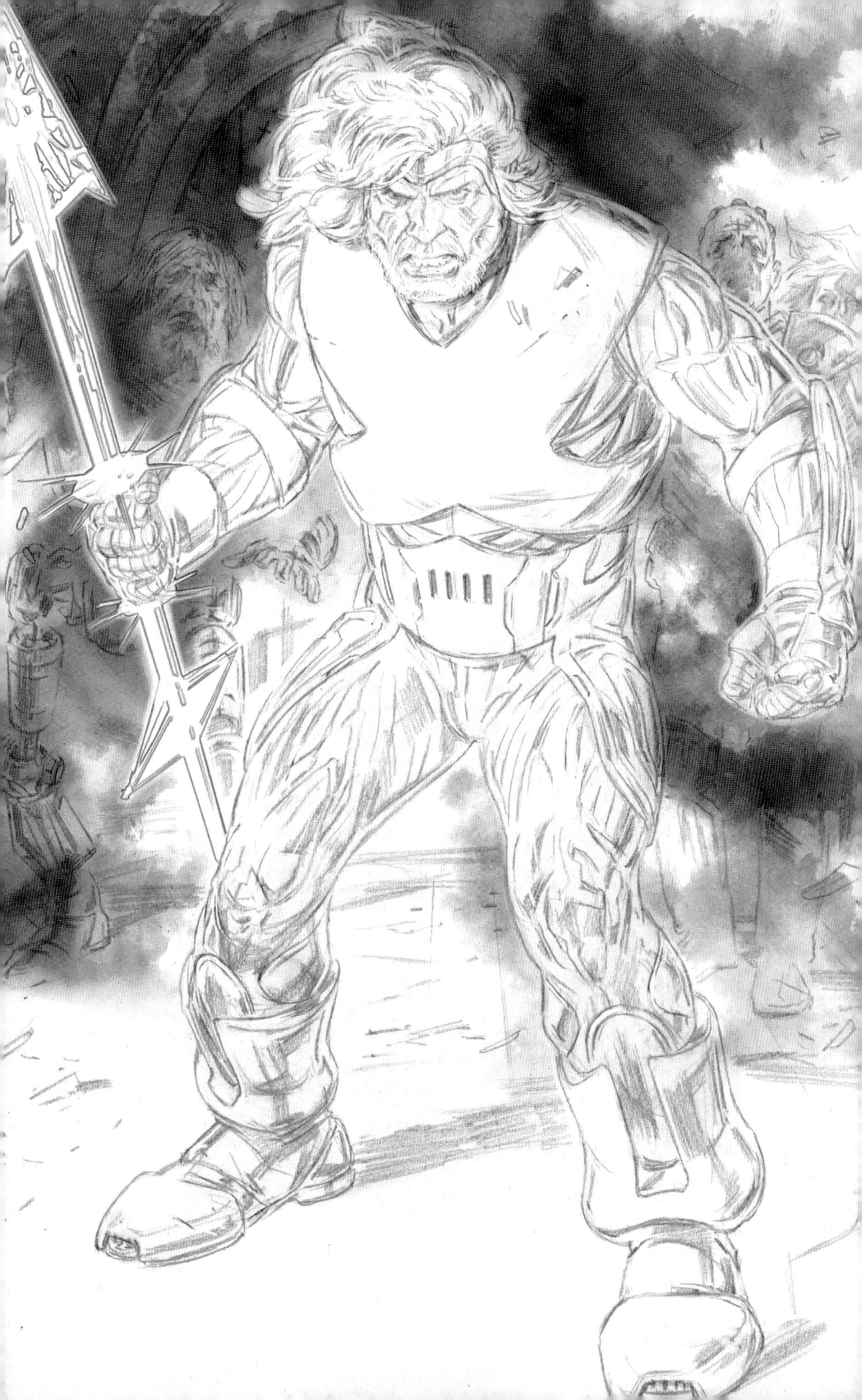

EXPLORE THE VALIANT UNIVERSE

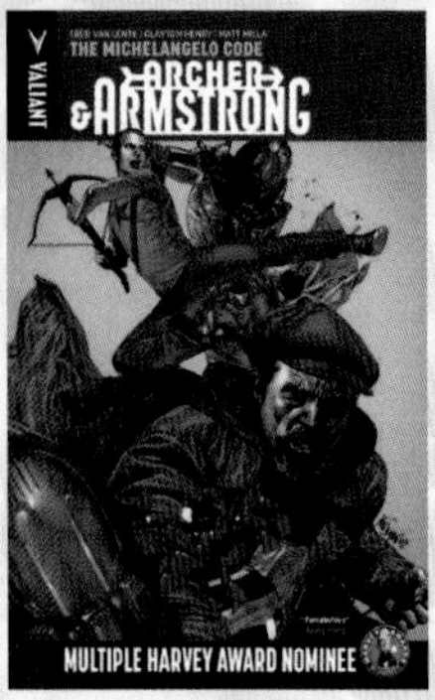
VALIANT
THE MICHELANGELO CODE
ARCHER & ARMSTRONG
MULTIPLE HARVEY AWARD NOMINEE

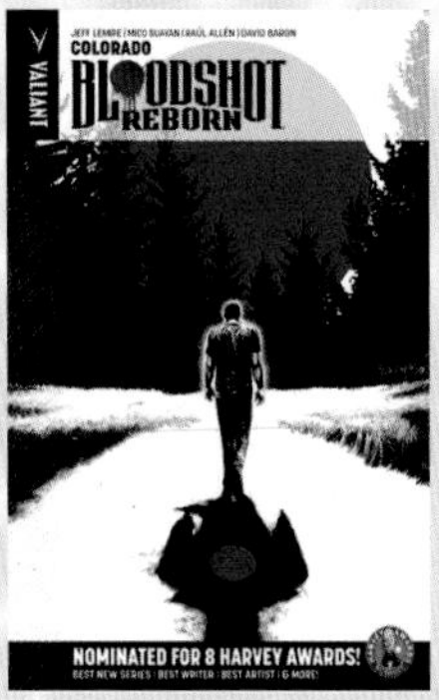
VALIANT
COLORADO
BLOODSHOT REBORN
NOMINATED FOR 8 HARVEY AWARDS!

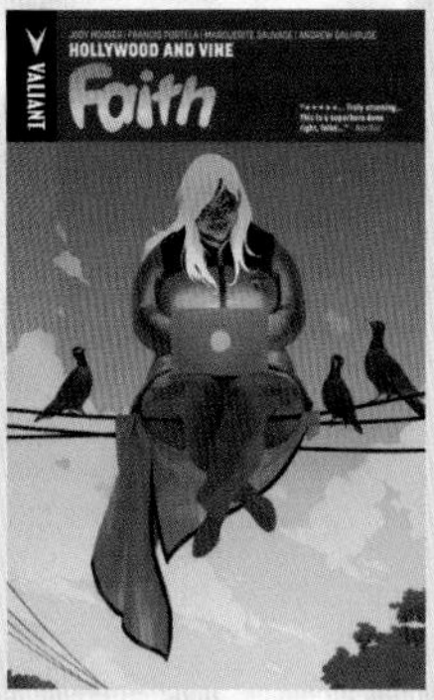
VALIANT
HOLLYWOOD AND VINE
Faith

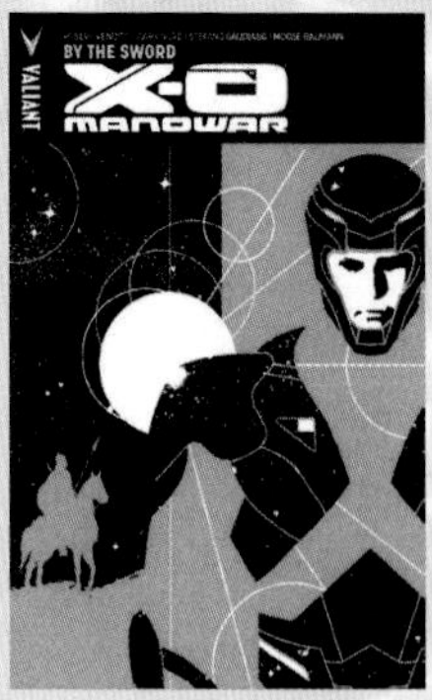
VALIANT
BY THE SWORD
X-O MANOWAR

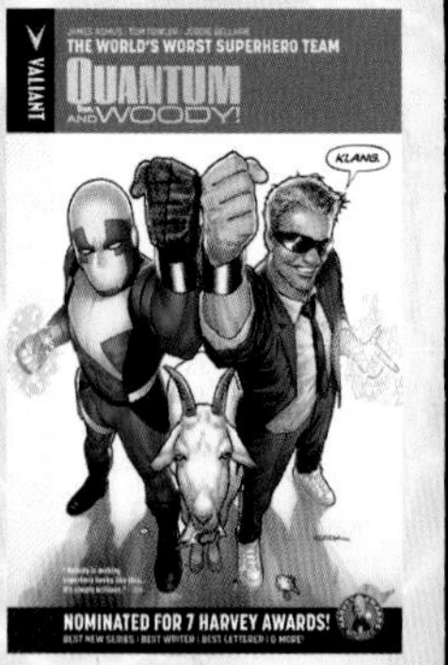
VALIANT
THE WORLD'S WORST SUPERHERO TEAM
QUANTUM AND WOODY!
KLANG.
NOMINATED FOR 7 HARVEY AWARDS!

4001 A.D.

4001 A.D.
ISBN: 9781682151433

4001 A.D.: Beyond New Japan
ISBN: 9781682151464

Rai Vol 4: 4001 A.D.
ISBN: 9781682151471

A&A: THE ADVENTURES OF ARCHER AND ARMSTRONG

Volume 1: In the Bag
ISBN: 9781682151495

Volume 2: Romance and Road Trips
ISBN: 9781682151716

Volume 3: Andromeda Estranged
978-1-68215-203-4

ARCHER & ARMSTRONG

Volume 1: The Michelangelo Code
ISBN: 9780979640988

Volume 2: Wrath of the Eternal Warrior
ISBN: 9781939346049

Volume 3: Far Faraway
ISBN: 9781939346148

Volume 4: Sect Civil War
ISBN: 9781939346254

Volume 5: Mission: Improbable
ISBN: 9781939346353

Volume 6: American Wasteland
ISBN: 9781939346421

Volume 7: The One Percent and Other Tales
ISBN: 9781939346537

ARMOR HUNTERS

Armor Hunters
ISBN: 9781939346452

Armor Hunters: Bloodshot
ISBN: 9781939346469

Armor Hunters: Harbinger
ISBN: 9781939346506

Unity Vol. 3: Armor Hunters
ISBN: 9781939346445

X-O Manowar Vol. 7: Armor Hunters
ISBN: 9781939346476

BLOODSHOT

Volume 1: Setting the World on Fire
ISBN: 9780979640964

Volume 2: The Rise and the Fall
ISBN: 9781939346032

Volume 3: Harbinger Wars
ISBN: 9781939346124

Volume 4: H.A.R.D. Corps
ISBN: 9781939346193

Volume 5: Get Some!
ISBN: 9781939346315

Volume 6: The Glitch and Other Tales
ISBN: 9781939346711

BLOODSHOT REBORN

Volume 1: Colorado
ISBN: 9781939346674

Volume 2: The Hunt
ISBN: 9781939346827

Volume 3: The Analog Man
ISBN: 9781682151334

Volume 4: Bloodshot Island
ISBN: 9781682151952

BLOODSHOT U.S.A.

ISBN: 9781682151952

BOOK OF DEATH

Book of Death
ISBN: 9781939346971

Book of Death: The Fall of the Valiant Universe
ISBN: 9781939346988

BRITANNIA

Volume 1
ISBN: 9781682151853

DEAD DROP

ISBN: 9781939346858

THE DEATH-DEFYING DOCTOR MIRAGE

Volume 1
ISBN: 9781939346490

Volume 2: Second Lives
ISBN: 9781682151297

THE DELINQUENTS

ISBN: 9781939346513

DIVINITY

Volume 1
ISBN: 9781939346766

Volume 2
ISBN: 9781682151518

Volume 3
ISBN: 9781682151914

Divinity III: Glorious Heroes of the Stalinverse
ISBN: 9781682152072

ETERNAL WARRIOR

Volume 1: Sword of the Wild
ISBN: 9781939346209

Volume 2: Eternal Emperor
ISBN: 9781939346292

Volume 3: Days of Steel
ISBN: 9781939346742

WRATH OF THE ETERNAL WARRIOR

Volume 1: Risen
ISBN: 9781682151235

Volume 2: Labyrinth
ISBN: 9781682151594

Volume 3: Deal With a Devil
ISBN: 9781682151976

FAITH

Volume 1: Hollywood and Vine
ISBN: 9781682151402

Volume 2: California Scheming
ISBN: 9781682151631

Volume 3: Superstar
978-1-68215-199-0

Volume 4: The Faithless
978-1-68215-219-5

GENERATION ZERO

Volume 1: We Are the Future
ISBN: 9781682151754

Volume 2: Heroscape
978-1-68215-209-6

HARBINGER

Volume 1: Omega Rising
ISBN: 9780979640957

Volume 2: Renegades
ISBN: 9781939346025

Volume 3: Harbinger Wars
ISBN: 9781939346117

Volume 4: Perfect Day
ISBN: 9781939346155

Volume 5: Death of a Renegade
ISBN: 9781939346339

Volume 6: Omegas
ISBN: 9781939346384

EXPLORE THE VALIANT UNIVERSE

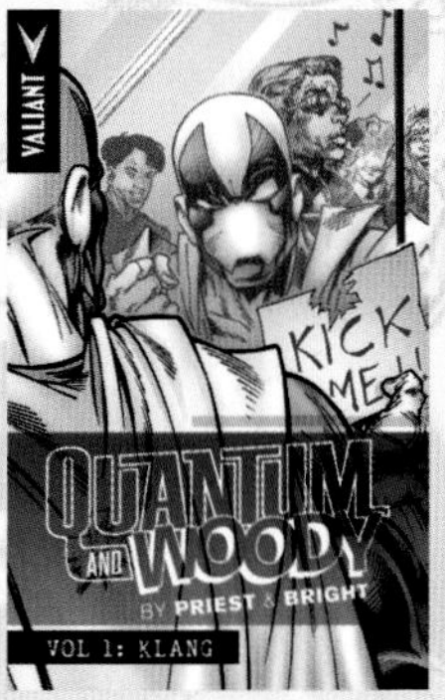
VALIANT
KICK ME
QUANTUM AND WOODY
BY PRIEST & BRIGHT
VOL 1: KLANG
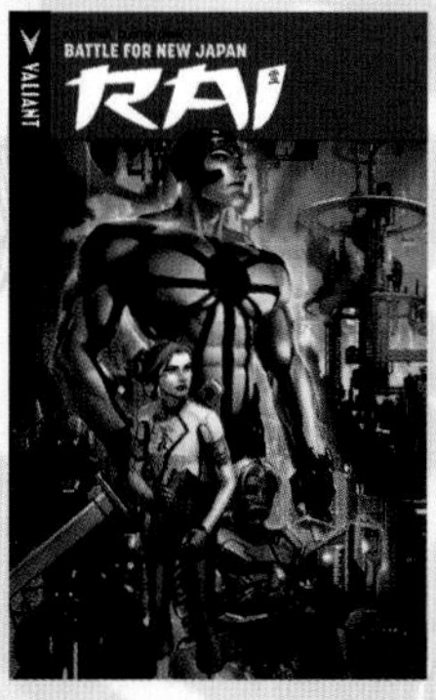
VALIANT
BATTLE FOR NEW JAPAN
RAI
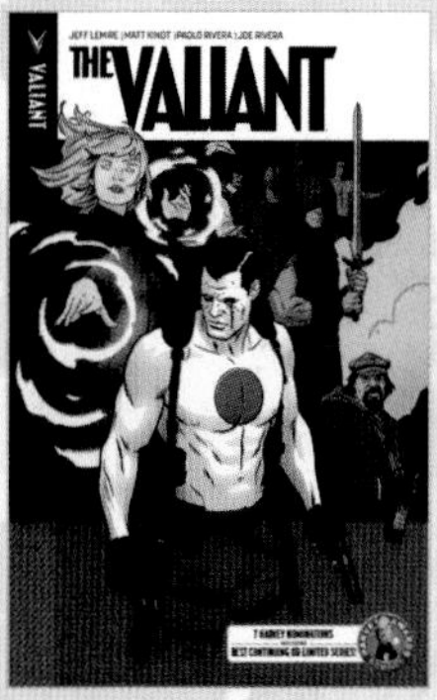
VALIANT
THE VALIANT
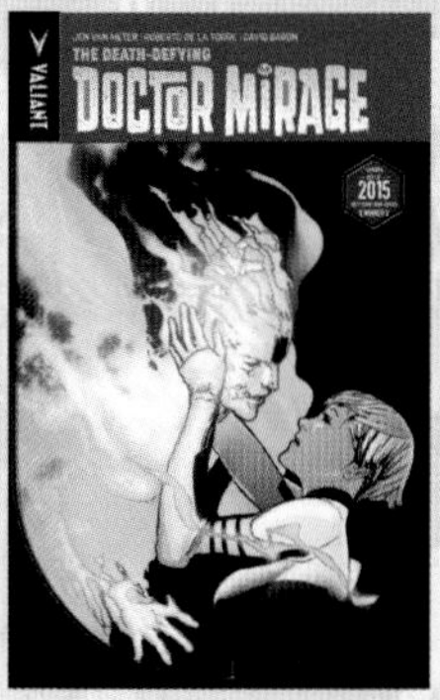
VALIANT
THE DEATH-DEFYING
DOCTOR MIRAGE
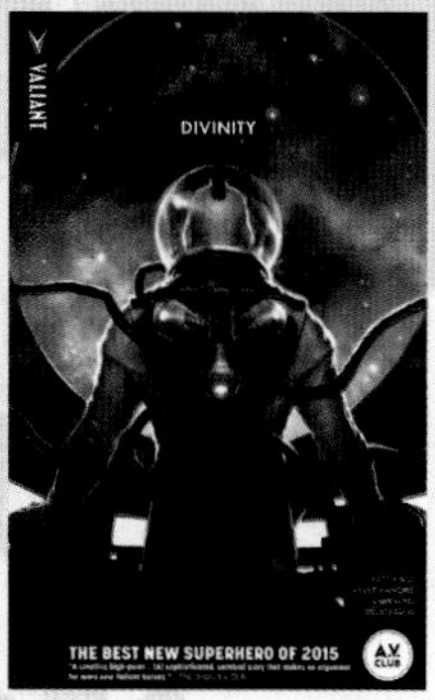
VALIANT
DIVINITY
THE BEST NEW SUPERHERO OF 2015

HARBINGER RENEGADE
Volume 1: The Judgment of Solomon
ISBN: 9781682151693

HARBINGER WARS
Harbinger Wars
ISBN: 9781939346094
Bloodshot Vol. 3: Harbinger Wars
ISBN: 9781939346124
Harbinger Vol. 3: Harbinger Wars
ISBN: 9781939346117

IMPERIUM
Volume 1: Collecting Monsters
ISBN: 9781939346759
Volume 2: Broken Angels
ISBN: 9781939346896
Volume 3: The Vine Imperative
ISBN: 9781682151112
Volume 4: Stormbreak
ISBN: 9781682151372

NINJAK
Volume 1: Weaponeer
ISBN: 9781939346667
Volume 2: The Shadow Wars
ISBN: 9781939346940
Volume 3: Operation: Deadside
ISBN: 9781682151259
Volume 4: The Siege of King's Castle
ISBN: 9781682151617
Volume 5: The Fist & The Steel
ISBN: 9781682151792
Volume 6: The Seven Blades of Master Darque
978-1-68215-211-9

QUANTUM AND WOODY
Volume 1: The World's Worst Superhero Team
ISBN: 9781939346186
Volume 2: In Security
ISBN: 9781939346230
Volume 3: Crooked Pasts, Present Tense
ISBN: 9781939346391
Volume 4: Quantum and Woody Must Die!
ISBN: 9781939346629

QUANTUM AND WOODY BY PRIEST & BRIGHT
Volume 1: Klang
ISBN: 9781939346780
Volume 2: Switch
ISBN: 9781939346803
Volume 3: And So...
ISBN: 9781939346865
Volume 4: Q2 - The Return
ISBN: 9781682151099

RAI
Volume 1: Welcome to New Japan
ISBN: 9781939346414
Volume 2: Battle for New Japan
ISBN: 9781939346612
Volume 3: The Orphan
ISBN: 9781939346841
Rai Vol 4: 4001 A.D.
ISBN: 9781682151471

SAVAGE
Volume 1
978-1-68215-189-1

SHADOWMAN
Volume 1: Birth Rites
ISBN: 9781939346001
Volume 2: Darque Reckoning
ISBN: 9781939346056
Volume 3: Deadside Blues
ISBN: 9781939346162
Volume 4: Fear, Blood, And Shadows
ISBN: 9781939346278
Volume 5: End Times
ISBN: 9781939346377

SHADOWMAN BY ENNIS & WOOD
ISBN: 9781682151358

IVAR, TIMEWALKER
Volume 1: Making History
ISBN: 9781939346636
Volume 2: Breaking History
ISBN: 9781939346834
Volume 3: Ending History
ISBN: 9781939346995

UNITY
Volume 1: To Kill a King
ISBN: 9781939346261
Volume 2: Trapped by Webnet
ISBN: 9781939346346
Volume 3: Armor Hunters
ISBN: 9781939346445
Volume 4: The United
ISBN: 9781939346544
Volume 5: Homefront
ISBN: 9781939346797
Volume 6: The War-Monger
ISBN: 9781939346902
Volume 7: Revenge of the Armor Hunters
ISBN: 9781682151136

THE VALIANT
ISBN: 9781939346605

VALIANT ZEROES AND ORIGINS
ISBN: 9781939346582

X-O MANOWAR
Volume 1: By the Sword
ISBN: 9780979640940
Volume 2: Enter Ninjak
ISBN: 9780979640995
Volume 3: Planet Death
ISBN: 9781939346087
Volume 4: Homecoming
ISBN: 9781939346179
Volume 5: At War With Unity
ISBN: 9781939346247
Volume 6: Prelude to Armor Hunters
ISBN: 9781939346407
Volume 7: Armor Hunters
ISBN: 9781939346476
Volume 8: Enter: Armorines
ISBN: 9781939346551
Volume 9: Dead Hand
ISBN: 9781939346650
Volume 10: Exodus
ISBN: 9781939346933
Volume 11: The Kill List
ISBN: 9781682151273
Volume 12: Long Live the King
ISBN: 9781682151655
Volume 13: Succession and Other Tales
ISBN: 9781682151754

X-O MANOWAR (2017)
Volume 1: Soldier
ISBN: 9781682152058
Volume 2: General
ISBN: 9781682152171

EXPLORE THE VALIANT UNIVERSE

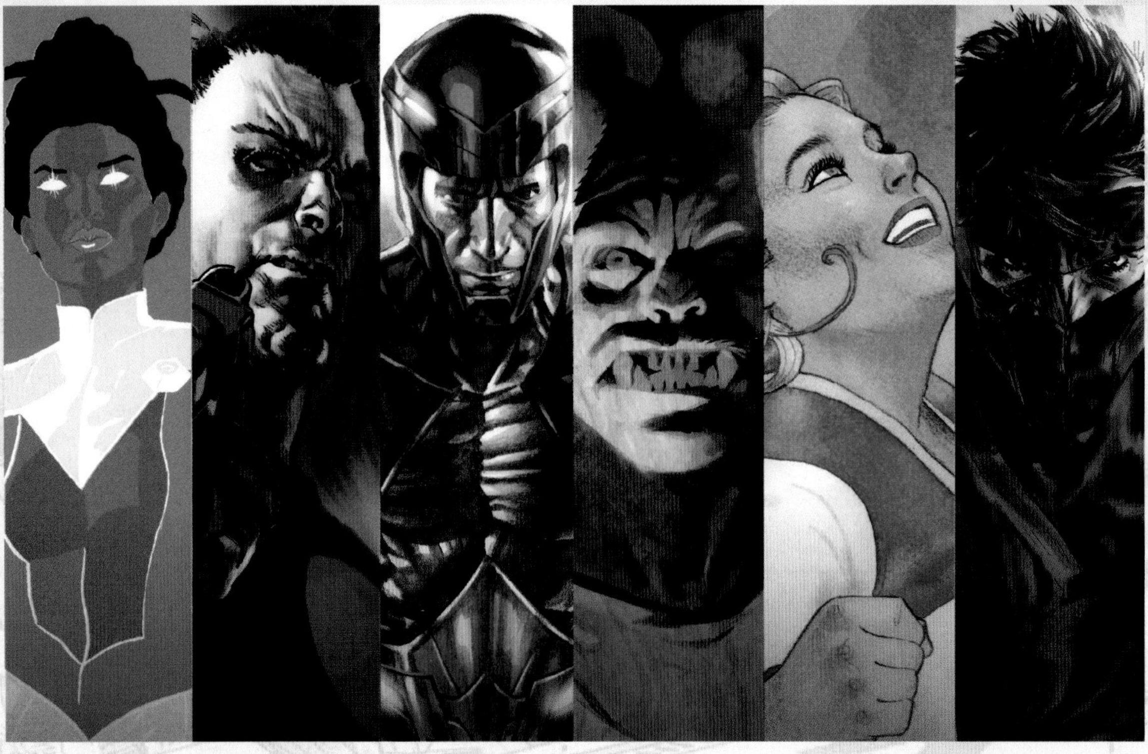

4001 A.D. DELUXE EDITION
ISBN: 978-1-68215-193-8

ARCHER & ARMSTRONG DELUXE EDITIONS
Book 1: ISBN: 978-1-939346-22-3
Book 2: ISBN: 978-1-939346-95-7

ARMOR HUNTERS DELUXE EDITION
ISBN: 978-1-939346-72-8

BLOODSHOT DELUXE EDITIONS
Book 1: ISBN: 978-1-939346-21-6
Book 2: ISBN: 978-1-939346-81-0

BLOODSHOT REBORN DELUXE EDITIONS
Book 1: ISBN: 978-1-68215-155-6
Book 2: ISBN: 978-1-68215-227-0

BOOK OF DEATH DELUXE EDITION
ISBN: 978-1-68215-115-0

THE DEATH-DEFYING DOCTOR MIRAGE DELUXE EDITION
ISBN: 978-1-68215-153-2

DIVINITY DELUXE EDITION
ISBN: 978-1-939346-92-6

FAITH: HOLLYWOOD & VINE DELUXE EDITION
ISBN: 978-1-68215-201-0

HARBINGER DELUXE EDITIONS
Book 1: ISBN: 978-1-939346-13-1
Book 2: ISBN: 978-1-939346-77-3

HARBINGER WARS DELUXE EDITION
ISBN: 978-1-939346-32-2

IVAR, TIMEWALKER DELUXE EDITION
Book 1: ISBN: 978-1-68215-119-8

NINJAK DELUXE EDITION
Book 1: ISBN: 978-1-68215-157-0

QUANTUM AND WOODY DELUXE EDITION
Book 1: ISBN: 978-1-939346-68-1

RAI DELUXE EDITION
Book 1: ISBN: 978-1-68215-117-4

SHADOWMAN DELUXE EDITION
Book 1: ISBN: 978-1-939346-43-8

UNITY DELUXE EDITION
Book 1: 978-1-939346-57-5

THE VALIANT DELUXE EDITION
ISBN: 978-1-939346-91-9

X-O MANOWAR DELUXE EDITIONS
Book 1: ISBN: 978-1-939346-10-0
Book 2: ISBN: 978-1-939346-52-0
Book 3 : ISBN: 978-1-68215-131-0
Book 4: ISBN: 978-1-68215-183-9
Book 5: ISBN: 978-1-68215-215-7

VALIANT CLASSIC

ARCHER & ARMSTRONG: THE COMPLETE CLASSIC OMNIBUS
ISBN: 978-1-939346-87-2

QUANTUM AND WOODY: THE COMPLETE CLASSIC OMNIBUS
ISBN: 978-1-939346-36-0

Q2: THE RETURN OF QUANTUM AND WOODY DELUXE EDITION
ISBN: 978-1-939346-56-8

VALIANT MASTERS: BLOODSHOT VOL. 1 - BLOOD OF THE MACHINE
ISBN: 978-0-9796409-3-3

VALIANT MASTERS: HARBINGER VOL. 1 - CHILDREN OF THE EIGHTH DAY
ISBN: 978-1-939346-48-3

VALIANT MASTERS: H.A.R.D. CORPS VOL. 1 - SEARCH AND DESTROY
ISBN: 978-1-939346-28-5

VALIANT MASTERS: NINJAK VOL. 1 - BLACK WATER
ISBN: 978-0-9796409-7-1

VALIANT MASTERS: RAI VOL. 1 - FROM HONOR TO STRENGTH
ISBN: 978-1-939346-07-0

VALIANT MASTERS: SHADOWMAN VOL. 1 - SPIRITS WITHIN
ISBN: 978-1-939346-01-8

X-O MANOWAR CLASSIC OMNIBUS
Vol. 1: ISBN: 978-1-939346-30-8

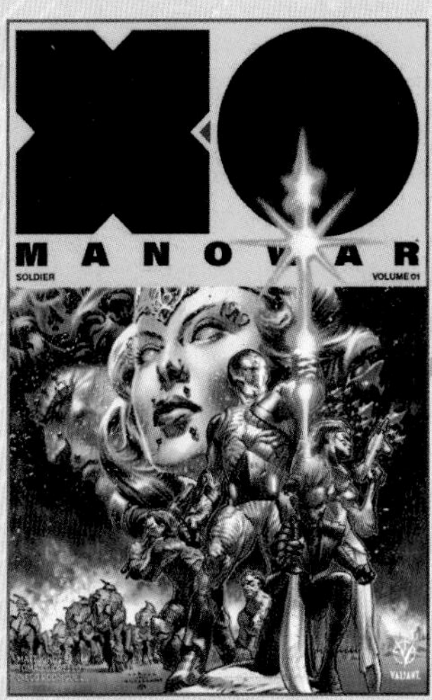
X-O
MANOWAR
SOLDIER
VOLUME 01

X-O Manowar (2017) Vol. 1: Soldier

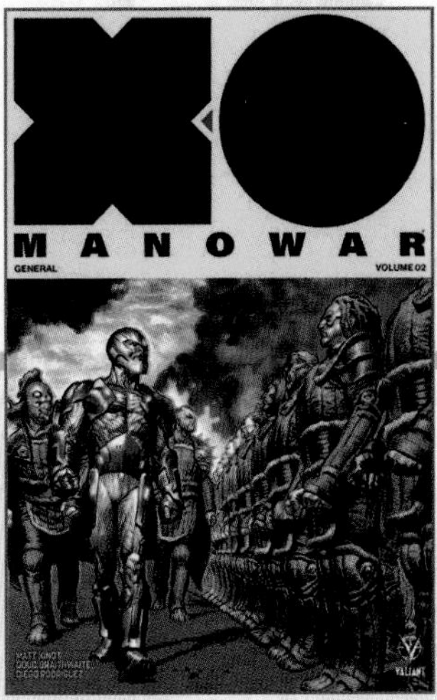
X-O
MANOWAR
GENERAL
VOLUME 02

X-O Manowar (2017) Vol. 2: General

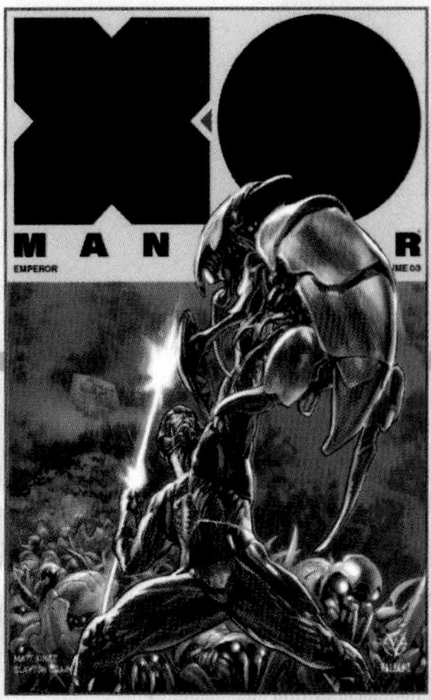
X-O
EMPEROR

X-O Manowar (2017) Vol. 3: Emperor

Read the origin and earliest adventures of Valiant's most enduring icon!

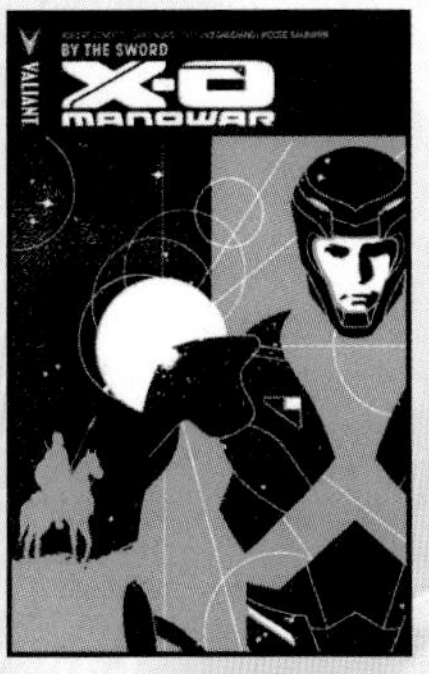
BY THE SWORD
X-O
MANOWAR
VALIANT

X-O Manowar
Vol. 1: By the Sword

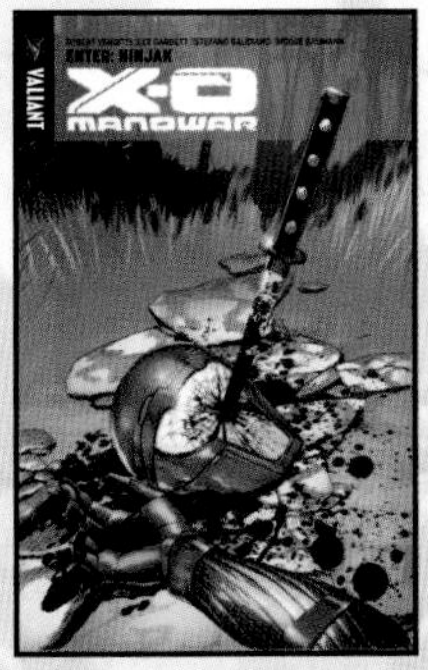
ENTER: NINJAK
X-O
MANOWAR
VALIANT

X-O Manowar
Vol. 2: Enter Ninjak

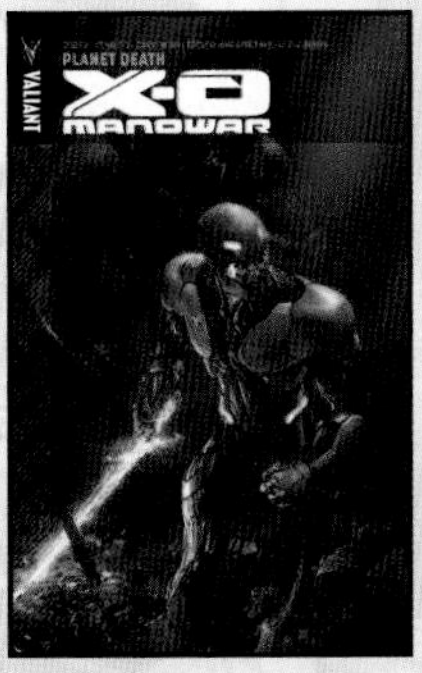
PLANET DEATH
X-O
MANOWAR
VALIANT

X-O Manowar
Vol. 3: Planet Death

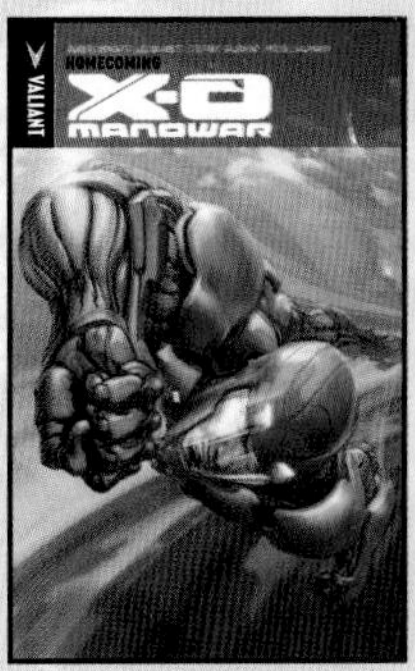
HOMECOMING
X-O
MANOWAR
VALIANT

X-O Manowar
Vol. 4: Homecoming

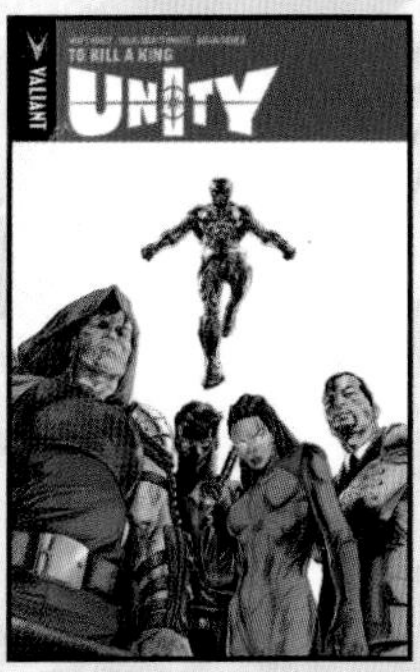
TO KILL A KING
UNITY
VALIANT

Unity
Vol. 1: To Kill a King

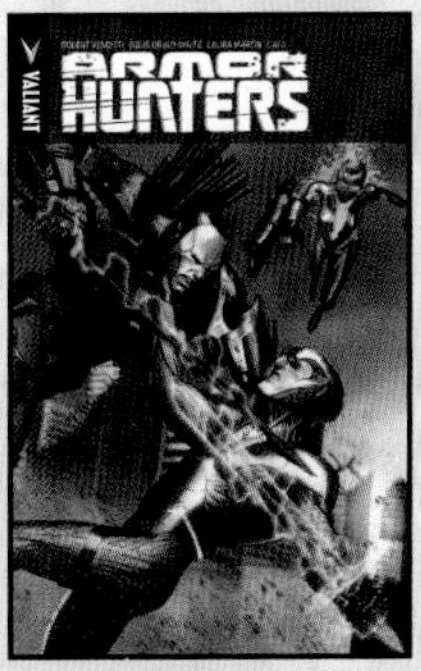
ARMOR
HUNTERS
VALIANT

Armor Hunters

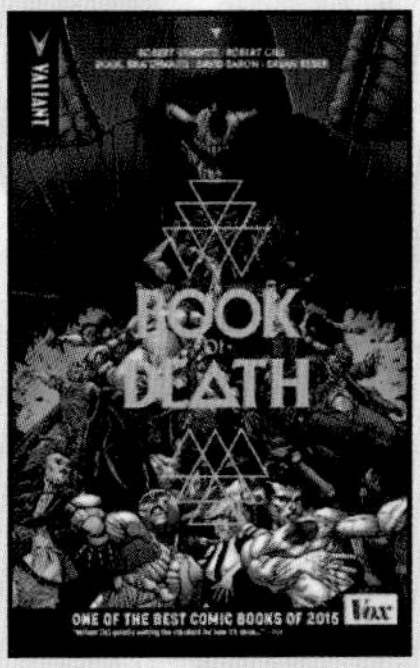
BOOK OF DEATH
ONE OF THE BEST COMIC BOOKS OF 2015
VALIANT

Book of Death

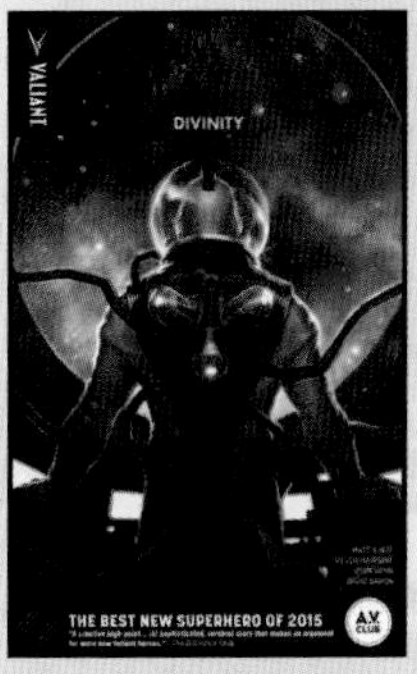
DIVINITY
THE BEST NEW SUPERHERO OF 2015
VALIANT

Divinity

X-O MANOR

VOLUME THREE: EMPEROR

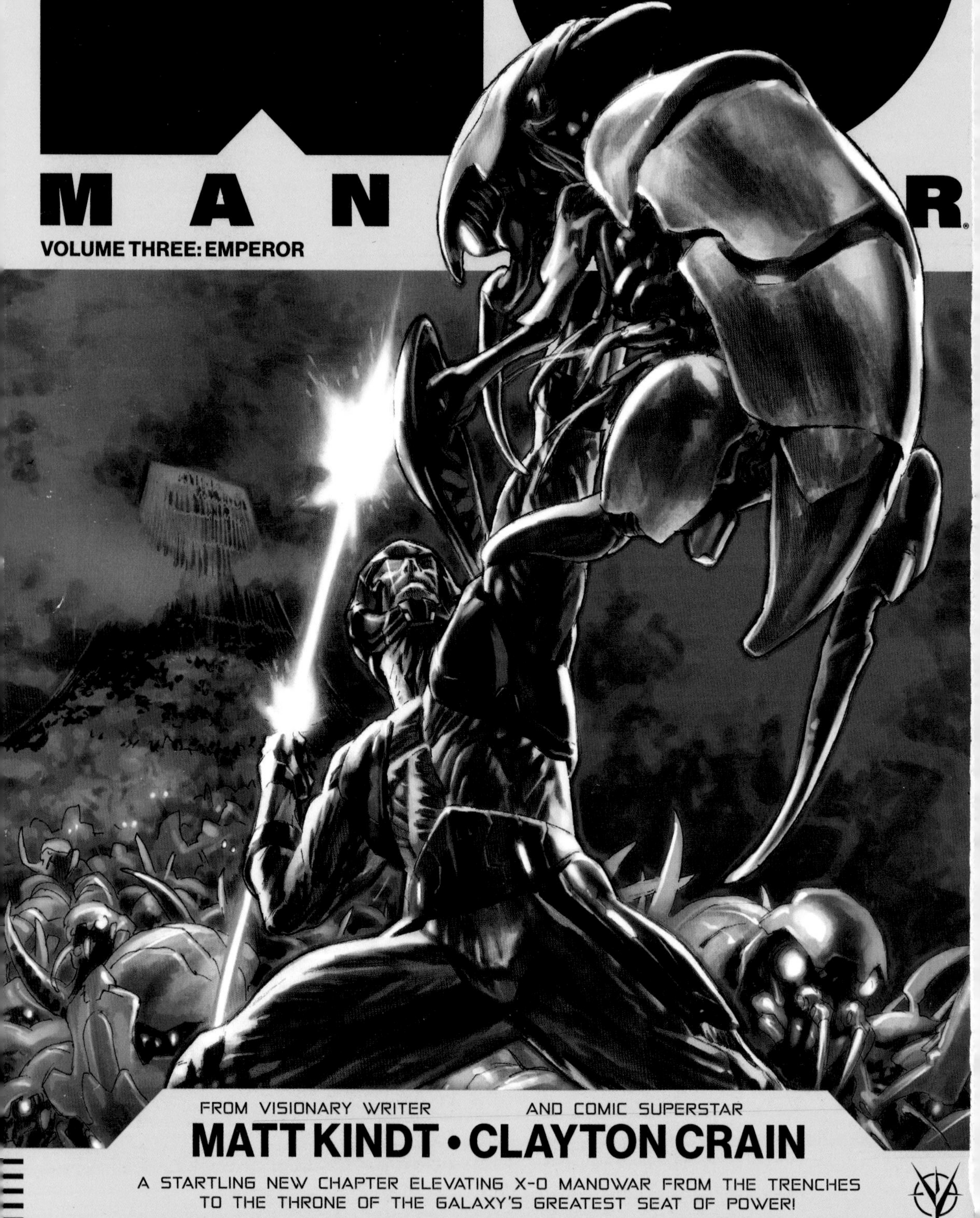

FROM VISIONARY WRITER   AND COMIC SUPERSTAR

MATT KINDT • CLAYTON CRAIN

A STARTLING NEW CHAPTER ELEVATING X-O MANOWAR FROM THE TRENCHES
TO THE THRONE OF THE GALAXY'S GREATEST SEAT OF POWER!

COLLECTING X-O MANOWAR (2017) #7–10 • ISBN: 978-1-68215-235-5